April De Angelis

PLAYS TWO

April De Angelis's plays include *Kerry Jackson* (National Theatre); *My Brilliant Friend* (adapted from Elena Ferrante's novels for Rose Theatre, Kingston, and NT), *House Party* (BBC4 and Headlong Theatre), *Gin Craze!*, a musical with Lucy Rivers (Royal & Derngate), *Extinct* (Stratford East), *Rune* (New Vic Theatre, Newcastle-under-Lyme), *The Village* (Stratford East), *Wild East* (Royal Court), *A Laughing Matter* (Out of Joint/NT/tour), *The Warwickshire Testimony* (RSC), *The Positive Hour* (Out of Joint/Hampstead/Old Vic; Sphinx), *Headstrong* (NT Shell Connections), *Playhouse Creatures* (Sphinx Theatre Company), *Hush* (Royal Court), *Soft Vengeance* (Graeae Theatre Company), *The Life and Times of Fanny Hill* (adapted from the James Cleland novel), *Ironmistress* (ReSisters Theatre Company), *Wuthering Heights* (adapted from Emily Brontë's novel for Birmingham Rep), *Jumpy* (Royal Court and Duke of York's Theatres), *Gastronauts* (Royal Court) and *After Electra* (Theatre Royal, Plymouth). Her work for BBC Radio includes *Visitants*, *The Outlander*, which won the Writers' Guild Award 1992, and *Cash Cows* for the *Woman's Hour* serial. For opera: *Flight* with composer Jonathan Dove (Glyndebourne), and the libretto for *Silent Twins* (Almeida).

APRIL DE ANGELIS

Plays Two

A Laughing Matter

Jumpy

The Village

Rune

Extinct

Gin Craze!
with Lucy Rivers

Introduced by the author

faber

First published in 2022
by Faber and Faber Limited
74–77 Great Russell Street
London WC1B 3DA

Typeset by Brighton Gray
Printed and bound in the UK by CPI Group (Ltd), Croydon CR0 4YY

A CIP record for this book
is available from the British Library

978–0–571–37823–4

2 4 6 8 10 9 7 5 3 1

Contents

Introduction

The six selected plays published here span almost two decades. All but the first two were commissioned by female artistic directors. That tells a story. There were almost no women running theatres when I started my career as a playwright back in the 1980s. Progress. Here are included one history play, one musical, one comedy, one short monologue, a contemporary adaptation of a seventeenth-century verse drama, and a longer monologue and cry from the heart about our perilous state: the climate and ecological emergency.

Starting at the end, *Gin Craze!* was a project I took to theatres rather than waiting to be asked, which suggests a newfound confidence after thirty years of playwriting. *Extinct* is a play that could only have been written in the Anthropocene. And two of the plays were written for the Theatre Royal Stratford East, proudly once the home of a heroine of mine, Joan Littlewood. During this time, I have collaborated with many wonderful artists. One of the joys of being a playwright is to come out of the solitary business of writing into the big family of the theatre and the rehearsal room.

A Laughing Matter

Max Stafford-Clark's Out of Joint theatre company asked me to find a classic play and write a response to it, so that both plays could be toured together. In the eighteenth century, there was a fashion for plays called 'sentimental' comedies. This species of play believed the stage must project a good example at all times, and conflict must come not out of malevolence but out of genuine, good-hearted mistakes.

Laughter was frowned upon as too 'low'. These plays were pretty woeful. One of the only plays to buck the trend was Oliver Goldsmith's refreshingly comic and lairy *She Stoops to Conquer*. However, the actor/manager of Drury Lane in 1767, David Garrick, Goldsmith's good friend, refused to stage the play for fear of a scandal. There, I thought, was a story. It was my first big, main-stage play, eventually performed at the National Theatre's Lyttelton. I had to compose lines for Dr Johnson, perhaps the wittiest man in history, which caused me some trepidation. Still, I loved writing the play: the bold language and larger-than-life characters who populated the eighteenth-century stage were great fun to bring alive. There was a lot of doubling – I learnt to contrive exits, so that an actor could come on again as a different character, which gave me a pleasing sense of connection to playwrights of the past.

Jumpy

Dominic Cooke read a scene I had written about a mother and daughter, which started with them arguing about homework and ended with the firing of a gun. He called me into the Royal Court and said, 'Write me the play,' so I did. I had just turned fifty and had a sixteen-year-old daughter. It was a case of write what you know. The extraordinary Tamsin Greig played Hilary, with Bel Powley as her daughter and Doon Mackichan as the best friend. It was directed by Nina Raine. Is there a more powerful story than that of bringing up a child and letting that child go? Weirdly, it's marginalised in theatre, and I wanted to push that mother/daughter relationship centre stage, powered by the explosive, rebellious energy of a teenager.

Rune

Theresa Heskins, the artistic director of the New Vic, Stoke-on-Trent, commissioned a series of plays to commemorate the discovery in 2009 of the Staffordshire Hoard, the largest ever find of Saxon gold and precious stuff by a first-time metal detectorist. Each writer had to choose an item from the hoard and write a short table play, to be performed as the audience sat in the bar before the main house opened. I chose to write about a rune. Stoke, Theresa told me, was one of the most deprived areas in the UK, and that started me thinking about what impact, if any, the discovery of the treasure would have on one teenage girl.

The Village

In 2018 Nadia Fall opened her first season at Theatre Royal Stratford East with a homage to Joan Littlewood, choosing a play that Joan had rediscovered, *Fuenteovejuna* by Lope de Vega. It was based on a true story of a fifteenth-century Spanish village, which, under the leadership of a young woman and rape victim, rose up to overthrow an oppressive, evil landlord. Nadia had the idea of setting the play in the contemporary India of right-wing nationalist Narendra Modi. The real rape and murder of a Dahlit girl by a group of nationalists, contesting her people's right to their land, was very much in our minds. As I began the adaptation of this verse drama it became clear that the poetry of the original was deep in its bones and our play needed to be in verse too. It was a nervous embarkation, which slowly found its confidence as we read the lines with actors. I had a vertiginous timescale from commission to first night – both in the same year – but I was thrilled to be working on this project. De Vega, I discovered, was one of only three survivors from his ship, part of the invading Armada fleet. Did that trauma lead him to deconstruct the elite patriarchy so effectively?

Extinct

In 2018, worried about climate heating, I went to a meeting of Extinction Rebellion and became an activist. I was on a steep learning curve, terrified for the future of the planet. In the middle of Lockdown, Nadia Fall asked me to write a show for one actor (Covid) on climate change. We decided it would mimic a TED Talk, but veer off into a story of the already impacted Global South. The director Kirsty Housley and I grappled with the show's structure and with the restrictions of staging anything during the pandemic, and the intrepid actor Kiran Landa took the job, which involved using a camera, getting into a cold bath and tipping 'crude oil' over herself, together with the huge ingestion of many facts. She reached out and touched the audience powerfully.

Gin Craze!

Michael Oakley directed two of my previous plays, *Playhouse Creatures* at Chichester and *Fanny Hill* at Bristol Old Vic. We talked about a third history project and landed on the eighteenth-century gin craze. Gin was a newly invented beverage, much more powerful than today's; a pint could kill you. We still talk about 'mother's ruin', a leftover from the moralising reaction to the 'craze', which saw the powerful afraid that they would lose their control over the poor, and especially the women, who enjoyed both hawking and imbibing the new liquor. In their tough lives, it was self-medication. As I researched, wonderful things happened. I discovered that the novelist Henry Fielding and his bluestocking sister Sarah were part of the gin story; and, as I began to write, I had the sense that these women of the street would be singing, and so it became a musical. Michael and I had the opportunity to visit the Orchard Project in America, and the lyricist and composer Lucy Rivers bravely joined us, never having met us before. We heard Lucy's first song one evening while sitting on a porch in Saratoga Springs. We were blown away. A wonderful moment.

With all these plays I wanted to put women's lives centre stage. I hope you enjoy them.

April De Angelis
June 2022

A LAUGHING MATTER

A Laughing Matter was first performed at the Yvonne Arnaud Theatre, Guildford, on 17 October 2002, with the following cast:

Edmund Burke / Sam Cautherley / Mr Cross
    Stephen Beresford
Charles Macklin / Sir Joshua Reynolds Nigel Cooke
Peg Woffington / Hannah Moore Monica Dolan
Mrs Garrick / Mrs Barry Fritha Goodey
Mrs Cibber Bella Merlin
Dr Samuel Johnson / Rev. Cumberland / Betty Flint
    Ian Redford
Oliver Goldsmith / Theophilus O'Ryan Owen Sharpe
Cedric Bounce / Mr Larpent Matthew Sim
James Boswell / Mr Barry / Duke of Kingston
    Christopher Staines
David Garrick Jason Watkins
Lady Kingston / Mrs Butler Jane Wood

Other parts played by members of the company

Director Max Stafford-Clark
Designer Julian McGowan
Lighting Johanna Town
Music Paddy Cunneen
Sound Neil Alexander
Choreographer Wendy Allnutt
Assistant Director Matthew Wilde

Characters

Samuel Johnson
Oliver Goldsmith
James Boswell
Edmund Burke
Joshua Reynolds
David Garrick
Mrs Eva Garrick
Lady Kingston
Reverend Richard Cumberland
Sam Cautherley
Mrs Susannah Cibber
Mrs Butler
Mrs Lavinia Barry
Mr Spranger Barry
Mr Charles Macklin
Hannah More
Cedric Bounce
Mr Richard Cross
Master Barry
Mr Theophilus O'Ryan
Peg Woffington
Betty Flint
Duke of Kingston
Old Man
Butcher
Vicar
Mr Larpent

Act One

Johnson A Club. One: An assembly of good fellows meeting under certain conditions for a common purpose. Two: A heavy tapering stick, knobby at one end. Used to strike with.

SCENE ONE: THE TURK'S HEAD

Goldsmith Gentlemen, I have written a comedy, but when or how it will be acted or whether it will be acted at all are questions I cannot resolve.

Boswell Gentlemen, we forget our toast. To the Turk's Head.

All The Turk's Head!

Johnson I find I no longer approve of our toast. We are not Turks. We must endeavour to discover a more suitable epithet.

Goldsmith Gentlemen. May I draw attention to the matter I flagged up some moments past?

Johnson No, Goldy, you may not. You must not be forever attempting to shine in conversation. You go on without ever knowing how you are to get off. You seldom come anywhere where you are not more ignorant than anyone else.

Burke If I remember correctly, Dr Johnson's pledge of old was to the king over the water.

Johnson It was, Mr Burke, until he threatened to arrive.

Burke You had not the stomach to be overrun by marauding Scots?

Johnson Scots, sir, will grab the flimsiest of straws to leave the land of their birth. Invasion of England would merely have provided them further excuse.

Boswell You are rather harsh upon my country fellows, I think.

Johnson A man cannot admire a nation whose national dish is oats. Oats in England, sir, are a cereal fed to horses. In Scotland they support the population. You may enquire of Reynolds here as to landscape.

Reynolds The landscape is perhaps a trifle severe for the English palette.

Johnson Just as your eye is blighted, so is the mind, for conversation has not yet been invented in Scotland. They are too busy chewing.

Boswell I object, sir.

Johnson You may object, Bozzy, or you may comfort yourself with this: although it is bad to be Scottish it is worse to be French. The French are a gross, ill-bred, untaught people; a lady there will spit on the floor and rub it with her foot.

Burke If we are to discover for ourselves a new pledge, we must go back to first principles. Why are we here?

Johnson Burke is the man, sirs, take up whatever topic you please, he is ready to meet you. We meet here to advance the cause of learning and furnish through our conversation understanding and enlightened thinking. We are at the helm, sirs, of an English renaissance. Which brings me to my matter.

Goldsmith Which brings me to my matter.

Johnson I have not finished, sir.

Goldsmith In essence.

Johnson Have I not shaken you off yet, Goldy? My point is this: that our toast, sirs, should be to England.

All England.

Goldsmith My point is that Mr Colman at Covent Garden has had my play twenty-two months. And, sirs, since I have been living off the expectation of it being performed, I am now brought so low as to face extinction. L–l–look at me one last time. I am a whisker away from the slab. Last night I ate my candle then lay in the darkness knowing my final hour must be approaching. Alas, this morning I woke as usual.

Boswell But what is your point, sir?

Johnson His point is he has no candle.

Reynolds You must apply to me for candles, sir. I shall furnish you gladly.

Boswell Perhaps your play is no good, sir.

Goldsmith I have examined all possibilities and that is the least probable. The truth is that your renaissance, sirs, has by-passed the English theatre altogether. We have no theatre to speak of.

Boswell That's odd. I could've sworn I was there last night.

Goldsmith What we have is a commercial venture. A different matter altogether.

Burke Now see here, Dr Goldsmith, we cannot allow you to cast aspersions upon commercial ventures – they are an expression of man's interests.

Reynolds It says something for a work of art that a man is prepared to pay for it.

Goldsmith If you are prepared to flatter, sir, men will pay you.

Boswell Ooh!

Johnson Now, Goldy . . .

Reynolds I flatter myself that I like to bring out the best in people.

Boswell Indeed you do, sir. I say that without flattery.

Johnson Knowing you as I do, Bozzy, that is highly improbable.

Burke Do you suggest Sir Joshua bring out the worst in his subjects?

Johnson It is reasonable to suppose that a man may desire to be presented in a good light as opposed to a bad.

Burke If it makes him content, should we not be happy for him?

Goldsmith It is not the b–business of art to content a man with his own flaws!

Reynolds You touch upon a philosophic point. Shouldn't art aspire to the ideal, since beauty instructs us in goodness?

Burke We would not wish to return to the barbaric impulses which lie within man's breast by always harking on his beastliness.

Goldsmith But it is a lie . . . gentlemen. An argument for lying.

Boswell A society must be encouraged in its aspirations.

Goldsmith You'd feel beastly if you'd been treated the way I had. My play has not received the serious . . .

Johnson We are back to Goldy's play. He must be headed off.

Johnson The theatre, I am not for it. A man is better off reading a play in the comfort of his own home.

Goldsmith You give yourself no concern about new p–plays as if you never had a thing to do with the stage. B–but you wrote a p–play once.

All *Irene.*

They giggle.

Johnson And the Sultan Mahomet. The theatre , sir, is a pointless activity. What does it benefit a man to sit squashed in unspeakable circumstances watching another prance and gesticulate upon a stage in clothes not his own? What does it give a man but a sore arse! A man of talent may do no better than leave the theatre well alone.

Goldsmith Gentlemen . . . I am reduced to eating my only source of lighting. Until I am assisted I will beat myself about the head with this book, the first volume of my own *Deserted Village.* (*He does so.*)

Reynolds Dr Goldsmith, please refrain. This is hardly the behaviour of a gentleman.

Johnson Goldy, you cannot treat books in that manner.

Burke Stop, sir, or I will be forced to set about you with my stick. (*He stops.*)

Goldsmith That's a b–big stick.

Johnson Have you not thought, Goldy, of taking your play to Mr Garrick? For if Mr Colman at Covent Garden will not have it, then perhaps his rival at Drury Lane may be persuaded.

Burke Excellent, Doctor.

Boswell You have hit upon it.

Reynolds A most satisfactory conclusion.

Goldsmith Garrick! Never!

Reynolds There's no pleasing Dr Goldsmith.

Burke What have you against Mr Garrick?

Goldsmith He is a scoundrel.

Johnson Garrick is a dear friend. Only I may disparage him.

Boswell But you have always kept him out of our club, sir.

Johnson Because he presumed he would be included.

Boswell Garrick is the greatest actor that has ever lived.

Goldsmith He has single-handedly destroyed the English theatre.

Burke I disagree, sir. By fine and considered management Garrick has saved our theatre from extinction.

Reynolds Garrick may be commended with rescuing Shakespeare from obscurity.

Johnson Sir, you lampoon the age. Some of us had acquaintance with him already.

Goldsmith But what of new plays! Is the credit of our own age nothing? Must our own time pass away unnoticed by posterity?

Reynolds I have painted Mr Garrick on two occasions. He doesn't stay in one expression long. The longer I painted him the further away I got. His face was best as a cloud.

Johnson What is a player but a shadow, sir?

Goldsmith A substantial shadow! P–puffed up with vanity.

Johnson No wonder, sir, that he is vain. A man who has a nation to admire him every night may well be expected to be somewhat elated.

Goldsmith But he turned down my first play and I wrote bad things about him.

Johnson Do you need me to come along and hold your hand, Goldy?

Goldsmith Yes p–please. I should like a b–big thing beside me.

Johnson Very well. Now let us call an end to the matter. I have no desire to extend it further. I should rather hear Bozzy whistle a Scotch tune.

Burke I propose a discussion on the nature of art.

Boswell All societies have art.

Johnson No, sir, some have pottery.

SCENE TWO: GARRICK'S OFFICE

Johnson Patron: one who countenances, supports or protects. Commonly a wretch who supports with insolence and is paid with flattery.

Garrick performs for Mrs Garrick.

Garrick
Give me another horse! Bind up my wounds!
Have mercy, Jesu!

At this point he operates a mechanism in his wig and his hair stands on end.

Soft, I did but dream.
Oh coward conscience, how thou dost affect me.

His hair subsides.

Even his wig can act.

Mrs Garrick Bravo, Mr Garrick.

Garrick You've seen it before, Mrs Garrick.

Mrs Garrick And it always alarms me. It's almost time for your ten o'clock. How will you be?

Garrick 'Surprised by visit', I think. Don't you?

Garrick I could do 'actor extremely surprised by visit'. (*He operates his wig in imitation of shock/horror.*) I suppose you'll be in the cupboard.

Mrs Garrick Of course!

Garrick You've spent quite a lot of time in there. It's only five-by-five. I feel quite bad about it.

Mrs Garrick Mr Garrick. What's got into you? I enjoy it. They'll be here.

Garrick (*taking a studious pose.*) Time's gone much quicker than I ever imagined.

Mrs Garrick What's the matter?

Garrick Nothing. We've had the most wonderful life. I just liked it when the end felt a long way off.

> *Mrs Garrick gives him a pat. They hear an approaching entrance.*

Lady Kingston (*off*) Mr Garrick.

> *Mrs Garrick goes into the secret cupboard. Lady Kingston sweeps in, followed by Reverend Cumberland.*

Genius and national treasure!

> *Garrick acts his 'surprised at work'. He then leaps to his feet and bows.*

Garrick Lady Kingston, I'm honoured.

Lady Kingston You know Reverend Cumberland?

Garrick Very well. How do you do, sir?

Cumberland Pleased to meet you again, sir.

Lady Kingston Well this is delightful. Now we saw your Lear last season and it was quite tremendous, Mr Garrick.

Garrick Thank you.

Lady Kingston It really was.

Garrick Thank you.

Lady Kingston And we've just been talking about it ever since. And it's so much better with your ending.

Garrick Thank you.

Lady Kingston The original is so depressing and may encourage people to hang their relatives.

Cumberland Her Ladyship was saying that your power to move was simply remarkable.

Lady Kingston Yes, I was. May I speak frankly? My husband, the Duke, is a good deal older than I and is in politics. Just recently I've felt a certain languor. Apprehending his complete indifference, I turned for solace to our parson who, it transpired, has written a play. My first thoughts upon the matter were, I must admit, what utter tedium. But Reverend Cumberland soon impressed upon me the very serious nature of such an enterprise. It is extraordinary, all these clergymen writing plays – you must be delighted.

Garrick I'm ecstatic.

Lady Kingston And it keeps them away from religion, which has led to so much trouble in the past. I'm so keen to get involved, Mr Garrick. The Reverend Cumberland has written a new weeping comedy called . . .

Cumberland *The Fashionable Lover.*

Lady Kingston *The Fashionable Lover.*

Cumberland It has no jokes in it.

Garrick Yes, I know. Reverend Cumberland kindly sent it me.

Lady Kingston This is what's so wonderful about what's happening in the theatre at the moment. There's a real sense of purpose.

Cumberland While weeping comedy has gained considerable ground on our stages, elevating tears above humour, it can go further. What is laughter but the wilful enjoyment of the misfortunes of others? Laughter divides us. Tears draw us together.

Lady Kingston I take culture very seriously. It is one field in which a woman may exert an influence and in so doing restore a reputation somewhat sullied by incessant gambling. The present Royals are sticklers for reputation. Do make use of me.

Garrick The theatre is always grateful of a presence such as yours, Lady Kingston.

Lady Kingston Mr Garrick, through a spotless reputation you've raised your profession to respectability. It has seen you admitted to the greatest houses in the land.

Garrick I have been most fortunate . . .

Lady Kingston You have. You must bring yourself and Mrs Garrick to Chatham. There's very good shooting.

Garrick I'm overwhelmingly flattered, ma'am.

Lady Kingston There's a revolution taking place in our country concerning polite behaviour. We can't just carry on as we did in the past. Table manners were appalling. My father-in-law once consumed half a pig and he didn't use cutlery.

Garrick Your Grace.

Cumberland I expect I'll be hearing news of my play shortly?

Garrick Drury Lane does produce one new play each season, Your Grace. We produced the Reverend's *The West Indian* two seasons past. It enjoyed considerable success.

Lady Kingston Excellent, Mr Garrick. Can I ask one more favour? A recitation?

Garrick Your Grace.

Garrick poses. He does an extract from Macbeth.
*A stunning alteration. A very physical performance of a
death scene.*

Before my body
I throw my warlike shield: lay on Macduff,
And damn'd be him that first cries hold enough!
'Tis done! The scene of life will quickly close.
Ambition's vain, delusive dreams are fled.
And now I wake to darkness, guilt and horror.
I cannot bear it! Let me shake it off.
Twa' not be; my soul is clogged with blood,
I cannot rise! I dare not ask for mercy.
It is too late, hell drags me down. I sink,
I sink . . . oh! . . . my soul is lost for ever! . . . Oh!

He dies.
  A pause. Lady Kingston is moved.

Lady Kingston And you wrote that yourself, Mr Garrick.
Marvellous.

Garrick A small addition to the original.

Cumberland Providing a welcome sense of moral
repentance.

Lady Kingston And the writhing is most affecting. Good day.

*She exits, followed by Cumberland. Garrick is still a
moment – to ensure that they have gone – then he
appears to double up in pain. Mrs Garrick rushes out of
the cupboard.*

Mrs Garrick You would do that one!

*She takes some smelling salts out of the bag at her waist
and gives them to Garrick.*

Did they even mention if there's a part for you in it?

She opens a drawer in his desk, takes out some medicine and spoons some out for him. He takes it.

Garrick Chatham, Mrs Garrick. Forty-six bedrooms and three French chefs. She owns Surrey.

Mrs Garrick Open up, Mr Garrick. (*She gives him more medicine. She then puts it away.*) I'm very glad we're retiring.

Garrick I've still a season to go, Mrs Garrick, don't rush me. His plays would be nothing much if we didn't spruce them up a bit.

A knock at the door.

Mrs Garrick But I expect there'll be a part for Sam in it.

They quickly put away medicine. Garrick composes himself. Mrs Garrick disappears.

Garrick Come in.

Sam Cautherley enters.

Cautherley Mr Garrick.

Garrick springs into action.

Garrick Mr Cautherley. (*He shakes his hand.*) You appear to have grown a few inches since the last time we met.

Cautherley I may have, sir.

Garrick Welcome home.

Cautherley Thank you, sir.

Garrick So you've seen a few great cities on your trip?

Cautherley Yes, sir.

Garrick What did you think to them?

Cautherley I liked them.

Garrick Rome, Vienna, Paris. Quite something for a young man.

Cautherley Yes, and I'd like to take this opportunity of thanking you, sir.

Garrick Well, a young gentleman isn't a gentleman these days unless he's been on his tour. Show me something, Mr Cautherley.

Cautherley I beg your pardon?

Garrick You must have seen something of interest?

Cautherley I bought you some artistic reproductions of the major sights.

Garrick No, no, no. I meant something particular you've observed. Actors are great observers of life, Mr Cautherley.

Cautherley I see. There were things I noted.

Garrick I should hope so – you've been gone a year.

Cautherley The cry of the fishwives at Dover. It sounded like one long wail. (*He demonstrates.*) Apparently they're saying, 'Half a pound of mussels straight out the pond.'

Garrick That's not the kind of thing I meant at all. If you're going to become an actor, I doubt you'll be playing a fishwife.

Cautherley An actor?

Garrick Not unless you're very disappointing. Think again, Mr Cautherley. Didn't you see anything useful?

Cautherley I did observe in Paris, among the gentlemen, that one glove only is removed and laid transversely across the knee, like so. (*He demonstrates.*)

Garrick Excellent, excellent. Mrs Garrick will be delighted.

Mrs Garrick enters from secret room.

Mrs Garrick Sam. (*She embraces him.*)

Cautherley Mrs Garrick!

Garrick My wife has spent twenty-four years eavesdropping in the interests of the English theatre. I'm sure you won't hold it against her.

Mrs Garrick It was all in a good cause.

Garrick Show her that thing with the glove.

Sam demonstrates.

Good, isn't it?

Mrs Garrick (*to Sam*) Wonderful. Because, you know, he's not as strong as he used to be.

Garrick Now, Mrs Garrick.

Mrs Garrick It's true, Davy. (*to Sam*) He suffers with the stone and I'm up all night with him and it takes ages to pass one. Little rocks. Awful.

Garrick Does he really have to know all this, Eva?

Mrs Garrick gets one of the rocks out from her handkerchief in her bag. She hands it to Cautherley . . .

Mrs Garrick Look. Really it is a rock.

. . . who can hardly bear to hold it but manages through politeness.

Cautherley Ah, yes.

Garrick No, no, no. (*Garrick retrieves the stone and gives it back to Mrs Garrick.*) Put it away, Eva.

Mrs Garrick (*to Sam*) Bent double. That is why it's so good you've come. To take some of the weight off his shoulders.

Garrick You're jumping the gun, Mrs Garrick. Now we've always said you had the makings of an actor. That's why I gave you lessons in the school holidays.

Cautherley I wish I was able to express my gratitude for the interest you've always taken in my welfare.

Garrick We were happy to do so, Sam. We had no children of our own.

Mrs Garrick You know the theatre is now a respectable profession for a gentleman.

Cautherley Yes, I know.

Mrs Garrick And it wasn't like that when we started out. It was a rake's paradise. Men would jump on stage and ravage a cleavage. Davy put a stop to that.

Garrick It spoiled the dramatic illusion. I've nothing against cleavages *per se*.

Mrs Garrick People aren't afraid to bring their daughters now. And daughters have as much right to a night out as anyone.

Garrick And then we sell more tickets. You see, the ladies will like you.

Cautherley Well, I don't know.

Garrick Don't be modest, Sam, they like a pretty face.

Mrs Garrick And a handsome figure.

Garrick You see, he's got the eyes. If it's one thing I had from nature it was the eyes.

Cautherley I just can't see myself being an actor, sir.

Pause.

Garrick Why not?

Cautherley I just can't see it, sir.

Garrick It's a profession that can bring great rewards.

Mrs Garrick Mr Garrick came from nothing. Look at him now.

Garrick Not quite nothing, Eva.

Mrs Garrick Soldiers. My father was an Austrian count.

Garrick (*correcting her pronunciation*) Count, Eva.

Cautherley I have been privileged to witness your genius, Mr Garrick. Your power to move and to terrify, to bring to life the greatest sentiments of the poets . . .

Garrick That's well said, Mrs Garrick.

Cautherley I could never get anywhere near that, Mr Garrick.

Garrick I've reason to believe you would be exceptional, Mr Cautherley.

    Pause.

But as you wish. (*He gets up to shake Cautherley's hand. As he does so, he pitches forward onto his desk in an attack of the stone.*)

Cautherley Mr Garrick.

Garrick (*writhing*) Good day, Mr Cautherley!

Cautherley Can't something be done?

Mrs Garrick Nothing, I'm afraid.

    Garrick does an elaborate show of it.

Cautherley Mr Garrick, I had no idea. Of course, if you think I have the potential to be an actor, then I will give it my very best shot.

Garrick Welcome to Drury Lane, sir.

    They shake hands.

Mrs Garrick I'll show you out, Sam.

Garrick (*calls*) We open Monday week!

    Mrs Garrick shuts the door behind Sam. Garrick as normal.

Very fine eyes.

Mrs Garrick stands as if protecting the door.

Mrs Garrick You've two more visitors, Mr Garrick. You've had quite a morning. Shall I ask them to come back tomorrow?

Garrick Who are they?

Mrs Garrick Dr Johnson and the other one. A writer. I think there's something moving in his wig.

Garrick I can't turn away Dr Johnson, we would never hear the end of it.

She shows them in.

Mrs Garrick I have something for you, Doctor.

Johnson Ma'am.

She leaves. Garrick poses himself holding a wooden box which he has on his desk.

Garrick Dr Johnson. Dr Goldsmith. What an unexpected pleasure.

Johnson Davy. We come to see you on an urgent matter.

Goldsmith My p–play. *She Stoops to Conquer, or The Mistakes of a Night.*

Johnson Dr Goldsmith is very poor and no one will put on his play so we have brought it to you.

Garrick That was very good of you.

Goldsmith Last week I ate my candle.

Garrick Is that the sort of thing that goes on in your play?

Goldsmith No, that wouldn't b–be funny.

Garrick Oh, I don't know.

Johnson Give him the play, Goldy.

Goldsmith does so.

Goldsmith The address of my lodgings is on the front.

Johnson Dr Goldsmith is a man of considerable talent although to look at him he appears something lunatic.

Goldsmith Thank you. I am horrible. I am forced into hack work; writing the *Animated History of Nature* in twenty-seven volumes. Did you know b–by the b–by that the great B–British Diving B-Beetle may b–be categorised as b–both a fish and a b–beetle. I'm forty-five. I remain a virgin. My great knowledge of its flora and fauna has failed to impress the women of B–Britain. My face continues to appal me. I have an eye disgustingly severe and a b–big wig. I by no means wish any of this to influence your decision on my play.

Garrick No, that would be unprofessional.

Johnson As you can see, Goldy's case is pressing. His play must go on as soon as possible.

Garrick Mr Colman has been considering it for Covent Garden I believe. What reasons does he give for hesitating?

Goldsmith He says it is low.

Garrick Is it?

Goldsmith It is funny, Mr Garrick. That, upon occasion, requires a little lowness!

Johnson You must explain the play a little, Goldy. Whet Davy's appetite for the thing. You must not be always twitching and shouting.

Goldsmith Very well. The hero Marlow is an idiot based on myself. He mistakenly believes he is staying at an inn and not the house of his father's oldest friend. There he tries to have his way with a barmaid.

Garrick Good Lord!

Goldsmith Don't worry – she's really the daughter of the house disguised as a barmaid.

Garrick That's worse, isn't it?

Goldsmith Marlow can't be honest with women of his own station – the curse of the middling sort – that is why Kate disguises herself – she stoops to conquer. Oh, and then there's Tony Lumpkin – the son. A wild, mischievous creature who really is . . . with a barmaid!

Garrick I'm not surprised at Colman's hesitation, Doctor. This play sounds as inflammatory as the last one. An audience likes to see moral flaws punished, not laughed at.

Goldsmith What's left. Tame stuff. It doesn't do the job that comedy does to p–point out our p–pomposity and hyp–pocrisy. It's sentimental bollocks! Good Lord – I'm the worst of the lot. I've fine clothes I can't afford – affectations of being a great writer when I've hardly tuppence to rub together. I see them whisper about me . . . my tight trousers and my monkey face. If I didn't laugh at myself . . . I'd be a madman.

Johnson Well said, Goldy.

Garrick I thought you'd grown disenchanted with the theatre, sir.

Johnson I have. I had hopes of it once, but they all came to nothing.

Garrick You are severe.

Johnson I have come enough, sir, to know that I had best keep away.

Garrick One wonders why you seek to promote your friend here.

Johnson Because he is my friend, sir. We come to you, Davy, because you've had a deal of success and can afford to be generous.

Garrick Thank you, I do credit myself with some modest success.

Johnson You are an actor, sir, let us remember. We may pass a pleasant half-hour with Mr Punch, but to reward him with a town house, another in the country and all with fine furniture beggars belief. There are others engaged in serious work who can barely scratch up a supper.

Garrick You must know, Dr Goldsmith, that Dr Johnson was once my schoolmaster and he has never quite lost that way with me. Let me run a few figures past you. Drury Lane. Twelve boxes, five shillings each. Pit, four hundred and fifty seats. Prices range from three shillings to two shillings six pence. Upper Gallery, two hundred and fifty seats. A shilling each. A full house may make in revenue three hundred and seventy-five pounds a night. Now bear in mind that Drury Lane employs over one hundred and eighty musicians, stagehands, actors. On top of that there is the general cost of running a building. There are invisible costs – we are suffering litigation as I speak from a young lady who was struck on the head by a lump of hard cheese dropped on her from the upper gallery. Profit margins are slimmer than might first appear. If a play gets a bad smell we certainly feel the pinch. Two in a row and we court disaster. And there are those, sir, who as in the past, would not shed a tear to see us go. I have a responsibility to my theatre, Dr Goldsmith. I can't just put a play on because a man is poor. I hope I may still be counted your friend, sirs.

Johnson We never see you, Davy. You do not come into a room but you have an excuse to get out of it.

Garrick You may say so, sir, but I am kept out of your club.

Johnson I doubt your wife would give you permission to come.

Garrick I can only hope my absence has been of some comfort to you.

Johnson On the contrary. You are a lively fellow, Davy, the first in the world for sprightly conversation. I regret that our paths have crossed so infrequently of late, for you might help alleviate my melancholy. There is scarcely a day I do not rise with it in the morning and take it to bed at night. A dismal dread of death.

Garrick I am sorry to hear it.

Johnson It is a shame we cannot see eye to eye on Goldy's play. I should have liked for us to be reconciled and that might have been the means to do it. See, an invitation. You were to have joined us at our club next week.

Garrick But I have always been kept out.

Johnson We had no reason before, sir, but now we are furnished with one.

Goldsmith Perhaps I could read a little of my play? Act Three. Kate disguised and Marlow. (*He reads.*) What a b–b–bawling in every p–part of the house, I have scarce a moment rep–pose. If I go to the b–b–best room –

Johnson We must read it, Goldy, or we will be here for eternity. (*Johnson reads.*) I go to the best room, there I find my host with his story. If I fly to the gallery, there we have my hostess with her curtsey down to the ground. I have at last got a moment to myself and now for recollection.

Garrick Did you call, sir? Did your honour call?

Johnson As for Miss Hardcastle, she's too grave and sentimental for me.

Garrick Did your honour call?

Johnson No, child. Besides, from the glimpse I had of her I think she squints.

Garrick I'm sure, sir, I heard the bell ring.

Johnson No, no. I have pleased my father, however, by coming down tomorrow I shall please myself by returning.

Garrick Perhaps the other gentlemen called, sir.

Johnson I tell you no.

Garrick I should be glad to know, sir; we have such a parcel of servants.

Johnson No, no, I tell you. Yes, child, I think I did call. I wanted . . . I wanted – I vow, child, you are vastly handsome.

Garrick Oh la, sir, you make one asham'd.

Johnson I never saw a more malicious eye. Yes, yes, my dear, I did call. Have you got any of your – a – what-do-you-call-it in the house?

Garrick No, sir, we have been out of that these ten days.

Johnson laughs.

Johnson You must not make me laugh, Davy, for I cannot continue if you do.

Garrick To see you laugh is a good thing, Doctor.

Johnson It is a creditable comedy, is it not, Davy?

Goldsmith (*to Garrick*) You would be fantastic in it.

Garrick May I take the invitation, sir?

Johnson gives it to him.

Goldsmith Does that mean you will do my p–play?

Johnson It is not fair to ask so direct, Goldy. Anyway, Davy must get his wife's permission.

Garrick No, sir, I make up my own mind. We may have had our differences but if *She Stoops to Conquer* continues to delight, you may be in luck, Dr Goldsmith.

Goldsmith (*gives a whoop*) I shall holla like a speaking trumpet!

Mrs Garrick Here, Doctor. A pudding. I supervised it myself.

Johnson A delectable meaty confection, ma'am. It shall glorify my table.

They exit. Mrs Garrick enters. She picks up play.

Mrs Garrick (*reads*) *She Stoops To Conquer or The Mistakes of a Night.* Did you tell them you had committed to Mr Cumberland's play?

Garrick suddenly folds up with pain.

(*sharply*) Davy!

He straightens up immediately.

Mrs Garrick You can't do them both.

Garrick No.

SCENE THREE

Johnson Playreading: An attempt by the artistic management of a theatre to avoid the responsibility of office. A low word.

The actors. Garrick and Goldsmith. Drury Lane stage.

Garrick (*concluding*) Tomorrow we shall gather all the poor of the parish about us, and the mistakes of the night shall be crown'd with a merry morning; so, boy, take her, and as you have been mistaken in the mistress, my wish is, that you may never be mistaken in the wife.

Actors politely applaud.

Goldsmith Thank you for your indulgence in allowing me not to read my p–p–play to you. Mr Garrick was uniformly excellent. Also I have to say the p–p–play is very good.

Garrick You are quite clear, Doctor, as to our purpose here today?

Goldsmith P–perfectly.

Garrick I am in the fortunate position of having to choose between two excellent plays. Reading each will assist me in my decision.

Goldsmith I'm sure you'll like mine the b–best.

Garrick Let me show you out, Doctor.

They exit.

Mrs Cibber Has he gone? I make the speech. Dear manager, dear, dear Garrick. And so on. Then we hand him the gloves. Who's got the gloves?

All You have.

Mrs Butler Nobody else got a look in.

Mrs Cibber And then he reads the card. Perhaps you would read it for now, Mr Cautherley.

Cautherley Shakespeare's gloves.

Macklin That's be the twelfth pair I've seen.

Mrs Butler He had a lot of gloves.

Mrs Cibber Your voice has an excellent timbre, Mr Cautherley.

Mrs Barry Yes, it has.

Cautherley Thank you.

Macklin Playreading. What a time-wasting shenanigan. (*He pulls out bottle and swigs.*)

Mrs Cibber I was under the impression that you were no longer fond of alcohol, Mr Macklin.

Macklin You were ill informed, Mrs Cibber.

Mrs Butler In all honesty I should put that in the book, Mr Macklin.

Macklin Stuff the book.

Mrs Butler Mr Garrick welcomed you back, Mr Macklin. Is this gratitude?

Mrs Cibber I'm just a little concerned that if we persist in not hitting it off it will communicate itself in that subtle way it does to an audience. If you'd wash, it might help.

Macklin Lonely men don't wash.

Mrs Cibber That's why they're lonely. It's a vicious circle. Smelly: lonely – lonely: smelly.

Macklin I am astounded afresh by your ability to see nothing whatsoever, Mrs Cibber. Garrick knows full well which play he wants. This is a political exercise to appease the loser!

Cautherley Mr Garrick is an honourable man. I am sure he will choose the best play.

Macklin So, Mr Cautherley, you're an actor.

Cautherley Yes, sir, I hope to be.

Macklin Garrick has embraced you. You must have something.

Barry Yes, he has my parts. I am juve lead male and this is my wife. Mrs Barry and I are a package.

Mrs Barry Oh, I don't mind doing it with someone different for a change.

Barry Lavinia!

Mrs Barry Audiences don't like seeing husbands and wives play together. They know we only row really.

Barry No we don't!

Macklin (*to Cautherley*) So you are to follow in the master's footsteps?

Cautherley I hope to, sir.

Macklin The thing you ought to know, Mr Cautherley, is that once upon a time Garrick was the newest thing that had ever been seen. I'll give him that. But, and this is a little known fact, there was another before him and it was he who invented the whole new style. He who really fired the dart that fatally struck the past. And do you know who he was?

Cautherley No, sir.

Macklin No, nobody does, and that is why I like a drink.

Cautherley You mean it was you.

Macklin Sharp as a whistle, Mr Cautherley.

Mrs Butler 1737.

Macklin My Shylock.

Barry You can be sure, not a day goes past but we have his Shylock.

Macklin But rarely on stage, ma'am, that is the point.

Mrs Butler Anyway, the damp's got your gaberdine.

Barry Mr Garrick will not choose Dr Goldsmith's play, it is too low.

Cautherley Low?

Barry It mocks gentility. All the characters live in the country.

Mrs Barry Someone has to live in the country, Mr Barry, else we'd never get any eggs.

Barry There must be other ways of getting eggs, Lavinia.

Macklin No, they must always come out of a chicken's arse.

Cautherley I often find plays rather tedious but I enjoyed this one.

Mrs Cibber I don't want to dampen your enthusiasm, Mr Cautherley, but I have similar concerns to Mr Barry. I prefer to play characters of spotless virtue, and in this way I avoid drawing attention to my unusual domestic arrangements.

Mrs Barry It was her misfortune to have two husbands simultaneously.

Mrs Cibber My first husband was deeply inconsiderate.

Mrs Butler He sold her to a gentleman for a night

Mrs Cibber He then fell in love with me and my first husband wouldn't leave me.

Mrs Barry So she had two.

Mrs Cibber Mrs Hardcastle is common and uncouth and she falls in a pond.

Mrs Barry I'm sure I would do either play, although Kate Hardcastle does get to kiss.

Barry Kate Hardcastle is a trollop.

Mrs Barry Can't you stick to your own part?

Mrs Butler Now you are poor seconds to Mr Cautherley, that's Lumpkin.

Cautherley Lumpkin is a mischief-maker but it's hard not to like him.

Barry Perhaps you're not a gentleman, sir, and so shouldn't mind playing him.

Mrs Cibber Mr Barry!

Barry I only know that he has come and taken my parts!

Cautherley I am quite content to give an account of myself, sir.

Mrs Cibber That will not be necessary.

Cautherley Mr Garrick acts as my guardian. I was found on the steps of this theatre. With a note pinned to me reading 'Gentleman'.

Barry I could pin a note to myself saying 'King of Sweden'.

Macklin Try actor first, sir.

Barry Ditto, sir.

Macklin Pup!

Mrs Butler Where's your company spirit, Mr Macklin?

Macklin In my bottle. (*Macklin advances.*)

Barry Stop him, Mrs Butler. He'll soon be in a state of advanced inebriation.

Mrs Barry Run, darling!

Mrs Butler Mr Macklin! This is definitely going in the book!

A general tussle to remove Macklin from Barry. Enter Garrick and Cumberland.

Mrs Butler Mr Garrick.

Actors part.

Garrick May I introduce you to the Reverend Richard Cumberland? The author of *The Fashionable Lover.*

Cumberland surveys the unseemly spectacle.

Cumberland Hello.

All Hello.

Cumberland Would you like me to describe the fountain of my inspiration?

Garrick Better not. Let's start. (*He signals to each actor in turn.*) Mrs Barry would play Augusta Aubrey. A young beautiful orphan. Mrs Cibber, Mrs Macintosh. A bitter, fading middle-aged woman of thirty-five or so.

Macklin No acting necessary.

Garrick Mr Macklin, Hamish Macleod. A Scottish gentleman. Mr Cautherley, Charles Millwood. A good young gentleman. Mr Barry, Lord Aberville. A rake who reforms. I should play Uncle Mortimer. A benign soul.

Mrs Cibber It seems a very uplifting sort of play with such a lot of good gentlemen in it. I appear to be the only unreformed character.

Cumberland And you are not on long.

Mrs Cibber Ah . . .

Garrick Reverend Cumberland has kindly agreed to give us a brief résumé of his play before he reads it.

Cumberland The hero, Charles Millwood, returns to London from his plantation on the Island of Tobago. He is a good-natured young gentleman and in the bustle of the dockside he inadvertently sets about one of the porters with his cane. Not used to such treatment the fellow pushes Charles into the water. He is pulled . . .

A buzzing sound (*Macklin*).

Garrick Let me explain, Mr Cumberland. We have developed a system over time where, if an actor feels there is a point to be raised during a reading, they make a small noise to alert the company's attention to the problem. I feel it is too early in the process for that, Macklin.

Macklin I was merely going to enquire whether Charles loses any clothes during his mishap?

Cumberland Ah, I hadn't thought.

Macklin For example, if he lost his breeches we could be in a very sensitive situation.

Garrick No one is suggesting for a moment that he loses his breeches.

Macklin Because you can't have an arse on stage, Mr Garrick.

Garrick No, but I have often been blessed with them in my company.

Cumberland Charles soon discovers the terrible truth of the loss of his papers from his breeches pocket. He breaks down in tears. The papers had been proof that Augusta Aubrey, the young woman he had never seen but had fallen in love with by correspondence, was really a wealthy heiress. Charles's Uncle Mortimer had always refused permission for him to marry Augusta because she was poor, and she submitted.

Buzz (Mrs Barry).

Mrs Barry Why would she do that?

Garrick Because she is essentially good, Mrs Barry.

Barry That will take a deal of explaining to you, so I suggest we avoid it at present.

Mrs Barry Apologise, Mr Barry.

Barry When you apologise to me for your behaviour last night.

Mrs Barry Your second entrance was entirely designed to upstage me.

Barry I was trying to refocus the performance.

Mrs Butler It's all in the book, Mr Garrick.

Barry She was too busy curtseying to some oaf in a box.

Mrs Barry It's my right to make new friends.

Macklin She's got a lot of them out there, Mr Barry.

Barry You were practically falling out of your dress.

Mrs Barry Oh!

Mrs Barry storms out.

Barry Lavinia!

Pause.

Garrick Please continue, Reverend.

Cumberland Hurrying to his uncle's house, Charles comes across the path of the most beautiful woman he has ever seen, whom he desires to –

Buzz (Macklin).

– get to know better.

Garrick Mr Macklin.

Macklin Sorry, Mr Garrick.

Cumberland Unknown to him, she and his cousin Augusta are one and the same person.

Mrs Butler I knew that.

Cumberland Now he is on the horns of a dilemma. Should he tell his uncle the truth about the papers he had concealed about his private . . .

Buzz (Mackin and Cautherley).

. . . down his trousers . . .

Buzz.

Garrick Can we restrain ourselves?

Cumberland . . . in his pocket. Or should he forget them and be free to propose to the unknown woman he wishes to . . .

Buzz.

Marry.

Garrick Mr Macklin.

Cumberland These constant interruptions, Mr Garrick.

Garrick I do apologise.

Cumberland You don't get them in church.

Mrs Cibber (*refers to Macklin*) He has been drinking.

Garrick Just put a cork in it, Macklin.

Cumberland Mr Garrick, I wish to withdraw my play.

Garrick From Drury Lane?

Cumberland No, from the actors. I feel you alone are the person qualified to make a decision on the future of my work. I wish to cast no aspersions on the present company, but actors are generally a pleasanter experience when viewed from a distance. Good day. (*He exits.*)

Macklin And bog off.

Garrick in some physical discomfort.

Garrick (*to the company*) I have always considered actors troublesome creatures and today you have gone further, if that is possible, in consolidating that opinion. Good day. Mr Macklin, I shall be reconsidering my appearance in your benefit.

Mrs Butler Never mind, Mr Garrick. No real harm done. You won't have to pay the actors for the afternoon.

Garrick Yes. Thank you, Mrs Butler.

Mrs Butler ushers out actors.

Cautherley I'm sorry, Mr Garrick. But it did seem an unlikely play.

Cautherley exits, Mrs Garrick enters.

Garrick Don't say anything.

Mrs Garrick I'm not saying anything.

Pause.

But now you're in the same position only worse. Dr Goldsmith's hopes are raised and you have offended Mr Cumberland. Lady Kingston has sent over a large cheese and a crate of claret.

Garrick Dr Goldsmith has influential friends of a different sort.

Mrs Garrick It's the great roles people want to see. You should be saving your strength for them. And the good thing about Shakespeare is he's dead, we don't have to pay him.

Garrick You have a new play in the repertoire otherwise writers attack you! Shakespeare was a new writer once.

Mrs Garrick Of course. But you must think practically. Dr Goldsmith's play is low. You don't want to be selling the patent for a theatre that has been torn apart by riots.

Garrick Goldsmith is a man of some genius.

Mrs Garrick Not as a playwright, looking at his last effort.

Garrick This one seems rather better than Cumberland's play.

Mrs Garrick But people like his sort of thing.

Garrick They did . . . the fashion for sentiment seems to be cooling a little. That's the trouble with getting older – you get less decisive.

Mrs Garrick Mr Garrick. The brochures are printed on Tuesday.

She exits. Hannah More enters, unseen.

Hannah Mr Garrick. We've met before. I was fourteen. I'd been taken to see *Hamlet*. I fainted. I was carried into your office. You were kind enough to enquire after me.

Garrick My dear young lady . . .

Hannah Then I read in a newspaper that this was rumoured to be your last season. And I had to come and tell you.

Garrick Tell me?

Hannah Of my extreme admiration. I am a writer.

Garrick Of plays?

Hannah Yes.

Garrick I'm not in a position to put on your play, madam, I won't even read it.

Hannah Mr Garrick . . .

Garrick I may never read another play as long as I live. Good day.

Hannah You mistake me, I would never try to influence a decision of yours. You are a great artist and the greatest man I've ever met. May I ask you to sign my bookmark, which I shall treasure with all my heart?

Garrick Very well. (*He signs it.*)

Hannah I have watched you many times and been moved to emotions I have never experienced.

Garrick But you know you must make an appointment next time.

Hannah This will be the brightest day of my life.

Garrick Oh dear. Have you come far?

Hannah Harrow. I walked. I couldn't afford a coach. I'm a schoolteacher. Today I claimed a cough and set off.

He gives her the bookmark.

Thank you. Your eyes, Mr Garrick, are the most piercing I have ever seen. And the kindest and most intelligent. And the most beautiful, I think.

Garrick Well, they are two balls side by side. So do you come to the theatre often?

Hannah I spend half my wages. I don't eat breakfasts. I have seen you play every part in your repertoire. I enjoyed you in Mr Kelly's *False Delicacy* and also *The Foundling* and *Wonder of Wonders*. But Lear is your greatest.

Garrick You seem very passionate about the theatre. Miss . . .?

Hannah More.

Garrick Perhaps if you leave your play with me, I may offer you some advice.

She gets to her knees.

Hannah I'm overcome with gratitude, dear Mr Garrick.

Garrick What are you doing?

Hannah Kneeling. Because to me everything that is beautiful in the world is before me now.

Garrick I repeat, I cannot offer you a production.

Hannah Just to breathe the same air.

Mrs Garrick enters.

Garrick This is my wife, Eva. Eva, Miss More.

Mrs Garrick We can always do with help. How are you with stuffing, Miss More?

SCENE FOUR: ROMANTIC COMEDY

Hannah alone in Garrick's office, tidying up files. Cautherley enters. Hannah looks up.

Hannah Can I help you?

Cautherley I came to see Mr Garrick.

Hannah Do take a seat.

Cautherley Will he be long?

Hannah I should expect so. There's a considerable amount of organising to do. Mr Garrick keeps everything. A copy of all his correspondence, of which he receives copious amounts. I hope you don't mind if I carry on. (*She continues to sort his files.*) Perhaps there's something I can help you with, Mr . . . ?

Cautherley Cautherley. No, no. It was Mr Garrick I particularly wanted to see.

She regards him.

It's about a part, Miss . . . ?

Hannah More. I am a writer. My best-known work is *The Trials of Percy*.

Cautherley Percy who?

Hannah Lord Percy.

Cautherley It sounds good.

Pause.

This part. I hope to persuade Mr Garrick to let me play it. I think I'd be rather good.

Hannah That's for others to say, I suspect.

Cautherley I don't mean to sound boastful. I'm just rather relieved. I owe Mr Garrick a great debt. I am his protégé.

Hannah You are?

Cautherley Yes. Mr Garrick has always looked after me.

Hannah You are very fortunate, Mr Cautherley, to have had Mr Garrick as a guardian. I was under the guardianship of teachers of religious instruction.

Cautherley You seem to have turned out all right.

Hannah What do you mean?

Cautherley You seem to have turned out . . . nice.

Beat.

Hannah Oh. Here's a letter you sent. (*She reads.*) Dear Mr Garrick. School is dull. I am not very happy. You've spelt it 'hoppy'.

Cautherley I'm not a good speller.

Hannah I was reading at the age of two. (*reading on*) One boy at school his name is Jeffries; I am to clean his shoes every morning before breakfast because his father is Lord Jeffries. Love, Sam. I don't read them as a rule. Mr Garrick is very exercised about which play he should put on. Which play do you prefer, Mr Cautherley?

Cautherley Dr Goldsmith's. It is a play in very good spirits.

Hannah To you, perhaps. But for middling people like myself it offends deeply. Mischief is rewarded and deception goes unpunished.

Cautherley But it's funny.

Hannah That is not a sufficient argument that justifies cruel and selfish behaviour. I'm sure Mr Garrick will refuse it.

Cautherley Mr Garrick used to say comedy is a spirit. Have you ever been for a walk in the countryside, Miss More?

Hannah Alone, Mr Cautherley?

Cautherley Perfectly alone.

Hannah Only once and I shouldn't have.

Cautherley Well, imagine that you're there now. It's a sunny day and suddenly you step off the path and find yourself in the shade of a wood. All the sounds are different. And you stop and you stare at a tangle of dark leaves and you can't be sure there isn't something there and it's not a bird and it's not a dog but you're sure there is something and the thought pleases you and it sends a shudder down your back. It's something old, something that won't do as you bid it. And do you know what it's doing?

Hannah No.

Cautherley It's laughing at the fool you're making of yourself staring at the bush.

Hannah slaps him.

Cautherley That's the spirit of comedy. It always tricks people into revealing themselves.

Hannah I'm sorry, Mr Cautherley, I shouldn't have struck you.

She kisses him. Garrick enters.

Hannah Your handwriting is very French, Mr Garrick.

Garrick Is it?

Hannah It has a natural curling elegance. (*She exits.*)

Cautherley I was wondering if I could have a word, sir.

Garrick Certainly, Sam.

Cautherley Mr Garrick, I've fallen in love.

Garrick Aaah . . .

Cautherley With a part. I wasn't sure I was an actor, sir, but this is a good sign, I think. I want to play Tony Lumpkin.

Garrick Lumpkin! But you are a natural Marlow, Sam. A young gentleman.

Cautherley But the actor who plays Lumpkin, sir, will have a lot of fun. He's always drinking and singing down the Three Pigeons. I hope you will indulge me.

Garrick Lumpkin is a different matter altogether, sir.

Cautherley You once played such parts,sir.

Garrick Not any more, Sam.

Cautherley Father-in-law has been calling me a whelp, and hound this half year. Now if I pleased I could be so revenged upon the old grumbletonian. But then I'm afraid – afraid of what? I shall soon be worth fifteen hundred a year, and let him frighten me out of that if he can.

Garrick Good, Sam. Yes. Yes. You've caught the spirit of it.

Mrs Garrick enters.

Sam was just expressing a preference for a certain part, Mrs Garrick.

Mrs Garrick So I heard. Actors can't choose their parts, Sam – if they did there'd be no one to play the messengers.

Garrick He has instinct.

Mrs Garrick Sam?

Garrick I had that. It makes all the difference . . .

Mrs Garrick I was an artist too, Sam, a dancer in the best theatres in Europe. It wouldn't have been proper for me to continue when I married Mr Garrick. There are considerations other than instinct. A dog has instinct.

Garrick Sam, would you mind?

Cautherley Mr Garrick, Mrs Garrick.

Sam exits.

Mrs Garrick Reverend Cumberland's play has no hint of impropriety.

Garrick He wouldn't know impropriety if it crawled up his cassock.

Mrs Garrick You can laugh, Mr Garrick, but you know how cruel scandal can be. People in scandals lose everything.

Garrick There's not going to be a scandal!

Mrs Garrick Good, because we'll retire soon. Then what would we do with ourselves?

Garrick Retired people get busier.

Mrs Garrick Not if they're being ignored. We'd just be staring at each other over the dining-room table. You've taken that boy from nowhere. He's your protégé. Do you want people to take him for a Lumpkin? If they see him in a low part, they'll ask why have you looked after him? People like to believe the worst.

Garrick I do have some responsibility to art.

Mrs Garrick You are the artist, Mr Garrick. Don't throw it all away in the end. Your reputation. Everything you deserve.

She exits. Contemplatively: Garrick goes over to a skip and pulls out a tobacconist's apron. He puts it on. He dresses himself as Abel Drugger.

SCENE FIVE: VERFREMDSDUNGSEFFEKT

Flashback. The rest of the company gathers. The cast of The Alchemist.

Macklin Where is Garrick?

Garrick Here, sir.

Macklin You have been with us . . .

Garrick Three days.

Macklin You are determined to follow the course upon which you have set yourself?

Garrick Yes, sir. But if I may be allowed to explain once more, Mr Macklin.

Macklin That will not be necessary.

Cross I have not had instructions from Mr Fleetwood . . .

Macklin I am manager in the absence of Fleetwood, Mr Cross. Where is Bounce?

Bounce Here, sir. Cedric Bounce. Low comedian. I was always Mr Drugger till this date, sir. But I am shifted about, sir, at Mr Garrick's convenience. He wished Mr Drugger.

Young Barry It is a low part.

O'Ryan Low indeed.

Bounce I specialise in those. My pratfalls are a joy. I inherited my father's extra-large shoes, sir, which till this day I was accustomed to wear on the wrong feet whilst playing Drugger.

Mrs Butler Shame.

Young Barry It is a shame.

Mrs Butler You see, even Master Barry thinks so.

Bounce What appliances do you favour, Mr Garrick? Buttock extensions or the comedy nose?

Garrick I favour nothing of the sort.

Bounce Nothing?

O'Ryan Nothing?

Flint It is the worst thing I ever saw.

Macklin We are in agreement with Mrs Flint. This is the matter, sir, we wish to call to your attention, sir.

Mrs Butler You have to make them laugh, otherwise they want their money back.

Woffington Mr Garrick is too tragic an actor to consider anything as unworthy as a laugh.

Macklin He prefers a good death. Show him your Drugger, Mr Bounce.

O'Ryan Oblige us, sir.

Bounce Surely, I pull a long face so. Hanging lip, you see. With my hair disarranged I look a regular booby. I come in. I fall over. I shake hands with the fire irons.

Mrs Butler Oh, it is priceless.

Macklin How shall you do it, Garrick?

Garrick I shall do as it says in the script: 'Enter'.

Macklin You must not let us down, Garrick.

Flint Coins.

Macklin If a play is shouted off, we actors are out of pocket.

Garrick Nowhere in the play does Ben Jonson indicate that Mr Drugger is a cretin. He is a tobacconist and that is how I shall play him.

Bounce It'll never work, Mr Garrick.

Mrs Butler I won't be able to look.

Barry I will look, for it is a very bad thing to take another man's part.

Macklin Mr Garrick, sir, remove your apron.

Cross I must protest, Mr Macklin.

Macklin I elect Mr Bounce to be Mr Drugger.

Garrick My name is on the flyers.

Mrs Butler He once killed a man in a mix-up over a wig.

O'Ryan Straight through the eye with a stick.

Macklin I am not to be lightly crossed.

Garrick It is curtain up in five minutes, Mr Macklin, and I shall be making an entrance.

Macklin Very well. We shall have to use force.

Flint Hit him!

Garrick I am ready for you.

Cross Mr Macklin, this is highly irregular.

Macklin Stick to writing your show reports, Mr Cross. Mrs Woffington.

Mrs Woffington takes out a pistol. Uproar from company.

Garrick Good Lord.

Macklin Play Drugger in the time-honoured way or Bounce takes your place.

Garrick Very well.

Macklin Mr Bounce, give him your shoes.

Gives them to Garrick, who puts them on.

Macklin And the nose.

Mrs Butler That's better.

O'Ryan That's funny.

General laughter.

Macklin Excellent.

Flint Like Bounce. Good.

Garrick gives a big sigh.

Young Barry What's wrong with him?

Garrick sighs again.

He doesn't like his shoes. Is that it?

Garrick shrugs his shoulders.

Maybe his nose pinches?

O'Ryan He's dejected.

Macklin He's acting.

Mrs Cibber Address him as Mr Drugger and perhaps he will answer.

Mrs Butler Go on, Master Barry.

Young Barry Are you Mr Drugger? The tobacconist?

Bounce He is not Abel Drugger. For Abel is a laugh a minute.

Garrick I have a little shop.

Mrs Butler That will be the tobacco shop.

Mrs Cibber They say Garrick becomes the part he plays. As if he's possessed.

Young Barry Shall we stick him with a pin?

Cross Leave him, Master Barry.

Garrick I sell pins. I go to see a man about my shop. I am an honest working man. I am not the quickest man in my street but I am honest and straightforward. Perhaps people will hoodwink me, but so be it. I live by principles and also by tobacco.

Macklin Enough of this.

Garrick I seek to know, sir, by alchemy, where to put my shelves and my boxes. And also my pots.

Flint It's not right.

Woffington We know you are an actor, sir, and so are we.

Garrick Very well. Must I go forth with these things on me?

Macklin You must.

Mrs Butler Oh dear. They don't look funny any more. They look sad.

Barry I think I may burst into tears.

Bounce They was always funny on me.

Mrs Butler That is because you are an idiot.

Cross Two minutes to curtain.

Garrick takes off the nose.

Macklin The nose, Mr Garrick.

Garrick does nothing.

Garrick Mr Macklin, for two years I have watched your every performance. I've learnt everything from you. You are sublime in your naturalness. You have affected a revolution!

Macklin That's true.

Garrick Your Shylock was a human being and not a comic turn.

Macklin But Drugger is a low character.

Garrick He is a working man, but we may still have sympathy with him.

O'Ryan The working man deserves sympathy.

Cross Curtain up.

Macklin What do you say, Mrs Woffington?

Woffington Working people work. Nothing would get done if they were as simple as they're made out.

Mrs Butler That's right, Mr Macklin.

Woffington Let him go on as he is. If he makes a a fool of himself he can disappear.

Macklin Well, well, perhaps we'll see how Mr Garrick does. Now you mustn't mind me, I've a temper that flares up upon occasion, that's all.

Garrick Thank you.

Cross Mr Garrick. The Prologue.

As he goes to exit, Mrs Woffington catches him.

Woffington My Rosalind was sublime in its naturalness, wanker.

Garrick Mrs Woffington. The flowers. I sent them. (*He exits.*)

Bounce Nothing beats a buttock extension.

The rest listen. We hear Garrick faintly speak the Prologue.

Garrick
I stand before you, men and women of the town . . .

Laughter.

Bounce If he is right, I have been wrong these twenty years.

SCENE SIX: POLITICAL THEATRE

Present: Mrs Cibber, Mrs Butler, Mrs Woffington, Betty Flint, Garrick, Macklin, Cross, Master Barry, Bounce, Mr O'Ryan.

Cross I call this meeting of the Drury Lane company to order. Speaker the first.

Mrs Butler Mrs Butler, dresser. I have begged Mr Fleetwood on my own behalf and that of my poor children that he should pay what he owes me but he always looks at me sadly and says it cannot be done. This has now continued for six months and if it had not been for the generosity of the actors I am sure we would all be dead. And although Mr Fleetwood says he is an honest man he is not starving as we are. I am now frightened to leave my house as it is put about that I am to be arrested for debt and thrown into a sponging house and then my poor children will starve for sure.

O'Ryan Theophilus O'Ryan, supporting actor. That is because he is a gambler.

Macklin Charles Macklin, actor. You can't hold it against a man that he gambles.

Mrs Butler Point of information. Charles Macklin and Mr Fleetwood are old friends.

Macklin Point of information. Not any more.

Mrs Butler I have nothing against gambling *per se*, but I do when it's with our wages.

All Agreed.

Flint Betty Flint, candle-tender. Newgate.

Mrs Butler The candle-tenders are in the same boat as the dressers. Some are thrown into Newgate for non-payment of debt and the rest will soon follow.

Flint Bill Williams.

Mrs Butler And Mr Bill Williams, prop-maker, has died of want, God rest his soul.

All Amen.

Flint Food.

Mrs Butler Betty Flint reminds us there was no one that made wooden food as good as he did. Mr Cross, the prompter has seen no wages since . . .

Cross Easter. But that is the business we are in, Mrs Butler.

Mrs Butler It is a bad business that will not pay its workers, Mr Cross.

Cross If it were not Mr Fleetwood, it would be someone worse.

O'Ryan Theophilus O'Ryan, supporting actor. I have personally applied to Mr Fleetwood on my own behalf and that of us all several times in recent weeks. Those being when his whereabouts were known.

Macklin His whereabouts are the Fox and Grapes on Argyll Street.

Mrs Butler Point of information. He is a bastard. I would go down to the Fox and Grapes only I don't trust myself not to beat him about the head with one of Mr Williams's wooden foodstuffs. Then my poor children would have the ignominy of seeing their mother transported. My question is this: will the actors withdraw their labour until the money that is owed us all is paid?

Macklin Charles Macklin, actor. What if we lose our jobs? Fleetwood can be a right petty bastard.

    Uproar from company.

Macklin What do you say, Garrick?

Garrick David Garrick, actor. I'm just listening, Mr Macklin. I've been with you barely a year.

Macklin You are our leading actor now, Garrick. We invite your response.

Garrick David Garrick, actor. It seems extraordinary that Mr Fleetwood should choose to treat our distinguished company in so cavalier a manner. Does he need to be reminded that he has some of the finest players in the country? Mr Macklin here began a revolution with his reinterpretation of Shylock that sent shock-waves across Europe. I have followed in his footsteps.

Mrs Butler We all enjoyed your Abel Drugger, Mr Garrick, and I for one said so at the time.

O'Ryan Mr Fleetwood cares nothing for the theatre. He throws away the money he should be spending on new costumes and scenery at the gaming table. No wonder our audiences desert us for Covent Garden.

Mrs Butler He is then forced to cut us to half-pay –

Bounce / Flint No pay, no pay.

Mrs Butler – and then to no pay whatsoever. We must demand what is owed us.

Garrick David Garrick, actor. We can do more. We can demand our own licence to play. When we have our own theatre we can pay ourselves and choose the plays we perform. When we do good work, people will respect us.

Some Hear, hear!

Woffington Peg Woffington, actor. There are only two licences and they have already been given!

Garrick The Lord Chamberlain will be told of Fleetwood's desertion. He will then grant a third.

Woffington The point of a licence is to limit the performance of plays to two theatres only. The government of this country is nervous of plays, which is why it introduced the principle of a licence in the first place. The law will not be changed on our account.

Garrick My dear Mrs Woffington, we have the moral imperative.

Woffington Point of information. David Garrick thinks he is in a play.

Mrs Butler Point of information. They're having a row.

Mrs Cibber It is strange to think that anyone would be scared of a play.

Cross Madam, please address yourself to the meeting in the correct manner.

Mrs Cibber Mrs Cibber, first singer. Sorry.

Master Barry Master Barry, child actor. And we must always be playing in pantomime 'cause it brings in the punters and I don't like the dogs in them for one bit me on the arm.

Bounce Bounce, low comedian that was. Presently stage-hand. Mr Garrick has only been in the business two minutes. What does he know?

Garrick We are in an intolerable situation. I know that, Mr Bounce.

Woffington It could be worse if we have to crawl back to Fleetwood.

Garrick Audiences don't come to see Fleetwood. I propose we refuse to play until we are granted our own theatre.

Mrs Butler Point of information. Mrs Woffington and Mr Fleetwood are very close. I'm not saying any more.

Woffington That is my business and nothing to do with this business.

Garrick We must all hope that Mrs Woffington will not let her personal interests prejudice her to the common good.

Mrs Cibber Mrs Cibber, first singer. It is indeed an honour, Mr Garrick, to hear our beleaguered profession dignified by your stirring rhetoric.

O'Ryan Theophilus O'Ryan, supporting actor. Specialising in supporting parts. I support Mr Garrick.

Woffington No wonder you put audiences to sleep, Mr O Ryan.

O'Ryan No need to get personal Mrs Woffington.

Cross Let us take it to the vote. Mr Garrick proposes we withdraw our labour until such time as a licence for an actors' theatre is granted us.

Macklin Charles Macklin, actor and revolutionary interpreter of Shylock. We did not trust Mr Garrick when he first came. To our shame we threatened him. I stood in his way then, but as his merit upon the stage is vastly superior to mine I will not stand in it now. I vote with Garrick.

Cross All in favour say 'aye'.

All (*except Woffington, Cross, Bounce*) Aye.

Cross Against.

Woffington/Cross/Bounce Nay.

Cross The motion is carried.

Macklin
Let no man break his word.
If every ducat in six thousand ducats
Were in six parts and every part a ducat
I would not draw them – I would have my bond.

Actors disperse, shaking hands, etc. Garrick keeps back Woffington.

Garrick We could do with a capital actress on our side.

Woffington I am on your side, Davy. I just think you're wasting your time.

Garrick Can't I persuade you?

Woffington They won't give actors a theatre.

Garrick I happen to have a personal letter from the Lord Chamberlain praising my Richard.

Woffington I have plenty of letters myself. I don't hold anything by them. You are funny, Mr Garrick. As if what we want ever matters to anything. Actors must be charming and win favour that way.

Garrick Can I see you later?

Woffington I might be able to fit you in.

Mrs Cibber approaches.

Mrs Cibber Mr Garrick!

Woffington walks off.

I was wondering if I might have a word with you. Time will sit very heavily upon me now there is no theatre to come to.

Garrick We'll have our own theatre soon.

Mrs Cibber No one talks to me outside the theatre. I'm a disgrace. I will meet no one except my two husbands. Perhaps I may be forced to drown myself!

Garrick It should only be a matter of weeks, Mrs Cibber. Surely you can avoid ponds in the meantime.

Mrs Cibber And I won't see you any more, Mr Garrick.

Garrick Well, I shall be around and about.

Mrs Cibber That's what I thought, and I thought that if you had some spare time, you might consider giving me some advice on acting. I would be very grateful. I do have rooms in town. If you're passing, I should be glad to see you. (*She hands him a key.*) That might make the whole situation quite bearable.

She exits.

SCENE SEVEN

Night. A room. It soon becomes clear that someone is being amorous. Grunts, etc. Someone gets up.

Duke Thanks.

He stumbles out. Garrick gets out from under bed.

Garrick Never again. Why should I cower under the furniture?

Woffington Because you're an actor and he's the Duke of Kingston.

Garrick We wouldn't be in this situation if you could restrict the number of your gentlemen callers.

Woffington He pays for the room.

Garrick Our room!

Woffington It's my room.

Garrick I want us to live like a normal, respectable couple with a plaque outside our front door saying, 'Mr Garrick and Mrs Woffington'. It should be like saying 'solicitors' or 'dentists'. It shouldn't be an invitation for every randy aristocrat to pop up for a free shag.

Woffington The theatre is an unreliable source of income.

Garrick I tried to change that, but you wouldn't come in with us.

Woffington It's a good thing I didn't. Look where it got Mr Macklin.

Garrick Everybody blames me, don't they?

Woffington Well, Macklin blames you. But then he lost his job.

Garrick If actors were respectable, people might have listened to us.

Woffington Your man'll be back in a minute.

Garrick Will he?

Woffington For his gloves.

Garrick Perhaps I'll tell him what I think of him.

Woffington You're all talk. You'll be diving under the bed the minute he walks through the door.

Duke calls off, 'Woff.'

Garrick I can't stand the noises he makes.

Woffington Get under the bed.

Garrick I'm grateful for your concern, madam.

Woffington Go on!

Enter Duke. Garrick dives under the bed.

Duke I forgot my gloves. Why don't you beat me for being a bad boy?

Woffington That's what you deserve. A great kick.

Duke I like the sound of that. Will you do it, Woff?

Woffington I'm sorely tempted.

Duke That's what I love about you, Woff: you're fiery. I look in your eyes and I see fire, fire, fire. Burn me. Drip wax on my tenderest places.

Woffington I'll get a candle.

Garrick crawls out from under the bed.

Garrick Here. (*He holds out a stump of candle.*) It was sticking in my back.

Duke Who's this?

Garrick My name is Garrick.

Duke Garrick?

Garrick The actor.

Duke What were you doing under our bed?

Garrick I was hiding, sir.

Duke Were you?

Garrick And then I decided it was behaviour ill becoming a gentleman.

Duke But not an actor.

Garrick The two are indistinguishable in my book. I have decided to give Mrs Woffington here an ultimatum. She must choose between the two of us.

Woffington What?

Duke How dare you come into my bed, actor?

Woffington It's my bed.

Duke Placing your stinking carcass between my sheets.

Woffington They're my sheets.

Duke Waving your stinking pizzle at my whore!

Woffington Oh, for God's sake!

Duke hits Garrick round the face.

Duke You putrid actor.

Garrick I own that is my profession.

Duke I may have to shoot you.

He picks up his gun.

Apologise.

Garrick What for?

Duke For being an actor, actor.

Woffington He stays here sometimes.

Duke In my room.

Woffington It's my room.

Duke I think you'll find I own the street. I'm giving you an ultimatum, Mrs Woffington. Get rid of him and the others and I'll sign you over five hundred pounds per annum. For life.

Woffington For life?

He turns to Garrick.

Duke Richard the Third, wasn't it?

Garrick Yes.

Duke You have apparently abandoned the rhythmic incantations and soporific rocking motions of your predecessors.

Garrick I have.

Duke Isn't it arrogance to presume that you can transcend a tradition that has served the public for centuries?

Garrick It seemed to me to be the right thing.

Duke I saw your Richard. You certainly execute the passions most poignantly and easily.

Garrick My journey to this point has not been an easy one, Your Grace. I was born in Birmingham.

Duke Definingly unpropitious.

Garrick Of a large and impecunious family. My dad was garrisoned in Malta and always forgot to write. I used to stand on the table and clown about to try to cheer Mum up.

Duke A charming picture.

Garrick I was hoping it might persuade you not to shoot me.

Duke Oh that. (*He puts gun away.*) I am only sorry that we had to become acquainted in such circumstances. I am a great theatre-lover and can only consider it a sadness I could not be of service to you in what might have been a most illustrious career. I'm sure Mrs Woffington must have pointed out to you the great advantage of being talked up in certain circles.

Woffington Look at you, chatting away. You'd think you'd known each other for years, when the truth is you've both been fucking the same woman.

Duke It does happen. I shall see you at the theatre tomorrow.

Woffington You will not. Because I choose Garrick.

Duke I shall retire for the time being and let the heat out of the moment. But the last thing a rising actor needs is a powerful enemy like myself. I leave you with this thought, Mr Garrick: what's the point of being the greatest actor of your generation if you don't survive to prove it?

Interval.

A BALLETIC INTERLUDE

Voice Madam Violetta. The Austrian Violet.

Mrs Garrick appears dressed in violet and partly as a violet. She performs a short burst of eighteenth-century ballet. Applause as she finishes.

Mrs Garrick Thank you, everybody. I am very happy in your country. Everything here is very pleasant. I am most happy to the Duke and Duchess for taking care of me. I shall be available for social engagements. On my first time of dancing in England I wear long knickers, but I quickly see that this is not the fashion and now I wear short knickers. Thank you.

Act Two

Garrick's office.

Johnson To enlighten. To illuminate. To supply with light, to instruct, to furnish with increase of knowledge, to cheer, to exhilarate, to gladden, to supply with sight, to quicken in the faculty of vision.

Garrick Have a look at this. (*Picks up a retractable knife. Stabs himself.*) Marvellous, isn't it?

Johnson In the sense of a thing beyond belief, Davy, certainly.

Garrick How is work on the dictionary going?

Johnson Tardily, protractedly, in a snail-like fashion.

Garrick I'm sorry to hear it. May I enquire about the Prologue?

Johnson You may, sir.

Garrick Do you have it, sir?

Johnson I do have it. For I possess it, sir. I entertain it, I have grasped the meaning and point of it. I have suffered it, endured it, created it.

Garrick May I see it?

Johnson No, sir, you may not. For it is in my head.

Garrick I long to hear it. I'm speaking it tonight at the opening.

Johnson Indeed, sir, I hope you are, for that was the purpose in my composing it. The meat of it, sir, is thus: that a new era is dawning for the stage over which you will preside.

Garrick That's very good.

Johnson That is nothing, sir. For had you heard the pungent and rigorous versification in which I have crafted the sentiments, you could then claim satisfaction.

Garrick I await it, sir!

Pause.

Johnson Ah.

Garrick Yes?

Johnson I have it not, sir. As in one that lacks possessions. I have had it all and now no longer.

Garrick Does that mean you have forgotten it, sir?

Johnson Forgotten, sir, as we must all be. Neglected, put away, immured, sir, in the grave.

Garrick Do not alarm yourself, Doctor!

Johnson I am not alarmed. I am mortally terrified!

Garrick (*calling*) Mrs Butler!

Johnson It is the pall of my melancholy, Davy, that has fallen across me.

Mrs Butler hurries in.

Garrick Take the Doctor here on a short walk, Mrs Butler. His nerves are troubling him.

Mrs Butler He's very large, Mr Garrick. What if he tries to escape?

Johnson Madam, there is no escape.

Garrick Perhaps exercise, sir, will refresh your memory.

Garrick returns to rehearsal with knife. Peg Woffington enters.

It's not for personal use, you understand.

Woffington I'm here because you want to destroy me.

Garrick Don't go all dramatic on me.

Woffington To take away my work.

Garrick That is a typical Woffington overreaction.

Woffington That is a typical Garrick obfuscation.

Garrick It's standard practice for a new manager to create a new repertoire.

Woffington With none of my parts in it.

Garrick We will, of course, be looking at new ways of including you in the season. This isn't personal.

Woffington You still love me and out of sheer bitterness you want to destroy me.

Garrick Peg, I'm about to be a happily married man.

Woffington I've met a lot of those.

Garrick I know. I made a list of all your misdemeanours. I found it the other day and had a good laugh.

Woffington I suppose you were clearing things out.

Garrick My wife and I will be moving into our new home.

Woffington You're not clearing me out of the theatre. Why have you cut *The Constant Couple*? Nobody does Sir Harry like I do. I've got the legs for it. (*She shows her legs.*)

Garrick Put those away.

Woffington They're only legs. Nothing to be scared of. You've seem them before.

Garrick If Sir Harry Wildair gets done again, he won't be played by a woman.

Woffington Why not? I made that part.

Garrick It is now considered vulgar for a woman to play a man.

Woffington Don't be a prick.

Garrick Unfortunately there are a lot of pricks that think the same way and they buy the tickets.

Woffington So what if I show my legs? Theatre isn't church. If it was, people would stop going.

Garrick Your theatre is finished. People are eager for change and I want to give it to them.

Woffington What kind of change?

Garrick Emotion, not cynicism. Dignity, not immorality.

Woffington I bet you never fucked her yet, have you?

Garrick No, because she's been well brought up.

Woffington I'd rather come from the gutter than from genteel poverty like you, forever sewing pockets over holes. I'd rather go naked.

Garrick Which you do with great frequency.

Woffington I don't know why God gave you your talent, because it's wasted on you. Always bowing and scraping and scared of what you want.

Garrick I got what I wanted.

Woffington Bastard. (*She picks up a knife.*)

Garrick That's retractable.

Woffington Typical. When I chose you, you ran off. That's what I don't understand – how you started out brave and ended up a coward.

Garrick After two years of putting up with you and your numerous infidelities, are you suggesting I should have stayed?

Woffington My lovers gave you an excuse. You wanted this theatre, not me.

Garrick Yes, I was tired of your world and its casual humiliations. It was cruel.

Mrs Cibber enters.

Mrs Cibber Mr Garrick?

Garrick Ah. Mrs Cibber.

Woffington I'll go to Dublin; the management there has a bit of sense. My life from now on doesn't look so bad: twenty-seven, beautiful, the toast of the Dublin stage. Yours looks a lot worse: married to a virgin and arse-licking your way around London.

Garrick Mrs Woffington is leaving us, Susannah. (*To Peg.*) May I offer you the usual sentiments?

Woffington Shove your sentiments.

Mrs Cibber Mr Garrick is careful to preserve the appearance of a dignified exchange. Some of us have a reputation to lose.

Woffington Yes, and some of us have a face like a dog's arse. (*She exits.*)

Mrs Cibber I've come to congratulate you, Mr Garrick, on your accession as manager.

Garrick Now Mrs Woffington is leaving us, Susannah, Drury Lane needs you more than ever.

Mrs Cibber I appear to have several new and demanding roles.

Garrick You are our leading actress, Mrs Cibber.

Mrs Cibber That's wonderful, although I may have to spend a few months in the country later in the season.

Garrick That's extremely inconvenient.

Mrs Cibber Yes. I've explained everything in this letter.

She hands him the letter. He takes it impatiently and reads silently. He looks up slowly.

Garrick A woman's condition? Well, I suppose congratulations are in order.

Mrs Cibber Not really. My first husband and I don't live as man and wife and my second husband is seventy-two.

Garrick Good Lord.

Mrs Cibber Yes, you can say that again. It really is the most frightful situation. But you were very distressed that day you left Mrs Woffington. Your acting advice took an unexpected turn.

Garrick Are you sure?

Mrs Cibber I shall spend a month in the country and then we must continue as if nothing ever happened. I know what it's like to live in the wilderness, Mr Garrick, and you would not take to it. And if you were not here, I could not be.

Garrick Yes, yes, I see. It's the right thing to do.

Mrs Cibber Before I go, may I say that I look forward to our playing in *King John* together. I am to be Lady Constance. I understand you had some concerns about me. I was primarily a musical person.

Garrick I have great hopes of your success. Even though your voice is naturally soft and inaudible.

Mrs Cibber Thank you. I wonder if I might steal a moment of your time. It concerns Lady Constance's screams of maternal agony at the loss of her son. Might I be allowed to ask what you think of the one I've been practising at home?

Garrick Very well.

Mrs Cibber Here goes.

She does a blood-curdlingly impressive scream.

Garrick That will do very well.

Mrs Cibber Mr Garrick.

She exits. Garrick sits silently for a moment. Johnson reappears with Goldsmith and Mrs Butler.

Mrs Butler He is restored, Mr Garrick.

Johnson I have it! The Prologue. And look who I bumped into, a young acquaintance of mine, a Dr Goldsmith. He has literary ambitions, like most Irishmen.

Mrs Butler He is rather foolish and has no money, but he seemed to lift the Doctor's spirits. It must be that to discover a fellow worse off than ourselves is in some way cheering.

Goldsmith I'm delighted that the theatre will b–be undergoing a renaissance in your hands, Mr Garrick. I look forward to the future with great interest.

Johnson
Hard is his lot that here by fortune placed
Must watch the wild vicissitudes of taste,
With every meteor of caprice must play
And chase the new-blown bubbles of the day.
Ah! Let not censure term our fate, our choice,
The stage but echoes back the public voice.
The drama's laws, the drama's patrons give,
For we that live to please must please to live.

Johnson exits. We resume the present. Hannah More enters, carrying a small tray of tea.

Hannah Mrs Garrick has sent me over with some tea.

Garrick Thank you, Hannah.

She sets up tea things. She looks at what he is reading.

Hannah Have you reached a decision yet, Mr Garrick?

Garrick I think Drury Lane may be ready to take its comedy with a little more gusto.

Hannah Oh. I hope you don't mind me speaking out. But I find Reverend Cumberland's play to have such elegant sentiments and elevated behaviour.

Garrick They are not much fun to act, Hannah.

Hannah But what is the point of Dr Goldsmith's play? Why should we want to see such characters on stage? They don't instruct us in decent behaviour. Art must have moral purpose, Mr Garrick. That's how God and art fit together.

Garrick I cannot believe that God has anything to do with some of the horrors that land on my desk.

Hannah And would Mr Cautherly be Tony Lumpkin?

Garrick I'd rather he played Marlow, but I want to encourage him.

Hannah But would it be beneficial to him, Mr Garrick? He's a young gentleman with his future before him. Lumpkin is a licentious pleasure seeker.

Garrick But it may set him on his path.

Hannah When I walked here that morning, Mr Garrick, I once or twice discerned bundles at the roadside. Desiring to rest a little I found myself beside one. It was a baby. Frozen.

Garrick It's a sad fact, Hannah.

Hannah How did those girls get their babies in the first place?

Garrick Perhaps Mrs Garrick . . .

Hannah Their morals, I meant. I found this . . . (*She brings out a letter.*)

Garrick What is it?

Hannah A letter. From Mrs Cibber.

Garrick That's ancient history. There's a fire in the green room. That's the place for it.

Hannah Reverend Cumberland's play is so wonderfully fresh and unjaded. So full of hope for a new future.

Garrick Yes, yes, that's true. That's a very thoughtful argument, thank you, Hannah.

Hannah Would you like sugar, Mr Garrick?

Garrick Six, please, Hannah.

Hannah I feel privileged to have had a chance to influence history, Mr Garrick. It brings me a little closer to you. (*She exits.*)

SCENE TWO

Johnson Melancholy. A disease supposed to proceed from an abundance of black bile. A kind of madness in which the mind is always fixed on one object. A gloomy, pensive, disenchanted temper.

The Turk's Head. A late stage in the proceedings.

Goldsmith So, sirs, in conclusion. There has never been an actor that combined such a happy facility to move and excite as Mr Garrick.

Boswell Goldy has had a change of heart.

Goldsmith He is unab–bated excellence!

Boswell He has had a complete change of personality.

Goldsmith And although he is small, he can dwarf the stage at will. That is his genius.

Johnson That is his platform shoes. Acting is nothing but trickery, sir; do not be taken in by it.

Boswell We must allow a great player some merit.

Johnson What, sir, a fellow who claps a hump on his back and cries, 'I am Richard the Third.' Nay, sir, a ballad-singer is a higher man, for he does two things: he repeats and he sings.

Boswell You can turn anything to ridicule, sir.

Burke Mankind has agreed in admiring talents for the stage. A great player does what very few are capable of. His art is a rare faculty.

Reynolds Who can repeat Hamlet's soliloquy, 'To be or not to be,' as Garrick does it?

Johnson Anybody may. The tea boy may do it as well in a week.

Reynolds He will not be paid one thousand pounds a year for it. That is a proof of great acting.

Johnson Is getting a thousand pounds a proof of excellence? That has been got by scoundrels.

Repulsive Old Man enters.

Old Man Excuse me, sirs, you expect one Garrick?

Johnson For the last hour, old man.

Old Man Well, he's not coming.

Boswell How are you privy to this confidence, sir?

Old Man I'm his hairdresser.

Reynolds Clearly a walking advertisement.

Old Man Point me in the right direction I can work wonders with a comb and scissors. I have an intelligence from Mr Garrick, if I can lay my hands upon it. (*He searches, finds it.*) 'To the Turk's Head club. A group of learned and ingenious men who meet to further the advancement of culture.' How do I know I have the right group?

Johnson You may take myself sir, Dr Samuel Johnson, as proof. Proceed, sir, what have you for us?

Old Man (*reads*) 'Sirs, forgive me. I have been called from London on unexpected business and must forego the pleasure of your company.' Read, sirs: he's had a better offer.

Burke You have no high opinion of your employer?

Old Man Has anybody?

Goldsmith P–perhaps it is the case that he has been called from London. Garrick is an extremely important man with a great deal of b–business to attend to.

Old Man blows his nose on a rag and wipes in on his sleeve.

Old Man Your name, sir?

Goldsmith Oliver Goldsmith.

Old Man I suppose you've not had the news, sir.

Goldsmith The news?

Old Man That Mr Garrick has passed your play over, sir. I have the playbill here. *The Fashionable Lover* – some veritable twaddle – opens on Tuesday.

Boswell I'll have to get tickets for that.

Reynolds Have a heart, Bozzy.

Goldsmith The b–backsliding b–bastard. Has Mr Garrick made clear his reasons?

Old Man Mr Garrick says your play mocks gentility, sir.

Goldsmith It mocks its affectations.

Old Man I have no time for affectations, sir. For example, you, sir, are ugly.

Goldsmith Very true.

Old Man Your coat is ugly.

Goldsmith I'd b–beg to disagree on that one.

Burke No, it is ugly.

Old Man Your wig is also quite repulsive. Yesterday I saw a dead dog, it is as if you had picked it up and placed it on your head, but only at the back.

Reynolds Hold off, old man.

Old Man Garrick is always huffing and puffing about politeness – he would consider it bad form to comment upon your coiffure in such a manner, but I stand up for the liberty of the Englishman to insult his neighbour.

Burke Without manners, sir, we are little more than beasts!

Old Man I was an actor once. I had a superlative act. I burped the alphabet while juggling five dogs. But Mr Garrick, sir, would have nothing of it. For it was too low.

Burke Indeed, old man, your act sounds quite missable.

Old Man I have heard him call Dr Goldsmith's play low. But what of that! What is so very wrong with the low? (*He farts.*) Pardon. Just because his play has a man fondling a woman at every opportunity! If a man's parts cannot rise in the theatre at the sight of an actress having her bubbies squeezed, it is a sad day.

Goldsmith I was making a political point.

The Old Man scratches his balls.

Old Man Make as many of them as you like.

Goldsmith (*to Old Man*) I wish you would not argue for me, sir, you are not scoring me any points.

Old Man I'll do a bit of my act, if you like. (*burping*) A . . . B . . . C . . .

Burke Take this man, gentlemen. (*He indicates Old Man.*) What an execrable creature.

Burke Imagine him as a play! Garrick chose not to take that path and must be commended.

Goldsmith Look at him again gentlemen. Is there not something human in him? His ridiculous pride in his burps and his dogs. We laugh at the faults in him and so correct them in ourselves.

Johnson After all, it is the end of comedy to make us merry.

Reynolds The danger is, to show such vulgarity is to encourage its emulation.

Goldsmith There is no danger in him!

Old Man Thank you, sir. I shall offer you a haircut on the house. (*The Old Man advances towards Goldsmith.*)

Goldsmith No, thank you.

Old Man grabs him.

Goldsmith Unhand me, sir. He has a grip of iron!

Reynolds Shake him off, Goldy.

Goldsmith I cannot. That is my eyebrow.

Old Man It will grow back.

Goldsmith Help!

Johnson Sir, it should be clear that your services are no longer required.

Boswell It appears there is great danger in a fool!

Garrick You make excellent sense, sir, as always.

Boswell It is Mr Garrick, how marvellous!

Reynolds Good Lord!

Goldsmith Garrick!

Garrick I had no hope of a hearing, sirs, I live in fear of the retribution of writers and so came in disguise.

Boswell A most amazing demonstration of your powers. Are you not amazed, Dr Johnson?

Johnson Nothing Davy does amazes me.

Goldsmith My hair does not resemble a dead dog.

Boswell It does now.

Goldsmith Your intention was to make a fool of me.

Garrick My intention, sir, was to show that there is some merit in aspiring to gentility and refinement.

Goldsmith It was not kind.

Burke But comedy is not kind, sir. That is Mr Garrick's contention, which he has proved admirably.

Goldsmith Very good, sir, I am a figure of fun.

Johnson Which is why we tolerate your company. May we say at last the topic of your play is dead? I have done my best for you, Goldy, and now you must be stoic. When life is not getting worse, it is generally unhappy.

Boswell Let us toast Mr Garrick.

Johnson I shall toast Goldy.

Reynolds That is not consistent, sir.

Johnson There is no great value in consistency. One may be consistently wrong. I desire to toast the loser for a change. That is the Englishman in me.

Goldsmith B–b–but I am not necessarily the loser, Doctor. I have a letter here from Mr Colman at Covent Garden. Hearing that Mr Garrick was to do my p–play he b–begs that I return it to him on promise of a production. I shall do so immediately. I second the toast to myself.

All Dr Goldsmith!

Reynolds Why, it will be something of a competition, Mr Garrick. The two plays simultaneously.

All drink except Garrick.

SCENE THREE: IN-YER-FACE THEATRE

Garrick's office. Cautherley is waiting. Hannah comes in.

Hannah Mr Garrick has decided to do *The Fashionable Lover.*

Cautherley Yes.

Hannah You could seem a little more cheerful, Mr Cautherley. Perhaps I could help you with your lines.

Cautherley No, thank you.

Hannah Mrs Garrick thinks you'll do very well. She's very fond of you. She's always talking about you. Your eyes, your hair, the way it flops down onto your forehead. You've got strong legs. Your hands. You're very sensitive, she says. She likes you. She wouldn't be surprised if the whole audience fell in love with you.

Cautherley Hmmm.

Hannah Charles Millward is a wonderful part.

Cautherley Is it?

Hannah He's tortured by his feelings and he struggles to find a way to express them. He longs to marry Augusta but he can't because she's too poor and so he struggles with duty and longing and he struggles all the time – he's always struggling but he can never put it into words. She's struggling too. She's in love with him but she mustn't say it or it would compromise his struggle so she struggles not to make his struggle more of a struggle. It's a struggle.

Cautherley He's a cunt.

Hannah I don't know what that is, Mr Cautherley, but I don't like the sound of it.

Cautherley Kiss me again.

Hannah I don't know what you're talking about. There won't be any more of that. That's why I begged Mr Garrick not to do *She Stoops to Conquer*.

Cautherley You did!

Hannah I know you won't like me now I've told you that, but I don't care what you think of me. That play is ugly. You have no idea, Mr Cautherley, of the joys of sensibility. I feel sorry for you. Do you see this flower?

Cautherley Yes.

Hannah I feel with this flower the heat of sun on its petals. The delicate roundness of a drop of dew, the bright garden throbbing with intensity around it.

Cautherley takes the flower and eats it.

Hannah Why did you do that?

Cautherley Just a joke.

Hannah Lumpkin!

Garrick enters.

Hannah Mr Garrick. (*She exits.*)

Garrick Drury Lane has to be good tonight, Mr Cautherley. *She Stoops to Conquer* opens at Covent Garden. We want to take the laurels.

Cautherley I don't see how we can, Mr Garrick.

Garrick Now don't take that attitude. Let's see what Mrs Butler has to say about how you've been doing. (*He opens ledger.*) Tuesday 8th September. *Macbeth*. Mr Cautherley fit

of giggles on seeing beards of witches. Failure to exit.
Friday 11th. *Antony and Cleopatra*. Mr Cautherley forgets
to bring on asp. Cleopatra suffocates herself with pillow.

Cautherley I don't think anybody noticed.

Garrick Saturday 12th. Lines lost. Cautherley makes up
bollocks. And so on. When I was your age, I walked to
London with sixpence in my pocket. I hung around the
theatre till they thought I was part of the furniture. I would
have died and gone to heaven if I'd had half the
opportunities you've had. Now I know you have promise,
sir, and I don't like to be proved wrong. So what is it that
makes you fail so miserably? Let's start with Charles
Millward.

Cautherley I don't like him, Mr Garrick.

Garrick What's wrong with him?

Cautherley He's in love all the time.

Garrick He's the romantic lead, Mr Cautherley. People
want to feel for somebody when they come to the theatre.

Cautherley Lumpkin. I could have played that part,
Mr Garrick. I had a feeling for it.

Garrick You have become a gentleman, sir, through your
character, as I have. That is why I recommend you leave the
Lumpkins of this world well alone.

Cautherley At school, sir, because I was no one they treated
me accordingly.

Garrick Well, that was very bad, sir.

Cautherley I used to dream of some way to get back at
them. Lumpkin does that.

Garrick I am sorry you were not happy at school, Sam, but
I cannot programme my theatre to satisfy a boyhood
grudge. You do see that?

Cautherley I know I am indebted to you.

Garrick Yes.

Cautherley I was very grateful to come to you in the holidays, sir. I remember you impersonated a turkey.

Garrick Did I?

Cautherley And a drunk, and Mrs Garrick.

Garrick I still do a very good Mrs Garrick.

Cautherley I only ever laughed when I was at your house. I remembered what you did and then I did it for the boys at school. I used to pretend I was your son, sir. Perhaps if I was I would not exercise you as I do.

Garrick People think I'll be selling the patent, but I'd like to pass this place on to a friend. I'm looking for that friend all the time, eh, Sam? Charles Millward is just one part. There'll be others you like better. Study hard, my boy, for seven years, and you may play the rest of your life.

Cautherley I won't let you down, Mr Garrick.

Cautherley exits.

SCENE FOUR

Backstage, Drury Lane.

Macklin These costumes, Mrs Butler.

Mrs Butler Yes, Mr Macklin?

Macklin They're a little overdone. Why am I covered in fur?

Mrs Butler It says 'fashionable' in the title, Mr Macklin.

Mrs Cibber It's too late to do anything about it now.

Mrs Butler The greater emphasis on design in contemporary theatre is due to paucity of content and you can't blame me for that. I only do the sewing.

Mrs Butler Five minutes, please. (*She exits.*)

Mrs Cibber We're on in ten minutes.

Cautherley enters.

Cautherley Yes. There are a great many lines to remember.

Mrs Barry One opens one's mouth and they come out.

Barry They didn't come out in rehearsal.

Cautherley It's the last scene I'm shaky on.

Barry You're home and dry by the last scene, love. I'd worry about getting there.

Macklin I share your concerns, sir, I'm expiring under the weight of dead animal.

Mrs Cibber Set his mind at rest, Mr Macklin. Go through his last scene with him.

Cautherley I'd be grateful, sir.

Mrs Barry I'm in your arms, I think.

Barry He said the lines, Lavinia.

Mrs Cibber Let us be quick about it.

Macklin Very well, we enter. (*He says the lines – a speed version.*) Give me thy hand Augusta. I was labouring for thy sake that I should restore the prostrate fortunes of an ancient house. I have toiled through eighteen years of wearisome adventure, crowned with success. I now return and find my daughter all my fondest hope could represent. I now bestow my treasure in faithful hands. What say you sir? Will you accept the charge?

They all look at Cautherley. A pause.

Mrs Barry That's your line, Mr Cautherley.

Barry There's a clue when he says, 'What say you, sir?'

Cautherley What do I say?

All You say, 'Yes.'

Cautherley Yes.

Garrick enters with Lady Kingston.

Garrick Company, let me call you together for a moment. Our patron would like to address us.

Lady Kingston So these are the actors. How fascinating.

They bow/curtsey.

Lady Kingston I would love to know something of the authentic behind-the-scenes life.

Garrick I'm sure we would be happy to oblige you.

Lady Kingston How splendid. And you all regard one another as family, I expect.

All Yes.

Lady Kingston I suppose because you work as an ensemble it is the greater good that motivates you.

All Yes.

Macklin When you get to my age, Your Grace, you realise that work is the only thing and you regret all the hours you have wasted in taverns.

Mrs Cibber When did you realise that, Mr Macklin?

Garrick Ha ha ha . . .

Lady Kingston I know I shall have good reason to be proud of you all and my association with Drury Lane.

Garrick We are deeply grateful for your interest, madam.

Cumberland As the author, I have prepared a short speech, which I propose . . .

Lady Kingston Nobody cares about that, Cumberland. Come on.

They exit.

Garrick Break a leg, everybody.

All Break a leg, Mr Garrick.

Mrs Butler (*off*) Scene One – beginners, Mr Macklin, Mr Garrick, Mr Barry.

They exit.

Mrs Cibber I'm not on for twenty-seven minutes.

Mrs Barry What's the house like, Mrs Butler?

Mrs Butler There's a good crowd in. Quite a few vicars.

Mrs Cibber That's always a comforting thought.

Mrs Butler Curtain up!

Mrs Cibber approaches Mr Cautherley.

Mrs Cibber Mr Cautherley. If there's any advice I can give you in a professional capacity, please don't hesitate to ask.

Cautherley That's very kind, Mrs Cibber.

Mrs Cibber I'm an old hand.

Cautherley You're a very fine actress. I can only apologise for what happened with your Cleopatra.

Mrs Barry I shall be going a step further with my restrained passion tonight, Mr Cautherley.

Cautherley Mrs Barry executes the attitude of restrained passion most excellently. I wish I didn't keep laughing.

Mrs Cibber My advice is to remember a time you were in love. Bring those feelings to mind and that will assist you in playing the part.

Cautherley I'm not sure I've ever been in love.

Mrs Cibber You surprise me, Mr Cautherley.

Cautherley Once I found a bird.

Mrs Cibber A bird?

Cautherley In the school grounds. I took it back to my room, but the next morning it was quite stiff.

Mrs Cibber And this is what you bring to mind when you are making passionate love to Miss Aubrey?

Cautherley Yes.

Mrs Cibber You must stop it at once. You must think of a person.

Cautherley Perhaps I could think of you, Mrs Cibber.

Mrs Cibber Mr Cautherley, I am out of the question.

Cautherley Why? I'll never be able to think of anyone else in time.

Mrs Butler Mr Cautherley, Mrs Barry.

They exit. A shout heard off. They listen. Re-enter Macklin.

Mrs Butler How is it, Mr Macklin?

Macklin A faction in the gallery doesn't appreciate characters of Scottish descent.

Mrs Butler Only the gallery. That's not bad.

Enter Reverend Cumberland.

Cumberland Perhaps you could tone down the accent, Mr Macklin.

Macklin With a name like Hamish Macleod?

A louder jeer: 'No Scots! No foreigners!'

Mrs Butler You've a fair number of foreigners in your play, Reverend Cumberland.

Cumberland That is intentional, ma'am.

Mrs Butler It is trouble, sir.

Cumberland Feeling with a person encourages us to transcend superficial differences.

Macklin No one supports the Scottish. It's a daft idea to have them in a play in the first place.

Mrs Butler Mr Macklin!

He begins to exit.

Cumberland Try smiling more, Mr Macklin!

Cautherley re-enters with Garrick.

Garrick How was that, Mr Cautherley?

Cautherley Someone called me a French arse. It was when I said I'd engaged in a contretemps.

Garrick You're doing extremely well, Mr Cautherley. And all of you.

Barry They said I was French, too, Mr Garrick, but I'm not, am I?

Garrick You should know, Mr Barry.

Barry You've got to tell them I've never been further than Barnstaple.

Garrick Calm down, Mr Barry. There'll be a few cuts tomorrow.

Cumberland Ahh . . . cuts . . .

Mrs Butler Mr Garrick!

Cumberland follows Garrick off. Mrs Barry enters.

Mrs Barry I've handled them!

Barry Yes, Lavinia, and so have half the audience.

Mrs Butler Mr Barry. Stage right.

He exits.

Mr Cautherley, Mrs Barry. Stage left.

They exit.

Hopefully we can now have a nice quiet night of it.

Sounds of jeering increase to a roar. A loud crash. Mrs Butler and Mrs Cibber react. Cautherley is brought on unconscious, carried by Garrick and Barry. Mr Barry is carrying a potato. Mrs Cibber gasps.

Mrs Cibber Will he be all right?

Garrick Put him here.

Mrs Barry He's out cold.

Mrs Barry It was a potato that struck him on the head, Mr Garrick.

Barry It was this potato here. They threw one at me too, Lavinia.

Mrs Barry I'll loosen his clothing.

Barry Lavinia!

Cautherley mumbles.

Garrick Do you know who I am, son?

Cautherley Mr Garrick.

Garrick Thank God.

Mrs Cibber Thank goodness.

88

Barry Yes, they threw one at me, too, Mr Garrick, but I ducked.

Garrick Good for you, Mr Barry. Your reflexes were working for once. The audience is a little restive tonight. They will subside shortly and we will continue with our performance.

A roar.

Cautherley Is it my line?

Mrs Cibber Poor Mr Cautherley. He can't go on. Mrs Butler must do it with the book.

Mrs Butler Fuck me!

Cautherley (*to Mrs Cibber*) Who are you?

Mrs Cibber Mrs Cibber, a fellow actor.

Cautherley You seem familiar. As if I knew you.

Mrs Cibber Mr Garrick, he has such a strange look in his eyes.

Garrick Not now, Susannah.

Macklin enters with a cauliflower.

Have you anything fresh to report, Mr Macklin?

Macklin Yes. A man has manoeuvred himself onto the chandelier and has commandeered vegetable projectiles.

Garrick What else did you ascertain?

Macklin I ascertained that the audience are fed up with *The Fashionable Lover* and are diverting themselves with anti-French feeling and nationalistic fervour.

Mrs Cibber I'm sure the religious gentlemen are getting a great deal from the performance.

Macklin Last thing was they have set about the anti-French faction with cushions.

Garrick Cushions?

Macklin Untimely ripped from the new seating arrangements.

Garrick Good God.

Macklin Yes, Mr Garrick, you have a riot on your hands.

Mrs Butler A lot of what people enjoy about the theatre is riots.

A loud crash.

That'll be the chandelier.

Garrick Six hundred pounds. I'll have to go and speak to them.

Mrs Cibber It might not be safe.

Garrick I cannot let them tear the theatre apart, Mrs Cibber.

Garrick exits. Cumberland re-enters.

Cumberland What is it that offends them?

All The French.

Macklin The play is unrelieved by laughter. They have no outlet for hatred and have turned on each other.

Mrs Cibber You wouldn't think religious gentlemen could make such a mess of a cushion.

Cumberland exits. Loud jeers and chanting from audience: 'Monsieur! Monsieur! On your knees, Garrick! Apologise! Pardon, pardon!'

Macklin There is nothing for it but to call a meeting.
I propose immediate cancellation of this bourgeois frippery.

Mrs Cibber Do we have to bother with all the paraphernalia, Mr Macklin?

Macklin Point of information. Yes.

Mrs Butler Since my promotion I disagree with meetings in principal. I answer only to Mr Garrick.

Macklin Charles Macklin, actor. Presently playing Hamish McLeod. We are in a right turkey.

Barry I thought it was going to be all right at first. I got a laugh when I came on.

Mrs Butler Point of information. It was the costume that got a laugh, Mr Barry.

Mrs Barry Anyway, now they want to kill you.

Barry Thank you, Lavinia.

Bounce Bounce. Second stage hand. It starts with cauliflowers and ends with murder. I've seen it before.

Barry I'm not voting against the management, it's old-fashioned.

Macklin You'd do it quick enough if you had to go out there and apologise.

Barry Mr Garrick wouldn't do that. This is the eighteenth century.

Garrick re-enters. Cries of 'No French, no Scottish! No foreigners! Pardon! Pardon!'

Mrs Cibber Here is Mr Garrick.

Garrick Mr Barry. It might help if you declare yourself an Englishman.

Barry I vote with you, Mr Macklin.

Garrick There's nothing to be afraid of, Spranger. If you apologise for sounding French, the show can continue.

Barry I have withdrawn my labour, Mr Garrick, and so has Lavinia.

Macklin And so have we all, pending the cancellation of *The Fashionable Lover.*

Mrs Butler It is mutiny, Mr Garrick.

Garrick Lady Kingston has been signalling me from the royal box. She is greatly anxious for the show to continue.

Barry (*pointing to Cautherley*) It's him they want. Charles Millwood. It's because he does French things with his glove.

Mrs Butler That's right, Mr Garrick.

Cautherley I'm happy to face them, sir.

Mrs Cibber The poor boy is not himself . . .

Macklin He has been struck by a vegetable, which I cite as evidence supporting my proposal.

Garrick Mr Cautherley has graciously agreed to apologise to the audience for their misapprehension. I'll be there with you, Mr Cautherley.

Cautherley Thank you, Mr Garrick.

Mrs Cibber There is an untamed mob out there who have failed to be persuaded to good manners. We cannot risk sending Mr Cautherley before them. My conscience is weighing very heavily on me, Mr Garrick.

Garrick Does it have to be today, Susannah?

Mrs Cibber To let a new company member face the crowd. I would prefer to do it myself.

Barry But you're not French.

Mrs Barry No one is, Mr Barry, or we would send them out there.

Garrick Ready, Mr Cautherley.

Cautherley Yes, Mr Garrick. (*He begins to exit in the wrong direction.*)

Garrick Other way, Mr Cautherley.

Mrs Cibber I won't let you go.

Cautherley But I must, Mrs Cibber.

Mrs Cibber holds on to him, as he begins to exit. A tussle.

Garrick Let him go, Susannah. He's not a child.

Mrs Cibber Yes, he is, Davy

She releases him. Cautherley stares at them both.

Macklin I have a suggestion. I have some sketches and impersonations in my repertoire. The material comprises a short comic entertainment which might cheer the audience up a bit.

A huge roar.

Mrs Barry Let them have comedy, Mr Garrick. That is what they deserve.

Banging on door.

Mrs Butler They're at the gates, Mr Garrick!

Macklin Let me go on and entertain them, Mr Garrick.

Garrick Very well. I'll make the announcement. Macklin will keep them at bay a while, but they've paid for a full evening's entertainment and they'll expect us to give it to them. Company, we must prepare for *Lear.*

All *Lear (etc.)*

Garrick (*starts to exit.*) Oh and Macklin, make it funny.

Macklin exits. Company hurries to prepare. Hannah attends to Cautherley's wounds.

Hannah Mr Cautherley, let me see to your head. I've improvised some bandages. My petticoat. You should now spend three days in a darkened room.

Cautherley I can't, we've a show to put on.

Hannah I've changed my mind about the theatre, sir. I've been entertaining a groundless hope that it might be converted into a school of virtue. Tonight's events prove me wrong. Your life was put in danger. Allow me to convince you sir, of the waste of life it would be to continue here.

Enter Garrick.

Hannah Mr Garrick. (*She exits.*)

Garrick Are you fit for tonight's performance?

Cautherley Yes, sir.

Garrick Good lad.

Cautherley I'm playing Edmund, sir, the bastard.

Garrick I know that, sir.

Cautherley Although he does know who his father is. He seems to live with his father, sir, in the same house. His father even seems to make a joke of it. 'His breeding sir, hath been at my charge. I have so often blushed to acknowledge him that I am now brazed to it.' It's very different, sir, from today. 'I grow, I prosper, now gods stand up for bastards!'

Garrick Yes, not so loud, Mr Cautherley.

Cautherley At least he knew who his father was, sir. An earl. I shouldn't mind an earl in the least. Mrs Butler says it was actors.

Garrick Have you your costume for this evening, sir? Mrs Butler's very exercised today.

Cautherley Yes, Mr Garrick.

He exits. Laughter offstage. Mrs Butler enters.

Mrs Butler Here's all the Lears we've got. (*calling off*) Bounce! The screen!

She places pile of Lear costumes down. Bounce appears with a screen for Garrick to dress behind.

Bounce I should have retired last year, Mrs Butler.

Bounce exits.

Garrick Thank you, Mrs Butler. I'm sorry it's such short notice.

Mrs Butler We like the classics, don't we, Mr Garrick? They tend to be less trouble than new plays.

Garrick Yes, and you can trust that the theatre will still be standing at the end of the evening.

Garrick emerges as Lear.

Mrs Butler Very nice, Mr Garrick. You'll have to excuse me. I've an emergency with Edgar's tights.

A loud burst of laughter and applause.

It all seems to be going swimmingly.

She exits. Garrick swigs his medicine. Macklin hurries on, dressed as a woman.

Macklin Mr Garrick, have you got a moment?

Garrick Good God! Mr Macklin! Why aren't you on stage?

Macklin They were eating out of my hand, Mr Garrick. So I threw in my most hilarious impersonation. Lady Kingston.

Garrick And?

Macklin She's going to kill me. I need money. I need clothes. I need to escape.

Garrick You're staying here! You're playing Gloucester in fifteen minutes. I'll send a note of apology round to Lady Kingston's box immediately. Take those clothes off, man!

Macklin Thank you kindly, sir.

Garrick Enough of that, Mr Macklin.

Garrick exits. Macklin begins to take off his dress. A Voice off: 'Mr Garrick!' Macklin grabs a Lear costume and darts behind screen. Lady Kingston enters.

Lady Kingston I know you're there, Mr Garrick. Don't think you can hide from me! I'll have you closed down this minute! Charles Macklin has just ridiculed me on a public stage.

Macklin He was quite good, apparently.

Lady Kingston He was poisonous! He slanderously insinuated that I wish my husband dead and have taken a young lover. I demand a public apology immediately! I cannot talk to you behind that screen, Mr Garrick.

Macklin emerges dressed as Lear.

I know you have sympathy with my predicament. You are a respectable man as well as a great actor.

Macklin I'm not that good. I've just taken all the great parts for myself.

Lady Kingston Nonsense. It's not the part, Mr Garrick, it's what a man does with it. Your performance always sets one's pulse racing. I demand satisfaction.

Macklin But I'm an old man.

Lady Kingston I need to feel you are behind me in this matter.

Macklin Very well, we'll do it behind the screen.

Lady Kingston The screen? So that's your price is it, you loathsome toad? You were with Macklin all the way. Let's get this over with, shall we?

She goes behind screen. Macklin tries to escape but on hearing Garrick's approach ducks into the skip.

Garrick (*off*) Tights are the least of my problems, Mrs Butler. (*to Macklin, whom he presumes is behind the screen*) Have you taken the dress off?

Lady Kingston I've barely had a moment, Mr Garrick.

Garrick I find your persistent female impersonation in the worst of taste. Put these on for now.

He hands her Lear costume.

Lady Kingston Male apparel, your taste sinks very low.

Garrick Hurry up, and talk like a man.

Lady Kingston As you wish.

Garrick This whole episode is extremely embarrassing.

Lady Kingston One wonders why you feel impelled to go through with it.

Garrick I have business with Mrs Butler.

Lady Kingston Her too.

Garrick exits. Macklin climbs out of skip to escape but Lady Kingston catches him.

You are dragging this out most unpleasantly. We could have had this over and done with in five minutes if Lord Kingston is anything to go by.

Macklin If t'were done when 'tis done, then it were well t'were done quickly.

Lady Kingston Shakespeare too, Mr Garrick, Well, that's a first.

They go behind screen. Cautherley and Hannah enter. He heads for skip to search for his costume.

Cautherley You appear to be following me about.

Hannah I'm concerned for you, Mr Cautherley.

Cautherley It's only a small bump, Miss More.

Hannah There's a post advertised in the *Hertfordshire Gazette*, teaching young foundlings. You could come with me, Mr Cautherley.

Cautherley Have you seen my costume lying about? It'll be black. I'm playing Edmund, the bastard.

Hannah Mr Cautherley, I'm trying to save you.

Cautherley I wish you wouldn't bother.

A noise from behind screen.

Wait there. Miss More, somebody may be hurt. (*He goes to look behind the screen. He starts visibly.*)

Hannah What is it, Mr Cautherley?

Cautherley Nothing. I think perhaps my head. I need a little air.

He exits, she follows. A crescendo of grunts behind screen. Macklin emerges.

Lady Kingston Well, Mr Garrick. Shakespeare certainly is our greatest poet. I now understand your great admiration for him.

Garrick (*offstage*) Do it yourself, Mrs Butler.

Macklin hears this and dives into skip. Mrs Cibber and Mr Barry enter with Garrick.

Mrs Cibber We're short on blood, Mr Garrick, and the jelly won't have set for Gloucester's eyes.

Barry My tights have gone for a walk.

Garrick Improvise! We don't want to keep the audience waiting any longer than we have to.

Mrs Cibber and Mr Barry exit.

(*To Lady Kingston.*)You have caused me a good deal of bother.

Lady Kingston I have?

Garrick Lear is my most taxing part and I've had to sort you out on top of it.

Lady Kingston It wasn't that bad, was it?

Garrick It was a waste of my time.

Lady Kingston Oh!

Garrick I'll prepare the public apology. But first I've the actors to see to.

He exits. Macklin climbs from the skip. Lady Kingston catches him.

Lady Kingston I think I take precedence above the actors, Mr Garrick. The apology can wait. Let's try the afterpiece in here.

Macklin I'm not the performer I once was, Lady Kingston.

Lady Kingston Your modesty verges on affectation, Mr Garrick.

She climbs into skip with him. Enter Hannah and Cautherley.

Hannah Does your head feel a little clearer, Mr Cautherley?

Cautherley Yes. Thank you.

Hannah Allow me to convince you, sir, of the profound satisfaction to be had in bringing hope to abandoned young children.

Cautherley It's here somewhere.

Hannah Their little faces, Mr Cautherley.

Cautherley I feel very sorry for them, but I'm an actor.

Hannah The theatre has not been as kind to you as you think.

Cautherley You exaggerate profoundly, Miss More; the theatre is no longer a hotbed of immorality. (*He opens skip. Shuts it hastily.*)

Hannah What is it?

Cautherley Probably nothing.

Hannah I insist you take another look, Mr Cautherley.

He does so.

Well?

Cautherley I think that potato may have inflicted more damage than I at first imagined. Air . . .

They exit. Enter Garrick. Checks behind screen. Sees Macklin gone. Sits down, takes medicine. Barry, Mrs Cibber and Mr Larpent enter.

Mrs Cibber You've a visitor from the Lord Chamberlain, Mr Garrick.

Barry He was in row seven. I can't go on without my lucky tights, Mr Garrick!

Garrick Pull yourself together, Mr Barry.

Mrs Cibber and Barry exit.

Larpent Garrick?

Garrick Here, sir.

Larpent I am Mr Larpent, the new man at the Lord Chamberlain's office. Tonight Drury Lane hosted an impromptu comic performance that was not submitted to us for prior inspection.

Garrick It was a one-off and it won't happen again.

Larpent You broke the law, sir. By rights we could revoke your license and throw you in gaol.

Garrick I had to calm the audience somehow. Entertaining them seemed the only option.

Larpent That was extremely irresponsible of you, sir.

Garrick I apologise. It won't happen again.

Larpent And this next, *King Lear*. Shakespeare isn't it? I don't know that one.

Garrick I've reinstated some of the original but it still ends happily. It's about a king, sir, a venerable old gentleman. The tragedy is deservedly celebrated. No play so much agitates our passions.

Larpent Our passions? I thought you said he was an old fellow.

Garrick I refer to pity and fear, not low behaviour.

Larpent Good, because none of us would wish to see venerated age compromised in sordid dalliance.

Hannah and Cautherley enter.

Hannah Mr Garrick. Mr Cautherley has been seeing things behind that screen and in that basket.

Barry His costume, perhaps.

Hannah Two old gentlemen doing things.

Larpent Two old gentlemen?

Cautherley They were going at it like the clappers, sir.

Garrick Trust me, Mr Cautherley, this is the result of your condition. He's been hit on the head by a vegetable.

Basket shakes.

Larpent There does appear to be something moving in that basket.

Garrick I think I can explain. Come on out, Mr Macklin. He prefers to rehearse in private.

Macklin I'm all rehearsed out, Mr Garrick.

Hannah There!

Cautherley That's one of them.

Hannah I knew a potato couldn't be responsible for the things he saw.

Garrick Mr Macklin is alone in that basket! I've been with him all evening! Your suggestions are absurd!

Larpent But you said there was only one king, sir?

Garrick He is the old king's identical twin brother.

Larpent And these old gentlemen lived morally upright lives?

Macklin They hardly ever left the castle, sir.

Larpent I am experiencing severe qualms about the suitability of *Lear* for performance. There appears to be a worrying proliferation of kings. What they get up to is a further disturbing question.

Audience slow-handclap.

Mrs Cibber The audience are growing restless, Mr Garrick. There's a vicar with his shirt off! (*She exits.*)

Garrick You can't ban Shakespeare! We've nothing else, and our audience is turning on us!

Larpent I have no choice, I'm afraid. The Lord Chamberlain comes down very heavily on this sort of thing.

Lady Kingston emerges from basket.

Lady Kingston Shakespeare is just what the British public needs!

Larpent There's another one!

Cautherley Two sir!

Hannah As you saw. Two hideous aged accomplices.

Larpent Explain this, Garrick!

Garrick It's quite simple, there are three brothers.

Lady Kingston I am Lady Kingston. I own Surrey.

Garrick I believe it is Lady Kingston.

Lady Kingston Shakespeare, Mr Larpent, is one way in which a woman may repair a reputation somewhat ravaged by scurrilous afterpieces. I know your mother, remember.

Larpent The only way I could ever condone it would be to categorise it as a musical. We tend to be more lenient with those.

Garrick *King Lear* definitely slots into that category.

Macklin Let's give him a number, Mr Garrick, and get it over with.

Garrick Very well. You begin, Mr Macklin.

Macklin After you, boss.

Garrick Blow wind and crack your cheeks.

Macklin I've been stuck in that basket it seems like weeks.

Lady Kingston I don't know the words. What is it about?

Garrick You cataracts and hurricanoes spout!

Macklin I once was a king but they chucked me out.

All Fa la la la. Fa la la.

Larpent That certainly clears matters up, thank you, Mr Garrick.

Lady Kingston You may escort me to my box, Mr Larpent. How is your mother?

They exit. Enter Goldsmith and Johnson. They sing.

Goldsmith *and* **Johnson**
Let school masters puzzle their brain
With grammar and nonsense and learning,
Good liquor I stoutly maintain
Gives reason a better discerning.

Mrs Butler (*off*) Beginners please.

Johnson Goldy's play is a great success, Davy!

Goldsmith They laughed, Mr Garrick.

Johnson I had to give them a bit of help at first.

Goldsmith He roared like a rhino! It is very bad manners to celebrate in so public a fashion. But I can't help it. (*He dances.*)

Mrs Butler (*off*) Scene one. Ancient British Court on stage. Tights or no tights, Mr Barry.

Mr Barry, Mrs Cibber take up positions in wings.

Johnson There was an excellent moment in Goldy's play when Mr Hardcastle tells of a battle and no one will listen to him for they think he is an inn-keeper . . . ha ha . . .

Goldsmith That's a great moment! How's your night going, Davy?

Mrs Butler (*off*) Curtain up!

Garrick steps forward.

Garrick Success. The termination of any affair, happy or unhappy. Success without any epithet is commonly taken for good success.

Mrs Garrick All three Persian rugs are not Persian.
They are in the style of Persia and were purchased in
Bermondsey at thirty shillings for the original production of
Tancred and Sigismunda.

Garrick Shite, in other words. (*Garrick operates his wig.*)

Mrs Garrick That's not coming with us.

Garrick That is a glorious piece of engineering.

Mrs Garrick writes in her ledger.

Mrs Garrick Tatty wig coming.

Garrick It's theatrical history, Mrs Garrick. Sheridan can
have the building, but he's not having history.

Mrs Garrick I shouldn't think he'd want it. It's got fleas.
Mr Sheridan has done us the favour of purchasing the
patent, so we may retire with peace of mind.

Garrick He is our successor. We may wish him modest
achievements. (*He picks a coat out of the skip, tries it on.*)
Look at this, Mrs Garrick. (*He sports Goldsmith's jacket.*)
He sold it to wardrobe. I always meant to get it back for
him. (*He puts it on. He imitates Goldsmith.*) Now M–Mrs
Garrick, who c–could I be?

Mrs Garrick They're making a fuss of him because of his
play.

Garrick It'll die down. That's what fashion's like. It's fickle.

A knock at the door. She regards the secret door.

Mrs Garrick One last time.

She disappears into the secret room. Enter Dr Johnson.
Garrick continues with his impersonation of Goldsmith.

Garrick Ah, Mr G–G–Garrick, wh–why won't you p–put on my new p–play, you b–bastard?

Johnson So, you've heard.

Garrick Heard?

Johnson I'm presuming your bad taste is intentional. Our dear friend Goldsmith died this morning.

Garrick Died?

Johnson Four a.m. He accidentally poisoned himself with his own medicine. There's an irony in there somewhere, but I'm too upset to discover it.

Garrick He had an appointment to see me this afternoon.

Johnson He won't be coming.

Garrick I had good news for him. Mr Sheridan is anxious to commission him on my advice.

Johnson Dr Goldsmith, sir, has finished with earthly tasks. You had your chance to couple your name with his, sir, and you missed it. He has written the only play worth mentioning in fifty years.

Garrick That is an overstatement.

Johnson Only because you did not do it, Davy. Otherwise you would be agreeing with them heartily. His name is on everybody's lips. The town has declared him a genius.

Garrick A genius?

Johnson I do not condone what they are saying about you. Take my advice and ignore the whisperers.

Garrick The whisperers?

Johnson Those who accuse you of not joining your name to his. The greatest actor of the age with the greatest writer.

Johnson We are lonelier since he left us. I have others to see. Give my regards to Mrs Garrick. But I forget. She can hear me.

Garrick We'll meet soon.

Johnson That is not always in our hands, Davy.

He exits. Mrs Garrick enters. She points to Goldsmith's jacket.

Mrs Garrick Dr Johnson should have that. It's only right.

Garrick takes it off hurriedly. She goes to the door.

Garrick The whisperers!

She comes back.

Mrs Garrick It's Sam.

Garrick Sam!

She exits. Garrick composes himself. Cautherley enters.

Cautherley Mr Garrick.

Garrick Mr Cautherley.

Cautherley I want to apologise, sir, for leaving the company so abruptly.

Garrick It is customary for actors to give a month's notice. I had to cast a Banquo and Benvolio with very little grace.

Cautherley I'm sorry, sir.

Garrick But I'm glad you've come back, Sam. I've been wanting to talk to you.

Cautherley I don't want you to think I'm not grateful for the past, sir.

Garrick Did I ever tell you how I researched the part of Lear, Mr Cautherley?

Cautherley No, Mr Garrick.

Garrick I knew a man who killed his own child by accident. He was playing with her at a window when she slipped from his grasp and was dashed to death on the cobbles below. The poor man went mad with grief. He never left the room again but would sit in a chair staring at the window and every few minutes would rush to it with a cry as if reliving the dreadful moment over and over again. I used to visit him and it made me very sad, but there was also a part of me thinking: excellent, I can use that. The part of us that is an artist, Sam, can be quite hard, is what I'm trying to say. I know you have heard things while you've been here. Rumours.

Cautherley Rumours? I don't listen to them, sir.

Garrick I think you ought to know about your parents.

Cautherley I would not like to learn anything, sir, that compromised my respectability now I'm to be married.

Garrick Married!?

Cautherley To Miss More. We're going to start a school, sir.

Garrick To Miss More! Mr Cautherley. You are an actor, sir. You can't run a school. Don't give up, Mr Cautherley. Believe me, you have natural talent.

Hannah enters.

Hannah A school for poor and abandoned children, sir. A worthy cause.

Cautherley I shall be glad to be useful. I shall shake your hand, sir. I doubt we'll have much time to visit.

Lady Kingston enters with everyone.

Lady Kingston Mr Garrick.

Mrs Cibber Dear manager, dear, dear Garrick. How can we let this momentous day pass without acknowledging in some way your extraordinary achievements, your overwhelming talent.

Garrick This is a speech.

Mrs Cibber Please accept this token of our gratitude and esteem.

She hands Garrick the gloves. Garrick takes them, reads the card.

Garrick Shakespeare's gloves. Will you look at that, Mrs Garrick?

Mrs Garrick Lovely.

Mrs Cibber No one is aware of the sacrifices you've made. We might not have a theatre today, had you not ensured the respectability of our profession.

Applause.

Lady Kingston Mr Garrick, I hear you will be dining your way round the best homes in England performing a selection of after-dinner pieces. Perhaps you would oblige us?

All Yes. Oh yes, do, Mr Garrick, *etc.*

Garrick
Howl, howl, howl! O you are men of stones!
Had I your tongues and eyes, I'd use them so
That heaven's vault should crack. She's gone for ever.
I know when one is dead and when one lives.
She's dead as earth.

A frisson runs through the crowd. He is performing the prohibited version.

'A plague upon you, murderers, traitors all!
I might have saved her, now she's gone for ever.'

Lady Kingston Mr Garrick. That is the wrong version.

Cibber We want the ending you rewrote so movingly.

Johnson The cruelty of the original cannot be countenanced by civilised people, Davy.

Mrs Garrick Give them what they want, Mr Garrick.

Garrick My apologies.

Mrs Cibber Perhaps I can oblige you. (*She arranges herself as Cordelia.*)

Garrick
    I know when one is dead and when one lives.
    The feather stirs! She lives. If it be so
    It is a chance which will redeem all sorrows
    That I have ever felt.

Mrs Cibber
                            Oh happy time.

Garrick
    All Nature pause, and listen to the change.
    Cordelia shall be a queen; winds catch the sound,
    And bear it on your rosy wings to Heav'n –
    Divine Cordelia, all the Gods can witness
    How much thy love to Empire I prefer!
    Whatever storms of Fortune are decreed
    Truth and virtue shall at last succeed.

Mrs Garrick Bravo.

Lady Kingston Magnificent.

Garrick Thank you. Thank you. (*He loves the praise. He soaks it up. He bows.*) Thank you, thank you, thank you.

JUMPY

Jumpy was first performed at the Royal Court Jerwood Theatre Downstairs, Sloane Square, on 13 October 2011, with the following cast, in order of appearance:

Tilly Bel Powley
Hilary Tamsin Greig
Mark Ewan Stewart
Lyndsey Seline Hizli
Frances Doon Mackichan
Roland Richard Lintern
Bea Sarah Woodward
Josh James Musgrave
Cam Michael Marcus

Director Nina Raine
Designer Lizzie Clachan
Lighting Designer Peter Mumford
Sound Designer Paul Arditti

Characters

Hilary

Mark
her husband

Tilly
their daughter

Frances
Hilary's friend

Lyndsey
Tilly's friend

Bea

Roland
Bea's husband

Josh
their son

Cam
a student

A teenage girl, Tilly, walks across the stage. She is dressed in
a short skirt, heels, bright colours. She is listening to an iPod.
    We hear the music: Florence and the Machine.
    She does not see her mother, Hilary, who watches her,
tired, carrying two shopping bags. Hilary puts down the
bags, takes out a bottle of wine, screws off lid and pours
herself a glass.

ONE

Mark and Hilary.

Mark So you got on the Tube?

Hilary Yes.

Mark You took the escalator down?

Hilary Yes.

Mark And you weren't thinking anything in particular?

Hilary Nothing. Except –

Mark Except?

Hilary Nothing.

Mark It must have been / something.

Hilary No. / Well.
    I was remembering the time I took the dog to Hyde Park.
For some reason I couldn't remember the rules about dogs
and escalators and I thought, Christ I'm going to have to
carry it.

Mark He wouldn't have liked that.

Hilary No. He wondered what the hell was going on. He hadn't left ground level for a considerable number of years. It was a nightmare. I was sweating, the dog was doubting.

Mark That's what you were thinking this morning?

Hilary Yes.

Mark You got on to the Tube, sat down. And then.

Hilary It wasn't immediate. It starts with a random thought. I don't want to tell you what it is in case it's viral.

Mark Tell me. I'll be immune.

Hilary There's this thought that there's a lot of earth above my head –

Mark I wouldn't think that.

Hilary – that I was in a tunnel bored deep down.
    And above me earth, heavy, dark, between me and –

Mark The top.

Hilary Yes.

Mark Air.

Hilary Yes.

Mark Outside.

Hilary Yes. And this feeling became.

Mark What?

Hilary It reached a level
    Of panic
    Which was unbearable
    And I thought if I don't get off this train –

Mark What?

Hilary I'll die.

Mark That's not good if you have to go to work every day.

Hilary I know. It's shit. It took me two and a half hours to ride five stops. After work I had to get a cab home.

Mark How will you be tomorrow?

Hilary No idea. Might try my bike. Stress.

Mark Yes.

Hilary Job stuff.

Mark Yes.

Hilary Worst-case scenario it happens to us both. Your business bottoms out. I get made redundant. And there are fuck-all jobs out there.

There's no point worrying.

Fifty sounds too old to put on an application form.

I might lie. No one would know. I don't look fifty. I don't act fifty. I could get away with forty-three. Don't you think I could get away with forty-three?

Pause.

Mark Depends.

Hilary On?

Mark If the person you're talking to happens to be forty-three they might think you look a little older.

Hilary What's the likelihood of saying I was forty-three to a person who happens to be forty-three?

Mark Quite high.

Hilary What would it have cost you, Mark, to say I look forty-three? If it made me happy?

Would it have cost you the earth?

Mark It'll muck up your CV. You could drop a year, two at most. What's the point?

Pause.

Hilary What time is it?

Mark Eight-eighteen.

Hilary Are you going to walk the dog?

Mark Yes. I'll take it round the block.

Hilary We don't work in car plants. Didn't mind when they went – too many cars on the road anyway, melting the icecaps, but a bloody Educational Reading Support Unit. How dare they?

Mark It might not come to that.
  Don't think about politics when you get on the Tube.

Hilary She has no idea.
  We mustn't tell her.

Mark What?

Hilary Anything. Telling her stuff like losing our livelihoods will only destabilise her further. Give her more fuel for disturbance to turn into her own brand of exquisite torture to inflict on us, her parents.
  What I'm hoping, Mark, is that what happened today was just a wobble.

Mark I think it is.

Hilary You know what else I was thinking? That time we took Tilly and her friends down to Brighton for the day right at the end of primary school and in the back of the car they were playing a game. They closed their eyes and took it in turns to tickle the inside of each other's arms, wrist to elbow, and Tilly said that's the equivalent of a quarter of an orgasm.

  Beat.

Would we have said that when we were eleven? I wouldn't. An orgasm.

  Beat.

Hilary You'd still have been playing with your Scalextric.

Mark I may have looked like I was playing – I was cognitively developing.

Hilary Where are you going now? I'm still talking.

Mark Dog.

He exits.

TWO

Tilly, Lyndsey (pregnant), Hilary.

Lyndsey Hello, Mrs Winters.

Hilary Hello, Lyndsey. Call me Hilary. I'm a Ms actually, anyway.

Tilly Ms. Like the sound you make before you vom.

Hilary Well, that's who I am.
Goodness, look at you, Lyndsey. When did that happen?

Tilly You want to know *when* it happened?

Hilary No, I didn't mean –

Lyndsey Lloyd Park, ten-thirty p.m., September 2nd 2008.
I remember everything because.

Hilary What?

Tilly Nothing. Is it your business?

Pause.

Hilary Your boyfriend. Is he still – involved?

Lyndsey No.

Hilary That's a shame.

Lyndsey He would be, but he's dead.

Hilary Dead?

Tilly Mum, I don't really think she wants to talk about it.

Lyndsey It's all right. I've come to terms with it.

Tilly It's cool of Lyndsey to keep this baby because Keiron got stabbed.

Hilary Oh God.

Lyndsey His mum's pleased. It's something to look forward to.

Hilary Well, I'm really sorry, Lyndsey, what a lot to go through. That's awful.

Pause.

What about your GCSEs?

Lyndsey I'm taking them this year. Then a year out then I'm going back to college.

Hilary Good. As long as it's your decision. The baby.

Tilly Who else's decision is it going to be?

Hilary I always remember you, Lyndsey, from the school plays.
The Lion King. You stood out. A hyena.

Tilly It's Lyndsey's decision.

Hilary I'm just saying there might have been pressure on Lyndsey, that's all, to keep it. It's not inconceivable.

Tilly Keiron got another girl pregnant as well. And she's having hers – so it was Lyndsey's choice.

Hilary Keiron fitted a lot in.

Tilly He died, Mum, it's not funny. At the bus station, Walthamstow.

Hilary Yes, I remember seeing all the flowers.

Lyndsey Me, his mum and his sister went down there every day. We used to hurry down there like we were late to meet someone. Stupid. In the end the council took them all away. The bouquets. When they went brown.

Hilary Perhaps you and this other girl expecting his baby, could be friends, support each other?

Tilly God no, she's got a monobrow.

Hilary What's that got to do with it? What she looks like? What A-levels do you want to do, Lyndsey?

Lyndsey A BTEC in Beauty Therapy.

Pause.

Hilary Well, people always want to be beautiful.

Lyndsey I'll be able to fit work in round having a kid.

Tilly Let's go.

Hilary Where are you two off to?

Tilly The Oak.

Hilary What is the attraction of that place?

Tilly Cheap booze.

Lyndsey It's my birthday.

Tilly Sweet sixteen.
There's loads of us going. And some guys from Forest School. I'll be really late.

Hilary I'll pick you up.

Tilly We're getting the night bus.

Hilary You've got GCSEs in a month. Don't forget.

Tilly A month. Yeah. I can't stay in every night like you.

Hilary Watch your drinks. Don't let anyone put anything in your drinks. You can have two drinks.

Tilly Down there they're too mean to waste drugs on other people.

Hilary It's not going to be people you know. Ruby, the woman that walks Pete's dogs, it happened to her – she woke up in a hotel room – had no idea how she got there – Rohypnol.

Tilly All right!

Hilary Well, it happens.

Lyndsey No one would bother to drug me, I'm too fat.

Hilary You're pregnant, / not fat.

Tilly Let's go.

Lyndsey Couldn't lift me.

Hilary Have a wonderful birthday, Lyndsey.

Tilly Laters.

Hilary Good luck.

Lyndsey Thank you.

Exit.

Hilary Tilly!

She returns.

Have you got any money?

Tilly I won't be buying the drinks.

Hilary Who'll be buying them?

Tilly shrugs.

(*Giving her some money.*) Take this – buy your own. And buy one for Lyndsey. A soft drink. Give me a hug.

Tilly I can't.

Hilary Why didn't you tell me about the baby?

Tilly I did.

Hilary Was she using contraception?

Tilly God. Please. I don't want to hear you say that word.

Hilary Be careful. Have fun.

Tilly Bye.

Hilary Do you think she really wanted to?

Tilly What?

Hilary With that boy, Keiron?

Tilly Don't be gay.

Hilary I'm fine with you going out but it has to be balanced by work because you need, you need –

She has gone.

Exams.

THREE

Hilary and Frances.

Hilary Lovely to see you. You're looking wonderful.

Frances You too. We got that over with – now can we have a drink?

Hilary I love this. Our second Friday of the month. A great institution.
What I thought we'd do is just drink and eat crisps.
If we get desperate we could order a pizza.
I've been getting those rocket pizzas.

Frances Fast delivery.

Hilary Cheeseless, lightly strewn with a kind of plant growth. The guilt factor of pizza and the brownie point of a green salad.

Frances You sign up for something you don't really get, sounds too much like my life.

Hilary You know we mustn't fall into that trap.

Frances What trap? Why haven't you opened a bottle?

She opens a bottle.

Hilary This is what we do every time. It's like we're wound up and plonked down and there we go down the same route. What year is it? It could be last year. Any year. We have to stop whingeing.

Frances I'm not going to sit here being positive. That would be insane.

I got on a train the other day with a writer.

Hilary Yes?

Frances Used to be an actor – we'd been in a show together years ago. He was 'beyond gender' in his work, he was telling me. That's all right for him. He's a bloke. Gender is burying us alive. Old women. Our only chance is to run a country or some vast significant organisation like Sainsbury's. That's all that's going to save us from invisibility. Being a woman and getting old is a disaster.

Hilary Don't be defeatist. No one's saying it's easy.

You had that availability check. David Hare play. What happened with that?

Frances They never saw me. Checked my availability and when they found out I was available they thought, God, no. If no one else wants her, we don't.

Hilary They didn't do that. That's just negative thinking.

Frances I went up for a film the other day. A war thing.

Hilary Great.

Frances To play an ageing German prostitute.

Hilary Right.

Frances I won't get it. There were a host of us dressed as old tarts just panting for the part. The bus home had its moments.

Hilary Did you finish your decorating?

Frances Yes.

Hilary Aren't we going to talk about it?

Frances No.
Decorating is false consciousness. You think you're improving your life, you're slapping paint on walls.

Hilary No, I don't accept that. In the seventies they painted everything white. A new start.

Frances The seventies were brown and orange. Most people weren't even born then.
The seventies – no one bothers with it now.

Hilary Rubbish. The woman's movement. Glam rock. Do I have to go through a list of our achievements?

Frances attempts to balance a glass on her head or does some writhing movements.

What are you doing?

Frances Something interesting. You're being boring.

Hilary I'm biking to work now, did I say?

Frances Good for the arse.

Hilary It also gets me to work.

Frances Get any comments?

Hilary No. Fortunately.

Frances Pity.

I used to love that. Being a young woman being sexy on a bike.

Hilary You hated that, we both did.

Frances I thought I hated it, I was wrong, now I miss it. I wouldn't get on to a bike now. I'd get withdrawal symptoms.

I was in a bar the other night. Being witty, laughing, being absolutely bloody brilliant actually. The stuff I was coming out with – I wish I could have recorded it for posterity. You know you get those nights.

Hilary Well –

Frances And I was getting admiring glances. I could feel that. On the surface of my skin.

Hilary You can't feel that.

Frances A woman's second sense, come on.

I was looking fucking amazing too. What a package. I never let myself go.

Hilary Neither have I.

Frances Persevered with vaginal toning.

Hilary Never top of my list.

Frances This man my age, looked older, and not as attractive as me, okay though, worth a punt, I could sense him at the edges of my force field being drawn in by my verbal magnetism.

Hilary Really?

Frances So when it was time to take a waz I walked past him, bit of a squeeze, packed bar. Thought I'd give him the full impact of my many charms at close quarters. I smiled, looked him straight in the eyes. Dead. Not so much as a flicker. Total reptilian blank. Or rather – actual distaste.

Hilary Well, you didn't know anything about him. Maybe someone he knew had just died?

Frances Yeah, that's what I do when I get news of a death, go straight to All Bar One.

Hilary It doesn't matter.

Frances No. Fuck him.

Hilary Yes. Some tossy / estate agent.

Frances Contracts lawyer. It does matter.
I haven't got a pension.

Hilary Got the flat.

Frances I've always thought of sexual attractiveness as an extreme fallback position. If I was starving. Do I look better like this?

Holds the sides of her face – like a facelift.

Hilary You look more surprised.
You're having some kind of crisis.

Frances It's called being fifty. You must be having it too.

Hilary No. Actually. Definitely not. No. No. There's more to life. You know.

Frances Going to a gallery – evening classes.
Feels like someone's stolen something from me.
But I don't want to hog. Your go.

Hilary Did I tell you about the other day?

Frances What?

Hilary When I came home and found – well – Tilly was home from school.
I'd got back early. She was supposed to be revising. She was just sitting there on the sofa and when she saw me come in her face changed but I ignored that because

I couldn't see a reason for it so I pushed it to the back of my mind and then down the stairs came this boy.

Frances A boy?

Hilary Fifteen years old. Both of them. They'd nipped home – found a 'window'.

To be honest I actually felt sick.

Frances Well, they're all so lush, aren't they? Flawless and bursting with hormones.

What was he like, the boy?

Hilary In his boxers. Tall, skinny. Hair hanging over his face. He grunted.

Frances I love that look. They haven't become men yet. Does he play the guitar?

Hilary I didn't ask.

Frances Let them get on with it.

Hilary She was letting me know she wanted my help. She wanted me to find out.

Frances Doesn't sound like she needed any help. Young love. I'm bloody jealous. Is it ever that good again?

Hilary Of course it is.

Frances The best we can expect of life now is avoiding the worst. I'm scared.

Hilary Scared?

Frances holds out her glass.

Frances Wine. I don't like looking ahead. Do you?

FOUR

Roland This is terrific, isn't it, Bea?

Pause.

We really appreciate you taking the time. I'm sorry we've got such a short 'window'.
It's . . . we've had this . . . dinner planned for – well, it's a shame.

Hilary That's fine. Honestly. Thanks for seeing me at such short notice.

Roland Great, great. We've got forty-five minutes.

Bea Less than that.

Roland Well, yes, a bit less, you're right.

Bea The traffic.

Roland Yes.

Bea Thirty-five minutes. More like.

Roland Well, let's crack on with it then.
You did the right thing. Didn't she, Bea? We completely understand.

Bea Well –

Roland What?

Bea We don't think as one, Roland.

Roland We understand. That's what I'm reassuring Hilary about.

Hilary I just thought it needed attending to –

Roland Totally. We love Tilly . . . She's a lovely girl. Feisty. But polite. Well done.

Hilary I found them. I came home that day earlier – they were both there. Tilly and Josh. They were truanting. And it was obvious . . . that they'd been –

Bea It was obvious? Why?

Hilary Because they weren't wearing any clothes. He was in boxer shorts, Tilly was in an old shirt.

Bea It doesn't mean they'd had sex.

Roland We're not arguing. We agree they did. I thought Josh was looking bloody pleased with himself. I wasn't having sex when I was fifteen. Lucky sod.

Bea You have no idea.

Roland Of course. It's serious. But there are no bones broken.

Hilary Tilly told me later. I asked her and she said yes. They'd done it three times.

Roland Coffee?

Hilary No, thank you.

Roland I think we've taken our eye off the ball where Josh's concerned. I think we have to hold up our hands and say that. We've both had a lot on. Bea's at HSBC. I'm an actor. I've been horribly busy.

Pause.

What do you do, Hilary?

Hilary I'm in literacy. I manage a reading support unit. We work in schools. We see quite a few troubled teens.

Roland You know what you're talking about then. Obviously.

Bea Josh isn't troubled.

Hilary Tilly's on the pill now.

132

Roland Christ, she wasn't before?

Hilary No. Well, fifteen.

Roland No, no.

Hilary I feel we somehow need to monitor the situation.

Bea You mean keep some sort of chart?

Roland Of course not. She doesn't mean that.

Bea It's happened. It's done. There's nothing we can do now.

Hilary If they sleep together I want it to be at our house.

Roland Right.

Hilary It's just a way of containing it – sex means big emotions.

Bea It's the same for Josh.
  What if we said it can only happen here, for Josh, for the 'emotions'?

Roland But we're not saying that.

Bea Are we saying it's different for girls than boys? How Victorian.

Roland It is different. Isn't it?

Hilary It's a big thing for Tilly. I'm her mother. It doesn't hurt Josh to realise that.

Bea They like each other a lot. They've explored their sexual feelings. They've gone on a journey together.

Hilary I think Tilly's in love.

Roland I expect Josh is too. Only he's a bloke.

Bea What does that mean?

Roland Well, he won't know he is.

Bea Josh is very different from you, Roland. For a start I'm his mother.

Roland Well, look, let's not get on to, on to my mother.

Hilary So perhaps you could let Josh know.

Bea I don't feel comfortable doing that.

Roland I'll do it. Look, it's fine, we're agreed.

Bea It feels punishing.

Hilary It's about taking responsibility.

Roland It's fine. It'll be fine.

Bea You don't know that. You're taking something that's natural and saying it needs to be supervised.
It's not Josh's fault.

Roland No one is saying it is.
I mean, I think we have to hold up our hands here, Bea, and admit that boys want it more, at that age.

Bea That's nonsense. Total unreconstructed.

Hilary I think that probably is nonsense.

Roland Okay, I give in.

Bea I have to go and get changed.

Hilary Of course. Thank you for seeing me. I realise it's a shock for you too.

Bea exits.

Roland Everything will be sorted.

Hilary I'm her mother – you understand. Because really it's not the same for girls.

Roland I've never been a girl.

Hilary They have approximately three thousand images of airbrushed-over sexualised women pumped out at them every day.

134

Roland That is awful. Unless you're a bloke.

Hilary They feel they have to be sexual to be human.

Roland Oh yes, yes, yes.

FIVE

Tilly Why did you go?

Hilary Look.

Tilly What's it got to do with you?

Hilary Look.

Tilly It's got nothing to do with you.

Hilary Yes it has.

Tilly I'm sixteen.

Hilary Not for a month.

Tilly I can't believe you did that, you ruined my life.

Hilary Don't overreact. Don't be stupid. How could I have ruined your life?

Tilly They won't have liked you. What did you wear?

Hilary I don't know.

Tilly You didn't wear your jeans?

Hilary I don't think they cared what I wore. It was what I had to say that was important. What's wrong with my jeans? Aren't I allowed to wear jeans any more?

Tilly I'm just saying that was the worst thing you ever did.

Hilary Listen –

Tilly You had no right, no right to do that.

Hilary You'll see it differently soon.

Tilly I won't.

Hilary In a year even.

Tilly No.

Hilary When you're my age.

Tilly I'll be dead by then.

Hilary Don't be ridiculous.

Tilly When I'm that old.

Hilary Well, you say that now, that's what everyone says, but life's very precious, I can tell you. No one says, 'Oh, I'm a bit old, I have a grey hair, I'm finishing it all.'

Tilly I will.

Hilary I said to them that I'm happy for you and Josh to see each other but you're both fifteen and I want it safe, I want it here and I think actually he'll respect you more for that.

Tilly It's finished.

Hilary When did that happen?

Tilly When you ruined it.

Hilary When did that happen?

Tilly His name's all over my Humanities folder. It really hurts.

    Tilly exits.

Hilary Don't slam the door like that. Tell me. Tell me. What is so appalling about the idea of me in jeans?

SIX

Bedroom.
Hilary's phone beeps. She checks it.
She gets into bed beside Mark.

Hilary *Great Expectations?*

She picks up a book.

Where were we? Pip's met Mr Pumblechook.

Mark I think I'm going to sleep.

Hilary We'll never get through it at this rate. If you keep falling asleep. At night.
Immediately, like this. I could just read a page.

Mark What's the point? I'll be asleep the minute I close my –

Hilary Christmas. That's how long we've been reading this. We reckoned a couple of months. It's July. We're defaulting on our project.

Mark Don't call it a project.

Hilary Project is a good word.

Pause.

Projects stop you being bored. I used to be so scared of boredom as a kid I had a kind of phobia about it. Like I feared being thrown into a living grave and trapped there for eternity. Did you get that feeling?

Mark No.

Hilary Lucky you. We lived in a flat. You had a garden. Maybe that had something to do with it, being trapped in a flat with a depressed mother.

Mark Maybe you were an odd kid.

Pause.

Night.

Hilary I wasn't. The sixties. The dark ages. Women in nylons and stilettos. That's how my mum picked me up from school when it was snowing.

Her only concession to the arctic conditions was a headscarf. Femininity must be asserted over everything, even frostbite.

Pause.

Are you asleep?

Mark How could I be asleep? You're talking.

Hilary It's interesting though, isn't it?

Pause.

I told you about our core funding.

Mark Yes.

Hilary We haven't got any.

Mark You thought it might go.

Hilary It's still a shock when it does.

Mark You'll have to crawl up the arse of the commercial sector.

Hilary I'm not looking at it that way, Mark. That's a predictable way to go.

I'm heading down the road of creative partnerships.

Mark Excellent. Goodnight.

Hilary How's your work?

Mark It's not picking up.

Hilary I got a text.

From Tilly. She's bringing Josh back.

Mark To stay?

Hilary Yes.

Mark I want to go to sleep.

Hilary They're back together. Thank God. Which is good for Tilly.

Mark I don't want to hear anything.

Hilary You won't hear anything. There are walls. Walls.

Mark Goodnight.

Hilary Walls between us. Solid walls.

Pause.

You'd have to be really listening out for –

Mark All right.

Hilary You know, really listening.

Sound of two young people walking past the room and going into the next-door room. Laughter. Muted talk.

You can hardly hear a thing. The good thing is we have a wardrobe against that wall. Full of clothes. Muffling everything. A happy accident.

Quite loud creak of bedsprings.

I could hear that. Could you?

Another creak.

We have to let them know. We have to – if we laugh – they'll know we can. Come on.

She looks at him, she laughs.

Mark What are you doing?

Hilary Laughing.

Mark Laughing like a lunatic.

Hilary If you weren't going to join in, why didn't you let me know? Of course it sounds strange to laugh out loud when the other person is totally silent. Do you want him to think I'm eccentric?

Mark Who cares what he thinks?

Hilary He goes to Forest School.

Mark So what?

Hilary He's a nice boy. If he likes us – he'll be kind to her.

Mark He better be kind to her – He's in there –

A loud creak.

Hilary Well, this isn't the nineteenth century.

Mark We never brought girls home when we were fifteen.

Hilary Sixteen now.

Mark Whatever. We fumbled about in the cinema.
We waited till university to have full sex. It was all part of the learning experience.
Is it respectful – to bring back – into the next room – next to your parents?

Hilary Shh. They'll hear us talking about them.

Mark Don't tell me to shh in my own house.

Hilary Shh.

Another creak.
  She starts to laugh.
  He starts to laugh.

Mark What?

He reaches out for her.

Hilary No, no. What if they hear us?

He is hurt.

Mark We're not doing things right.

Hilary This is what happens now.

He turns over. Shuts his eyes. Hilary turns out the light. Creaks in the dark.

SEVEN

Roland, Hilary.
A silence. They both speak at the same time.

Both I do.

Laughter.

Roland It's a mess.
You must have felt something.

Hilary I think I was so caught up in –

Roland Yes, what you were –

Hilary Yes.

Roland But you could sense something? I felt as if it was blaring out of loudspeakers. These people are in meltdown.

Hilary I couldn't tell. Most couples appear to be on the verge of – some kind of dissatisfaction.

Roland Yes, that's very good. Yes.

Pause.

So after you came to see us – about the kids – I felt we hadn't told you everything.
Because we were in trouble – and he was reacting to us.

Hilary Josh.

Roland Yes. A kind of rebellion.

Hilary That makes sense.

Roland That's what he was telling us with Tilly. A kind of 'fuck you, I'm a man now'.

Between me and his mother it hasn't been good. I mean that's tangible. And then when I waded in and said – it's fine, but do it at Tilly's house, he walked away from it all – but really I was the one he was rebelling against because it was me telling him.

Hilary But it's okay now. They've sorted it out.

Roland Teenage boys and their fathers. Freud was right. Underneath it all they'd like to eat us and take our women.

Hilary They don't know how to cook, do they?

Roland You don't need to cook warm flesh. You just need sturdy teeth and a lack of consideration for others. Most teenagers qualify.

Hilary 'I only have a short window.'

Roland We made that up. About the window. I said to Bea, people know when you're lying. They just know instinctively. Did you know?

Hilary No.

Roland There goes another theory. Soon I'll be left with nothing.

Hilary Was there something specific?

Roland I could murder a drink.

Pause.

We, I, felt bad about what happened next. But it was when it was really hitting the rocks. I couldn't speak to Bea without shouting. I've moved out. Now I live with the sofa bed and our old kettle. Everything's crappy.

Hilary What 'happened next'?

Roland I said to Bea we should have told you.

Hilary What?

Roland Josh was really upset.

Hilary What about?

Roland He was with another girl and they were at a party.

Hilary Whose party?

Roland They're always at parties. And Tilly came – as far as I can make out he didn't know she was going – she didn't know he was – and then she went up to a bedroom with a guy – and then after that another guy . . . she was angry with Josh.

Hilary Oh God –

Roland I've been wanting to tell you. Josh told Bea. He was gutted.

Hilary When did this happen?

Roland Over a month ago – right when Bea and I were going through it.

Hilary She never told me.

Roland Well, you can understand that.

Hilary I'm her mother.

Roland I wouldn't take it personally.

Hilary Why didn't she tell me?

Roland It's okay. She's probably talked about it to her friends. They like their friends better than us. We like them better than our friends. That's okay. They move in packs. Day and night – every minute they want to be with each other. Can you imagine wanting to spend that much time with other people? I mean a few drinks, lunch, an evening. But every minute of the day? Phoning, eating, sleeping at each other's houses, they can't get enough. What happens to us that we grow so un-enamoured of each other? People turn your stomach, don't they? Their fucking issues and their vanity.

One minute there's the nappies, the Calpol, their inconvenient sicknesses, reading them the same story till it's tattooed on the back of your eyelids – though Bea did that mainly – you can't wait for them to go to sleep at night so you can get in a few glasses of wine – then this redundancy. How does that happen?

Hilary I'm not redundant.

Roland Maybe with girls it's different.

Soon we won't be parents. I'll say 'my son' and I'll be referring to some twenty-eight-year-old lunk who works for a living. That actually gives me a pain.

Hilary We shouldn't hurry time.

Roland Bea accused me of flirting with you. I told her she was being a maniac.

Hilary Like who would?

Roland I didn't mean that. I told Bea I was being friendly. I'm a tactile person.

And warm. I'm an actor, for God's sake, I don't know how to turn off the charm, that's how I make a living.

Where's Mark?

Hilary Scotland, visiting his mother.

Roland Didn't fancy it?

Hilary I didn't want to be poisoned. Every jar in the fridge is more than two years old.

She has a hardened immune system. Visitors aren't so lucky.

Roland That's what's in store for us all: mouldering. You have nice skin.

Hilary Clarins. I can't afford my skin.

Roland Bea had nice skin. It was her personality that stank. Am I genetically divorceable?

Hilary ?

Roland Do you think that sooner or later anyone would have ceased to love me? What am I talking about, 'love'. 'Like' would have been good enough. I would have put up with 'just tolerate long enough to sit down to dinner with'.

Hilary It doesn't sound like you've been having a very good time.

Roland Did Bea seem a little caustic to you?

Hilary I don't know. Maybe.

Roland Or just frigid? I was a fucking eunuch in that marriage. Am I repulsive?

Hilary I don't know. No.

Roland If I did flirt with other women can you blame me? I was literally starving in that department.

Hilary Was she having an affair?

Roland No. Why? Have you heard something?

Hilary No. No.

Roland I used to lie next to her, my whole flesh weeping to be touched. All I got was, 'You need to take a look at the bathroom grouting.'

Hilary It's odd what goes through your mind.

Roland She was punishing me for some crime I never committed. Being in a marriage with her. That's why I'm jealous of Josh.

Hilary Why?

Roland No one gets married at sixteen unless they're in the movie *Deliverance*.

Hilary Men have greater survival rates in marriage.

Roland Surviving. Is that what I've been doing?
  So how's your marriage?

Hilary It's fine.

Roland Don't fucking lie to me.

Hilary I mean obviously we're not – in the first throes of passion – it's not like it was.
  We tend to lead separate lives. A bit.

Roland Go on.

Hilary I suppose I'd be scared not to be in it.

Roland Thank you.

EIGHT

Hilary and Tilly.

Hilary How was school?

Tilly All right.

Hilary Did you have a good day? Tell me something that happened.

Tilly Christ, I just walked in the door.

Hilary Don't go upstairs yet.

Tilly Why?

Hilary Just sit down, have a cup of tea with me.

Tilly No.

Hilary Five minutes is all I'm asking.
  I want to talk to you.

Tilly God.

  She sits down.

Go on then, speak.

Tilly's phone goes. She gets it out and reads a text, laughs. Texts back. Hilary waits till this is over.

Hilary Having a daughter, well, it's a privilege.

Tilly's phone beeps again.
She scans phone. Texts back quite a long message. Hilary waits till this is finished.

It goes fast, though, really fast, and I don't want to waste this time we have together.

Tilly Is this going on much longer?

Hilary Why?

Tilly Because it's really dull.

Her phone beeps. She answers.

Hilary Can that wait?

Tilly No.

Hilary Of course it can. It can't be more important that this.

Tilly Well, it is.

She texts back.

Can I go now?

Hilary SIT DOWN!

Tilly Don't go all psycho on me.

She sits.

Hilary I want us to do more things together.

Tilly Like what?

Hilary I wanted to show you my album.

Tilly What album?

Hilary The blue one. I stuck everything in. Old bus tickets.

Tilly What's a bus ticket?

Hilary / What's –

Tilly I know. / Joke.

Hilary There's photos of me when I went to Greenham Common.

Tilly What?

Hilary A peace camp
A protest against American nuclear missiles being sited at Greenham. Women lived there.
For years. In tents. I went. It got very muddy.

Tilly Like Glastonbury without the music.

Hilary There I am.

Tilly Why are there are loads of men there?

Hilary They're women. They have short hair.

Tilly Not a good look.
Can I go now?

Hilary In December 1982 thirty thousand women from all over Britain came to 'embrace the base'.
Which we did. Nine miles of perimeter fence. You felt this incredible energy and also lots of confusion, women were saying, 'Are we supposed to hold hands now?'

Tilly Time's up.

Hilary I'm talking to you.

Tilly Five minutes, you said.

Hilary I didn't mean five minutes.

Tilly You're a liar then because that's what you said.

Pause.

148

Hilary Is there something you want to tell me?

Tilly What?

Hilary Something you want to tell me?

Tilly No.

Hilary Are you sure?

Tilly What?

Hilary I know what happened at the party.

Tilly What party?

Hilary The party where you went into a room – and – did you use a condom?

Tilly Oh my God.

Hilary We have to talk about this.

Tilly I'm sixteen. I don't have to talk.

Hilary No, I know. But if you want to.

Tilly I don't want to.
 What's the matter with you?
 Why don't you have a drink?

Hilary Listen.

Tilly Open another bottle.

Hilary I have two glasses a night.

Tilly Yeah.
 I'm going out.

Hilary You're not.

Tilly I'm not a prisoner.

Hilary It's a school night.

Tilly It's six o'clock.

Hilary Twenty past.

Tilly So. I'll be back in an hour.

Hilary Is that the three-hour-long hour?
Or the four?

Tilly Is this talking?

Hilary Let's not shout. This is emotional.
All I'm saying is – be safe, look after yourself. That's all I'm saying. Tell me.

Tilly What is it you want me to do? Do you want to tell me what to do?

Hilary Listen. You think 'I'm being a strong woman', that's a misinterpretation . . .

Tilly Like you're so happy.

Hilary What?

Tilly You heard.

Hilary It's never an hour, is it?

Tilly It's never five minutes, is it?

Hilary But did you want to do it?
What did you want?

Tilly Did I want?

Hilary Yes.
You must know. What you wanted?

Tilly LEAVE ME ALONE.

Mark enters.

I want to go to Lauren's for an hour.

Hilary She wants to go out. Tell her she can't go out.

Mark Hello.

Hilary Just tell her.

Mark How long for?

Hilary It's a no.

Tilly An hour.

Mark Okay. That seems okay. If it's an hour. That should be okay.

Tilly exits.

Bit of an overreaction.

Hilary She slept with some boys at a party. She hasn't told us.

Mark Hold on. Hold on. What?

Hilary That's it. That's all I know. Look at us, we're supposed to be a family.

She exits.

NINE

A beach
    Roland tampers with a shop-bought, for-one-use barbecue pack.
    Hilary enters.

Hilary Have you lit a fire before?

Roland I must have, I'm a man. I think with these it's just a matter of – firelighters. I can do that. A woman could do that. This was such a great idea. Inspirational. Thank you. Why is Frances so desperate?

Hilary She's not.

Roland She directs everything she says straight at me. Like bad acting.

Hilary She's good at connecting with new people.

Roland She wants me.

Hilary You should be so lucky. She's good at sex. She takes charge. She has toys.

Roland Are you trying to shunt me sideways on to your friend? Because it's you I like, not her.

Hilary Yes, but we're not going to happen. I'm married to Mark.

Roland But you told me –

Hilary What I told you . . .

Roland You didn't love him in that way.

Hilary We're outside.

Roland You said you were just going through the motions. For Tilly's sake.

Hilary You're very needy. Your marriage is over and you're grasping at me. My marriage is held together by habit, but that's okay.

Roland When you came to see me and Bea, I thought there's a woman that has passionate convictions.

Hilary Stop talking like this. You're making me anxious.

Roland Are you scared to leave Mark – because your job's on the line?

Hilary His job is on the line too. Nobody's job is safe nowadays.

Roland Mine is. Sometimes I turn work down.

Hilary I'm trying to remember why it is I like you.

Mark walks in with a cool bag. He has on shorts and a T-shirt.

Mark I'm fatter than I was last year. Look.

He grabs his tummy.

Roland You should sort yourself out with a longer T-shirt, mate.

Hilary Too short. Doesn't cover the top of –

Roland Then your spare tyre wouldn't –

Mark This is my favourite T-shirt. Darts. 1979. World tour. Winchester.
  I'm not eating more – some fats cells moved in and thought, this is good, this is permanent – we must tell our friends. And this process of accumulation is taking place independently of any responsibility on my part.

Roland Is Frances after me?

Hilary Don't assume she's out to get you because she's single and over forty.

Roland Fifty, isn't she?

Frances enters in a bikini, sunglasses.

Mark That's brave for Norfolk in September.

Frances Any chance to get my clothes off. I've only got five years left in this body.

Mark Then where do you go?

Frances It's hard to attribute mortality to me, I know I'm a goddess, but the decline of musculature is relentless.

Hilary Stop it.

Frances Then the ears lengthen, noses grow longer and the jawbone loses material.
  Our faces collapse.

Hilary Think Meryl Streep. We need a new attitude. Our lives are written on our bodies and our faces. Our experience. Who'd want to be a blank? Think of all the stories we have to tell each other?

Pause.

We have so many stories.

Roland Is it too early for alcohol?

Frances I thought you'd never ask.

Mark opens up the cool box, takes out beer bottles, distributes them.

I'm stunned with inertia when people tell me stories. And there's only one thing worse than hearing a boring story once and that's hearing it twice. There's an old girl at the home I do shifts in – she's always asking 'What's that called outside?' 'It's the corridor, Win.' I get so desperate to get back to people in basic working order I have to will myself not to run away screaming.

It's coming to us all.

(*To Roland, who has a towel round his waist.*) Don't keep us guessing. What have you got on under that?

Roland Trunks.

Frances Can't wait. Did you buy them yourself?

Roland My ex-wife bought them.

Frances You see this is my theory: only an older man would buy a young woman swimwear. (*To Hilary.*) I bet Mark never bought you yours, did he?

Hilary No.

Frances What's under your jumper then?

Hilary God, just an old costume.

Frances Let's see.

Hilary I'm not that warm actually.

Frances Not shy, are you?

Hilary We don't all get time to go to the gym like you do.
I've been helping Mark out in the shop every spare moment.

Frances How is the world of blinds?

Mark Slow. As it happens.

Frances Blinds was an odd turn for you to take, wasn't it? I was just thinking. For an art student.

Mark Needs must.

Pause.

Frances Are we going to catch the fish?

Mark I caught them earlier from Sainsbury's.

Frances Excellent. I don't want to see things die. (*To Roland.*) So, how is detoxing after decades of marriage?

Roland You're not one of those mad women who don't respect boundaries, are you?

Frances Yes.

Roland I thought so. It's pretty shit, actually. I was levelled. I was the shit on your shoe. There was no time of day I looked forward to.

Frances I've been there. It lasts about two months.

Roland Four in my case. Then I progressed to the taking-it-out-on-my-liver phase. Occasionally I'd have a few hours when I felt normal. Then it kicked in all over again. When I found out Bea was seeing someone else, I felt as though a knife was plunging into my groin . . .

Hilary The local lifeboat crew are singing *a cappella* tonight in the Grapes.

Roland I thought emotional pain was a metaphor till then.

Mark Where are the kids?

Hilary I woke them up. They should be here now.

Frances Did you get it checked out?

Roland What?

Frances Your prostate?

Hilary I shouted at them through a closed door – I think they heard.

Roland It was a metaphor.

Mark They'll still be sleeping.

Hilary I didn't go in – obviously.

Roland My balls were in perfect working condition, which was part of the problem.

Mark Pity for them to miss so much of the day.

Hilary You wake them up then.

Roland Getting sexual favours out of my ex-wife was akin to chipping at a glacier with a toothpick. I'm honest about that. Most people lie. Then it makes it harder for people like me to come out. You put up with abstinence because you think it's just you. You don't know it's practically every married couple in the Western hemisphere.

Hilary Are we going to swim?

Mark Swimming, in England. That's novel.

Hilary Who wants to be sluggish?

Frances I applaud you, Roland, for your honesty.

Hilary Let's go in. Come on.

> *She takes off her jumper. She is wearing a light-coloured costume – a bit risqué.*
> *The teenagers, Tilly and Josh, enter. They look like gods.*

Roland Hello, you two.

Tilly Oh my God, Mum, that's disgusting. You're practically naked. Put something on.

Mark Mum looks fine.

Roland Very good. Morning, Josh.

Josh makes an inaudible reply.

Frances That's not an old costume. You've gone out and bought that, you sex bomb. It's a flesh tone. That's why it looks so undressed.

Hilary puts her jumper back on.

Hilary Bit cold for swimming.

Tilly You can look now, Josh. It's safe.

She looks at package of fish.

Ugh. Josh doesn't like fish.

Roland Don't you, Josh?

Hilary There's salad.

Tilly That's not food.

Hilary begins to get out the food.

Hilary I don't want you going funny about eating.

Roland Josh will eat anything.

Hilary Wonderful.

Tilly No, he wouldn't. He wouldn't eat a rat. He wouldn't eat another man's penis. Like that bloke near us who ate his friend's. They cooked it first.

Roland Obviously.

Frances God, it all happens in Walthamstow.

Hilary Why don't you try it? At least try some fish.

Tilly I've tried it. It's rank.

Hilary It's dieting that makes you fat.

Tilly You're always going on about your fat arse.

Mark *and* **Roland** She hasn't got a –

Hilary Anorexia is a mug's game.

Tilly Oh my God. We're going for a walk.

She exits. Josh follows her.

Frances Oops.

Hilary Mark. I was about to get her to eat fish.

Mark That was never gonna happen. Let her walk it off.

Frances Is she always like that?
I don't know how you put up with it.

Hilary Well, that's the thing, with children you can't take them back and exchange them.

Roland They have a lot of stuff we never did but they don't seem to like us more for giving it to them.

Frances My niece has a mobile, an iPod, driving lessons, a laptop. We had record players and people shouting at us to get off the phone.

Mark I used to play with a stick.

Roland Josh has six hundred and sixty Facebook friends. How many have you got?

Hilary Ninety-eight.

Frances Tragic.

Roland They don't need us.

Mark They may be angry with us. We're responsible for them being here.
It's dawning on them, as they look at us, it's not going to be a fairy tale.

Hilary You never stand up to her, Mark. I look like the bitch.
I'm going in.

She exits.

158

Frances That's why I never had children.

Mark I'll start the fish.

Roland They sleep the sleep of angels, you know.
No two a.m. horrors. Sometimes I lie there –
Wondering which is the next bit of me that's going to fall apart – I'm morphing into an old geezer. A hairy back, balding legs. Like an ostrich.
(*Looking in direction of Tilly and Josh.*) I wonder where they've gone.

TEN

The cottage, five p.m.

Tilly Why aren't they back yet? Josh pulled his 'help me' face as the car drove off. Why can't they just buy wood from a shop?

Hilary They wanted an experience with nature. Maybe you should have gone with him. Got some exercise.

Tilly Join the nightmare.

Hilary Being with his dad is not a nightmare.

Tilly Why does he say it is, then? I had stuff to do.

Hilary Urgent stuff like bleaching your non-existent moustache.

Tilly It's not non-existent. I inherited it from you. Only I have more pride.

Pause.

Am I going to get those things round my eyes? Like you've got?

Hilary What things?

Tilly Like you've been attacked by a cat.

Hilary Yes. They spring up overnight aged about sixteen. Try not to lose any sleep over it.

Tilly When are you two going away?

Hilary We are away.

Tilly Together. For a weekend. Without me. A week? Sacha's parents are always going away. They went to St Petersburg. She has great sleepovers.

Hilary Sorry. Not on the horizon. We're in Norfolk. Let's just enjoy that.

Tilly You and Dad would have such a good time. Get the old love-juice flowing, Dad. You know you want to.

Mark The Van Goghs in the Musée d'Orsay. We got to them half an hour before it shut and we weren't even looking for them – just stumbled into this gallery. Genius paintings.
    The portrait of Dr Gachet. Holding these healing herbs. Hallucinatory colours.

Hilary (*to Tilly*) Dr Gachet was . . .

Tilly I don't care.

Mark I could do that again.

Hilary Look what you're doing. Giving in to her. She just wants us away so she can have a party.

Tilly Sleepover.

Hilary We'd come back, our loo would be pulled off the wall.

Mark I wasn't giving in. I was thinking aloud.

Tilly Forget it, Dad, she doesn't want to go with you.

Hilary I don't like the idea of coming back and having no place to shit.

Tilly Your definition of home.

Roland and Josh enter.

Roland I just need to –

Josh His eye –

Hilary What happened?

Roland No fuss – I just need to –

Hilary Your eye?

Roland Ridiculous.

Josh Wood chip bounced into his eye. Bang on target.

Hilary Is that dangerous?

Roland A scratch –

Josh gets out his BlackBerry.

You're not –?

Josh Googling it.

Roland That's unholy.

Josh 'Many people are discovering the adventure of chopping wood. But even for the experienced woodsman or woodswoman the possibility of injury or even death should be taken into consideration for this seemingly simple task.'

Roland What – when I accidentally chopped at my own neck?

Josh 'Even the smallest piece of wood, flying off can cause major injury to the eye and medical attention would be needed almost immediately.'

Roland I can't listen to this. It's written by a fool who wants everyone to stay indoors.

Josh The Forestry Commission.

Hilary Let me see. Get a torch, Mark.

Mark exits.

Roland Just need to bathe it.

Tilly Josh. (*She indicates to him.*)

Hilary I'll see to it.

He goes.

Roland I was just trying some father–son bonding.
Maybe I'll lose an eye. All this liberal shit – we should just beat them senseless.
That's what my father would have done.

Mark re-enters
Hilary shines the torch into his eye.

That's hellish.

Hilary I can't see anything.

Roland Let me – get some water on it. It'll be fine.

Roland exits.
Frances enters.

Frances You know that thing I was telling you about?

Hilary No.

Frances Yes, that thing I've been going on about relentlessly for weeks only you've obviously just been pretending to listen.

Hilary Oh yes, that.

Frances Well what do you think?

Hilary Well, it's your call.

Frances (*to Mark*) I want to try this thing out, Mark, on some mates, it only takes five minutes, what do you think?

Mark Is it a starter?

Frances No.

Mark Well, fine.

Frances Good. I'll get ready.

She exits.

Mark Don't you want to go to Paris?

Hilary I have to start the dinner.

Mark Don't you want to go to Paris with me?

Hilary Can we afford it?

Mark With me?

Hilary God, do you want to do this now?

Mark What's the point?

Hilary What?

Mark The point in us. Is there a point?

Hilary Mark –

Roland comes in with a handkerchief held over his eye.

Roland 'You should have seen the other fella.'

Mark exits.

You like my jokes. With Bea they fell on stony ground. I can talk to you so easily.

The sound of my voice used to grate on Bea's soul. I could see her flinching. If we were having a dinner party and I launched on an anecdote – you have to do that sometimes at dinner parties, otherwise all you hear is that dreadful clicking of knives on plates – she should have been grateful to me – instead I could see something slide down behind her eyes.

She was postponing her life until after I'd finished and someone else, who wasn't her husband, would say something that might kindle a fire in her.

She was a fucking effigy.

Hilary You're not over her.

Roland I am now. Can we have some booze?

Hilary White's open.

Roland I'd kill for a red.

I did sleep with other women. By the end. It was a survival thing. And I was quite surprised. These lovely young women, interested in me.

Hilary Right.

Roland That's why life is so . . . You feel like shit and then – something can happen between people. The space between you becomes charged – all the little emotional tentacles reaching out. Imagine living without that.

Hilary Flirting.

Roland It's being alive and not being old.

He moves towards her.

Hilary How is the eye? It's quite red.

Roland Good when it's looking at you.

He touches her face. Moves away as Tilly and Josh enter, followed by Mark.

Tilly We need a lift to the station.

Mark Wait. I said it needed a discussion first.

Hilary No. No way. Dinner's in an hour.

Tilly If we don't go now there'll be no point. We'll miss the train. Chloe's sister's having a party.

Hilary Out of the question, sorry.

Tilly Dad says we can. It's going to be really good.

Mark No, that's not correct. I said a discussion.

Hilary Why did you say that? That just gives her leverage. We're away. For the weekend. What's so difficult to understand about that?

Tilly Yes, but we don't like it.

Hilary None of us like it, that's not the point.

Tilly Dad.

Hilary Say no to her for once.

Tilly We're bored here. You don't even really want us here.

Mark Sorry, love, it's a no. It's not so bad here with us?

Tilly It's marginally better than being dead.

Roland We can go for a walk after dinner. Josh, remember those great walks we had in France?

Josh I was eight. You lost me. It was pitch black. I almost fell into a river.

Tilly Please. We're dying here. It's so dull. It's just wine and talking.

Hilary No. What's wrong with you? It's a no.

Tilly (*to Mark*) Why do you always do what she says?

Frances (*off*) Can you do the music for me?

Tilly She doesn't even like you.

Frances (*off*) The music.

Tilly She treats you like shit.

Frances I'll switch it on, then.

She switches the music on.
And performs a burlesque routine.
Black leather, black balloon. Challenging.
Quite a lot of it directed at Roland.
Occasionally she stops and says things like 'And then
I do something here, but I haven't worked it out yet'.
She finishes, switches off the music.

I'd love some feedback. What did you think?

Roland I can't see any more. Both my eyes appear to have swelled up.

Frances That's an extreme reaction.

Hilary Oh God.

Roland Who said that?

Hilary Oh God.

Roland No. I know –

Josh It's your eyes, Dad. You should take it seriously.

Hilary (*to Mark*) Drive him to Casualty.

Roland It's actually fucking terrifying. Will I go blind? Oh Christ. It's a Greek tragedy right here in Norfolk.

Josh You're going to be okay, Dad. We're taking you to Casualty.

Tilly Can you drop us at the station after?

Mark Yes, love.

They start to exit.

Hilary (*as Mark leaves*) What are you doing? Does anything I do have an impact on anyone? Is anyone listening to me? No, Mark, I don't think there is a point.

He exits.

Frances Well, that was a resounding yes. What did you think?

Hilary I wasn't really concentrating.

Frances It's quite empowering about female sexuality. I'm definitely in control.

Hilary Do you think the kids should have seen it?

Frances I think it's an antidote to the pornographication of women. I control and playfully manipulate the gaze. The only thing was my balloon burst too early.

Hilary Yes, there's glitter all over the floor. Like there's been a party.

Frances exits, leaving Hilary alone.
Roland re-enters.

Roland I told them I needed a piss. I'm not blind yet. The walking wounded.

I wanted to –

He kisses her. They kiss.

– feel like I'm fifteen.

He exits.

ELEVEN

Hilary with a glass of wine.
Tilly and Lyndsey, looking remarkably glamorous and sexy.

Tilly We're going now.

Lyndsey Hi, Hilary.

Hilary Lyndsey. How are you? You've had the baby.

Lyndsey Yeah.

Tilly He's really cute. Dayne.

Hilary I'd love to see him.

Tilly She'd love to get her hands on him.

Lyndsey He's really nice.

Tilly She's got baby envy.

Hilary No, I haven't.

Tilly No, of course you haven't – baby lust. One little peek at his little fatty arms.

Hilary How's life, Lyndsey? We don't see you that often.

Lyndsey It's okay.

Hilary You're looking well.

Lyndsey Thanks.

Hilary Really wonderful.

Tilly She's such a skinny minny.

Hilary So where are you off to?

Tilly Town.

Hilary Stick together, won't you. Where?

Tilly This club Lyndsey's sister goes to.

Hilary What's it called?

Tilly You won't know it. Fabric.

Lyndsey It's got a bodysonic dance floor.

Hilary Has it? What's that?

Tilly Music pumping from the floor.

Lyndsey It goes through your whole body. Pumps through.

Hilary That sounds good.

Lyndsey It's really sick.

Hilary It sounds – sick. What sort of music does it play?

Tilly Mum. Don't be such a freak.

Hilary Do they let sixteen-year-olds in those places?

Tilly We have fake IDs.

Hilary Do you?

Tilly Got it online, twenty quid.

Hilary Right. Why don't you have a drink with me here first?

Tilly We're meeting people.

Hilary One glass.

Lyndsey They can wait ten minutes.

Hilary Least it'll be decent wine.

Hilary pours.

Lyndsey My sister hangs out with a footballer.

Hilary Do footballers go to this club?

Lyndsey I got an itinerary, where they all go. I downloaded it.

Hilary Is that what you want to do, Lyndsey? Meet a footballer?

Lyndsey Yeah. I'll get him to pay for my lipo.

Tilly Lyndsey wants lipo.

Hilary Oh my God, you don't.

Lyndsey I do.

Tilly Don't set her off.

Hilary You've got a beautiful figure.

Tilly It's no good, she wants lipo.

Lyndsey My fat legs.

Hilary It's a surgical procedure. It has a risk factor. You can't encourage your friend to have lipo, Tilly.

Tilly I'm not encouraging her.

Hilary You were never supposed to have a Barbie.

Tilly Oh my days, not this again.

Hilary I always swore you never would and then you had a party when you were six
 And got given two.

Tilly The happiest day of my childhood.

Hilary Barbie is an Aryan. Put together by eleven thousand Chinese women in Guangdong Province. She's a recipe for self-hatred.

Lyndsey I love your mum, she's so original.

Tilly Let's go.

Lyndsey I heard about you and Mr Winters having a trial separation. I'm really sorry.

Hilary That's okay. Thanks, Lyndsey. These things happen.
 Tilly?

Tilly What?

Hilary Life has to be a balance.
 Work and play.

Tilly I do work.

Hilary Because things get serious now.
 I mean, how you did so well in your GCSEs. You won't get by on that amount of work this time – A-levels are a different level.

Tilly Yes, they're A-levels. It's Saturday night.

Hilary Yes.

Tilly Get a life.

 Exits.
  Hilary sits drinking alone.

TWELVE

Spring 2010.
  Hilary, Frances.
  Hilary is changing in an adjacent room.
  Frances is dancing and finding songs on the iPod.
  Hilary comes in, wearing a dressing gown.

Hilary I haven't had a 'visitor' for four months.
  What happens now?

Frances I get myself a glass.

Hilary Is my cunt going to dry up?

Frances Wait till I get a drink down me, for God's sake.

Hilary It doesn't seem that long ago I got my first period.
That smear in the crotch of your pants. I ran in to my
mother, I said 'I've become a woman.' She looked at me like
I was insane. She took me to the bathroom and showed me
where she kept her 'towels'.
  Like I was being inducted into a cult.

Frances What did you do for Tilly?

Hilary I gave her a Topshop voucher. She didn't want a
fuss.
  I've hit a low point.
  I've let go of too many things at once. Periods, job's on
the line, Mark.

Frances In that order? It's not very flattering to Mark, is it?

Hilary It'll be Tilly next, then I'll be alone. I'm not sure
I want to do this.

Frances It'll cheer you up. Go on.

  She ushers Hilary into adjacent room.

There was a picture of Kim Cattrall in the papers the other
day, a full body shot and then a close-up of her chin, she

has a sagging chin and it said – even Kim cannot fight off the advancing years.

Hilary (*off*) Sexist tossers.

Frances And then I got to thinking. She's got the money – why doesn't she sort it out?

Hilary (*off*) So would you?

Frances Definitely.

Hilary (*off*) You could die. Under the knife. Like that woman that wrote *The First Wives Club*, Olivia . . . She was having her chin done. Maybe, you know, Kim wants to live.

Frances Come on. Let's have a look.

Hilary enters. Burlesque costume.

Hilary I don't like it.

Frances Therapy.

Hilary It's not working for me.

Frances Performing is a powerful place to be.

Hilary I just can't see myself doing it.

Frances Amateur night. You needed something. You were a mess. This is my suggestion. Please take it seriously.
We'll find you some music. You acted at university.

Hilary *The Duchess of Malfi.*

Music: Helen Reddy's 'I Am Woman'.

What is that? Post-feminist irony?

Frances Try the moves. (*Giving advice.*) Stick out your arse more. Try being suggestive with the duster.
I've just about forgiven you for the Roland thing.

Hilary What?

Frances I was in there with a chance. We had so much in common.

Hilary You weren't in there with a chance.

Frances Well, you would say that, that's your moral justification.

Hilary Nothing's happened, after that one time, he's all talk.

She breaks off.

It's making me want to cry.

Frances You liked my routine.

Hilary That thing you did in Norfolk? I was uncertain.

Frances And how's Mark?

Hilary Well, he's still living above the shop.

Frances Basically you've got two men sniffing around you and you're at my throat for considering a facial procedure. How unsympathetic.

Hilary Don't let's do this. Don't let's argue. Then we don't speak for weeks and one of us has to pick up the phone and eat dirt.

Frances I blame our mothers.

Hilary What for?

Frances That thing yours said to you.

Hilary What?

Frances She got pregnant with you and so she had to marry –

Hilary Before the pill it was a nightmare – imagine, medieval.

Frances Still a cow. Told you you'd ruined her life. Said that in cold blood.
    Don't know why you stood there and took it.

Hilary She's my mother, what could I do? Terminate the friendship?

Frances They gave us their love with a nip of poison. No wonder we hate ourselves, hate women.

Hilary We don't. I've changed the whole dynamic with Tilly.

Frances Yeah.

Hilary What?

Frances Like I've noticed how amazingly you get on.

Hilary This isn't working for me. It feels like a step back.

Frances I knew you were going to say that.

Hilary It's posh people's lap dancing. When we were at Greenham Common –

Frances We did a few day trips. Let's be clear – we weren't really a part of –

Hilary Because we were students. But we were part of – something bigger.
    Didn't you feel –
    Powerful? Kids' clothes sewn on to the fences.

Frances Thirty years ago. Your point is?

Hilary We should be living those ideas.
    I don't know if I have lived them.

Frances You're so sentimental. Grow up.

Hilary The practical thing of life is more tricky. But if you take the politics out, what's left?

Frances The interesting stuff.

Tilly enters.

Hilary Tilly. You're back early!

Tilly Yeah.
(*Refers to her costume.*) That's sad.

Hilary Yes, it is. You've let yourself down, Frances, I'm not joining you.

Frances I haven't got time for this.

Hilary I won't become a 'fuck-me puppet'.

Frances I'm ironically deconstructing it.

Hilary I'm worth more than that. We are, Tilly. I'm just going to –

She exits to change.

Frances (*calls*) I won't be the one phoning you. Bye, Tilly.

Tilly Has she gone mental-pausal?

Frances Probably.

Frances exits.
  Hilary comes back with dressing gown.

Hilary (*sees Frances has gone*) Oh God. (*To Tilly.*) Everything okay?

Tilly Yeah.
  It was boring. Just round someone's house. Wanna watch TV?

Hilary What are we going to watch then?

Tilly switches on TV.

We can have a cuddle.

Tilly sits obligingly and unusually next to Hilary.

This is nice. (*Refers to Tilly's programme choice.*) Not *Half Ton Teen!*
  Unbelievably gross and voyeuristic.

Tilly Makes me feel better.

Hilary You have a beautiful body. Just enjoy it – before –

Tilly What?

Hilary Nothing.

Tilly I'm not looking forward to vagina neck.

Hilary What?

Tilly shows Hilary what she means.

Please. Really. That is – no no. God. Vagina neck. That's hateful, can't you see that?

Pause.

Tilly On Facebook.

Hilary What? On Facebook – what?

Tilly There's stuff posted about me.

Hilary What?

Tilly Facebook-slut stuff. Because –

Hilary Oh no. No. Sweetheart.

She hugs her. Tilly lets her.

We'll get it taken off. Can you do that?

Continues to hug her.

It's not the boys that get called that stuff. You see how it works.

Pause.

I think you didn't really want to do it.

You were feeling rejected and you were reasserting yourself by saying 'I'm sexy, I'm desirable', but we add up to more than 'being sexy'.

People can be happy with vagina neck! We don't have to be fucked by a man to be human.

Tilly You're making me feel shit.

Hilary Sorry, love. Think next time: 'Is this what I want? Or is it because I want to be wanted, to feel my existence is validated?'

Tilly What? Like I'm going to think shit like that.

Hilary Do you know what validated means? It –

Tilly My period's late.

THIRTEEN

Lyndsey, holding a baby, Roland, Bea.

Roland He's a lovely chap.

Lyndsey Thanks.

Roland What do you call him?

Lyndsey Dayne.

Roland Is that his name?

Bea It's his name.

Mark comes in.

Mark Sorry – Hilary's on her way – work – some kind of crisis meeting.
Can I get you –?

Bea No, thank you.

Roland (*to Lyndsey*) Keep you up much?

Lyndsey He's very good. My mum helps.

Roland Does she?

Lyndsey Has him Saturday nights, some Fridays, every Wednesday.

Roland A big commitment.

Lyndsey She doesn't mind.

Roland All those late nights. At her age.

Lyndsey Thirty-six?

Roland That is – that is young. Well, that's good of her.

Lyndsey His dad's mum has him every other weekend.

Roland You've got it sorted.
We could do that.

Bea No, we couldn't.
It would be hellish to go back.

Hilary enters.

Hilary Thanks for coming. Lyndsey, your input will be really useful. Is Tilly still –?

Lyndsey Upstairs. I'll text her.

Hilary I haven't said hello properly. Is Josh –?

Bea Josh isn't coming.

Hilary Right.

Bea I've told him he doesn't have to.

Roland You told him not to.

Bea Because it's a bit like a military tribunal.

Roland I don't think it is.

Hilary I thought the idea was to get us all together.

Bea That might be damaging.

Hilary Damaging?

Bea We can give Josh's side of things better than he can.

Hilary Well.

Bea He's sixteen years old. He's still a child.

Hilary But he's old enough to –

Bea The guilt.

Hilary The guilt?

Bea Of this whole – It's designed, unintentionally, to make him feel – guilt.

Roland Make him face his responsibilities.

Bea From the man that had psychosomatic headaches every time I attended a pre-natal class.

Roland I didn't need lessons in deep breathing.

Bea No, that would be me.

Roland (*to Lyndsey*) We've split up. You might be able to tell.

Lyndsey Isn't that weird? You've split up and they've split up and mine's dead.

Roland Yes, that is weird.

Bea The pressure might make Josh agree to something he doesn't really want because –
    He's afraid to say what he really feels.

Hilary I'll tell Tilly not to come down. It's not fair she – On her own.

Bea What are we here for? Look, it's her decision, of course it is.
    Only from my point of view I think it's a disaster for Josh. To father a child at sixteen.
    What kind of father can you be at that age? And not being a good father, what effect does that have?

Roland Are you absolutely sure she's –

Mark We've taken three tests.

Roland So it's highly unlikely.

Hilary I told Tilly you wanted to have input into her decision. And Tilly agreed to get your input. So whatever is decided, she decides – with your input, our input, and Lyndsey's input – but if Josh isn't here, then obviously I can't let her come down alone, it's not fair.

Bea Then how will she get our input?

Hilary You could input to us and we could convey your input to her.

Bea It's more persuasive if it comes from us. This is our son's life.

Hilary She's not coming down if Josh isn't here. Lyndsey, would you mind –

Lyndsey I'll text her.

Roland We thought she was on the pill.

Hilary She was, then she stopped when they stopped and then it started again.

Roland Oh dear.

Hilary I mean, if we had a choice of course –
    I mean, Lyndsey, if you could turn back the clock.

Lyndsey What?

Hilary I thought Lyndsey could advise Tilly – because if you could, Lyndsey –
    Would you choose to have had a baby at fifteen?

Roland It's not that you don't love your baby. But if you could wipe the slate clean.

Bea Look, she's not going to admit to that.

Lyndsey I'm not wiping the slate clean.

Roland No, of course.

Lyndsey Of Dayne.

Roland No no no.

Hilary But in an ideal world of course –

Lyndsey What?

Hilary In an ideal world you might have delayed.

Lyndsey Dayne?
　Then he wouldn't exist.

Hilary He's lovely.
　Yes, in an ideal world, perhaps not for you, but for
Tilly – you can see that.

Mark Is she the right person to ask?

Bea Josh has other options.

Hilary Tilly has options.

Lyndsey I have options.

Bea You have less options. Let's be honest. I'm sure you've
faced that.
　Josh, like a lot of bright kids, has the capacity to go off
the rails, to be derailed.
　This could derail him. I know it could. The stigma, the
confusion of being a child with a child, the adult
responsibilities.

Roland Romeo and Juliet.

Bea Are characters in a play.
　I don't know why you are seriously giving her an option.

Mark You can't force –

Bea She doesn't understand fully the nature of the decision
before her. That should be impressed upon her. I'm not
saying forced. How did this happen?

Roland We know how it happened.

Bea I mean how was this allowed to happen? By us.

Hilary By me – are you saying?

Bea Do we think it's okay for girls to be hyper-sexual and not bring upon themselves the, okay, unfair consequences? Josh would be expected to go to a university but as the father of a young child, he won't be developmentally experiencing what he needs – freedom – to learn – to socialise.

Hilary The same for Tilly.

Bea Changing nappies. Wiping up sick.

Lyndsey She says Josh keeps ringing her, can you tell him to stop ringing her?

Bea He's upset.

Roland He should be here.

Bea I don't want him here. It's awful.

Mark We should get Tilly down here.

Hilary On her own, as if she's the guilty one? The girl who dared to have sex – the slut.

Lyndsey She's not a –

Hilary I was making a point, Lyndsey – I wasn't really calling her a –

   I can't force her to get rid of it – she has to want to.

Bea It won't last. Have you mentioned that? The relationship won't last. Perhaps she thinks this will cement something – it's the opposite. Lyndsey, are you with your partner?

Lyndsey No.

All He's dead.

Bea Oh God, yes, sorry.

Lyndsey It's all right. It was last year.

Mark I think Tilly has to be here.

Bea What was he seeking – some kind of love, attention?

Roland He was seeking sex. It's a drive. You missed out on it.

Bea It had a resurgence after you left.
We are happy to pay for the termination privately. That is something we can do.

Mark It's not a question of money.

Bea It's a gesture.
Does Tilly want a baby – at sixteen? Her life will be over.

Lyndsey My life isn't over.

Bea I shouldn't have said over. Severely limited.

Hilary Thank you so much for being here, Lyndsey. Whatever she decides she needs to know how tough it is.

Lyndsey I wouldn't turn the clock back.

Hilary Of course not. You must have feelings of frustration?

Lyndsey I do worry.

Bea Yes –

Lyndsey How I'm going to support him?
Will I meet someone who'll be a good dad to him? When I see on the news – stepdads who *starve* kids, put them in *black plastic bags* in the bath and the mothers stand by, I'm scared, but I won't like anyone like that, will I? Unless I change in some way, get *depressed*, I start taking *drugs*, my life spirals out of control, I end up homeless, a crack-whore – but apart from that I'm fairly positive.
Have you seen that film *The Road*?
The Road made me cry. If someone ate Dayne I'd go mental.

I can't afford to get down. Not now I've got Dayne. Who else has he got?

Bea Your mother. It's just this generation has everything now. Don't wait. We pick up the pieces.
   I won't do that.

Lyndsey starts to cry.

Mark We're talking about our grandchild here. We do know that.

Bea We don't know that it is.

Roland Very likely.

Bea There was that other time she – at that party – a stranger. I can't be the only one to be thinking it. It's the elephant in the room. Josh going through all this and it's not his.

Hilary Josh can't just walk away.

Roland No no.

Bea Roland, you asshole.

Hilary Josh fucked my daughter. He fucked her and now he thinks he can just walk away.

Mark Calm down, love.

Bea I'm here to advocate for my son.

Hilary Sorry, Lyndsey, have we upset you?

Lyndsey No.

She holds up her phone.

Tilly. She's been bleeding.

FOURTEEN

Home.
  Hilary is still in her coat. Her knee is bleeding.
  A Young Man walks into the room in boxer shorts.

Young Man You haven't got any milk?

Hilary There's no milk?

Young Man It's cool. I'll have juice.

  He pours himself some juice.

Hilary You are –?

Young Man Oh sorry. I'm a friend of Tilly's.

Hilary I'd figured that out.

Young Man Right, yeah. Cam.

Hilary Cam. I don't think I've heard of you. Where's Josh?

Young Man I've no idea. I've never heard of him.

Hilary Tilly's boyfriend.

Young Man Oh yeah – I think that finished.

Hilary When was that?

  He shrugs.

Young Man I don't know. Not that long ago.
  Your house is very hot. We crashed out.

Hilary She never said anything to me.

  Young Man shrugs.

Shouldn't Tilly be at school?

Young Man Inset day.

Hilary Right. Shouldn't you be somewhere?

Young Man Uni, reading week.

Hilary Tilly is sixteen – aren't you a bit old for her?

Young Man Twenty?

Hilary Yes.

Young Man It's not like Ronnie Wood territory.

Hilary I suppose not . . .

Young Man He must be well old. Fifty.

Hilary Older.

Young Man Yeah?

He notices her leg is bleeding.

What happened to you?

Hilary I got knocked off my bike.

Young Man Do you want a juice?

Hilary Yes. Actually. That would be good.

He pours her one.

Thanks.

Young Man You ought to clean that up.

Hilary Yeah.

Hilary gets stuff to clean leg.

Young Man I'll do it, if you like.

Hilary Okay.

He begins to clean.

I didn't know how thirsty I was.

Young Man Yeah?

Hilary I lost my job today.

Young Man That's a bit shit.

Hilary Yes, it is actually.

Young Man Here's to the next one.

Hilary Thanks.

Young Man You've been having a bit of a *Titanic* day.

Hilary Yeah.

Young Man I don't know your name.

Hilary Hilary.

Young Man Hilary. I saw your photo upstairs.
Tilly told me you were her mum. I didn't believe her.
I said you looked too hot to be her mum.

Hilary It's an old photo.

Pause.

What are you doing at uni?

Young Man Psychology.

Hilary What do you want to do with psychology?

Young Man I want to specialise in child psychology. I did a
placement in an adolescent unit.

Hilary Yeah?

Young Man Yeah. It was like amazing. There was this kid,
he had absolutely no friends. And every time the
psychologist asked him a question he just said – yes – like
that –
Really fast.

Hilary As if he wanted to stop.

Young Man Yeah, stop any – like –

Hilary Being seen.

Young Man Yeah. It was like he didn't even know how sad he was. He was just tucked into a little ball inside himself. Lost. The psychologist was saying the thing is, he just has to wake up. Somehow he has to wake up. To know how sad he is before he can –

Hilary Move on.

Young Man Yeah.

Hilary Well, that sounds –

Young Man Yeah.

Pause.

Well. I better –

Hilary Yes.

Young Man Thanks for the juice.

Hilary No. Don't go. I mean you don't have to go – yet –

He stops.

Young Man Okay.
Did you like your job? I mean, not everybody does.

Hilary I think it's important that people – you know – read.

Pause.

They just opened the car door just as I was . . . the cunt.

She begins to cry but wipes her eyes as Tilly comes down.

Tilly Mum?

Hilary Yes.

Young Man I better –

He goes.

Tilly Cam's helping me revise.

Hilary I'm not stupid.

Tilly What?

Pause.

He is.
Don't take it out on me that you and Dad aren't getting on.

She walks away, turns back.

Oh yeah, and we've run out of shower gel.

Hilary Can't you keep your fucking knickers on? You disgust me.

Tilly turns and exits.

FIFTEEN

Roland, Hilary, Tilly.

Hilary I'm really sorry about tonight.

Roland That's okay. That's okay.

Hilary I hate to think of you sitting in that bar.

Roland It's fine.

Hilary I've been having a crisis with Tilly. I've instituted a new regime.
She's got AS-levels in two weeks.
As far as I know she's done a completely inadequate amount of revision.
I couldn't leave her tonight because – she'd go out. Or be on Facebook.
She wouldn't actually apply herself. The only thing she applies with any diligence is eyeliner. Would you like a drink?

Roland Just water.

She gives him a drink.

Hilary Thought we'd made a breakthrough with *Othello*.
Talking about the women. Desdemona and Emilia
trapped on a fort with a load of bastards. But it was a
momentary breakthrough. Hostilities have broken out again.

Roland So Mark is –? He's still –

Hilary In the flat above the shop.
I'm going to make a pasta. Ever so simple. I'm sorry.
I thought we'd be eating out.

Roland That's fine. That's good. I like pasta. I'd rather be
here. I've gone off bars.

Pause.

Hilary So, how have you been?

Roland Rehearsing.

Hilary How's that?

Roland First week wonderful, third week crisis – usual
stuff.

Pause.

Hilary How's Josh?

Roland Oh he's – he's okay. Enjoying A-levels. It seems. He
went for Drama. That was his mother's genius idea. God
knows why. I could have taught him everything he needs to
know. Basically, get a good agent and don't take coke.

Hilary I was sorry about Josh and Tilly.

Roland I think it was all a bit of a shock. They wanted to
turn their backs on it.
Understandable.

Tilly enters.

Tilly Hello.

Roland Hello.

Tilly Are you gay?

Hilary Tilly!

Tilly We haven't seen that much of you. We thought maybe you've made a discovery. Are you?

Roland No, I'm a Buddhist.

Tilly That's actually more shocking.

Roland I went for that retreat, remember?

Hilary Oh yes. Yes.

Roland I have to say it's really been wonderful. Meditation. I've been working on my Calm Abiding. It's very important go inside and be still.

Hilary I ought to put on the pasta.
Why don't you lay the table?
Could you – please?

She shoves cutlery into Tilly's hands, who begins to lay the table.
Hilary exits briefly, re-enters.

The Berlin Wall came down over twenty years ago.

Roland Really. That went quickly.

Hilary Yes, I was watching a programme about it. Where does time go?
Do you know what the Berlin Wall is, Tilly?

Pause.

In 1945 . . .

Tilly Nobody cares.

Hilary Well, they might actually. They might have an interest in the world wider than their own wardrobe.

Tilly I don't want to go around looking like I've just been released from *Ten Years Younger* before the makeover.

Roland Dreadful show.

Hilary When I was your age I had an engagement with sexual politics.
My vision extended beyond my next outfit.

Tilly I know. I saw the photos. Roland, what do you call a blonde with two brain cells?

Roland I don't know if I should answer that.

Tilly Pregnant.

Roland That is actually quite funny.

Hilary Excuse me.

Roland Can I help?

Hilary I only have to –

She exits.

Tilly She's fucking doing my head in. I'm locked up here with a depressed mother
You like me, don't you?

Roland Yes.

Tilly Can I come and stay with you? I'll just have to throw some stuff into a bag. I'm only asking because I'm really desperate.

Hilary brings in a bowl of salad, puts it on the table.

Tilly Uncle Roland says I can go and live with him in Highgate.

Roland Well I –

Hilary I'm sure he didn't.

Tilly I can stay – he said I could if I packed a bag tonight. We're not getting on.
I can revise there.

Hilary No.

Tilly I knew you wouldn't let me.
You don't know her.
Do you know what she did the other day?
She followed me. She only went and followed me.

Hilary Look, I apologised for that. I overreacted.

Tilly We were walking along and one of my friends pointed and said, 'Look, isn't that your mum in that car?' and I looked and it was – how embarrassing was that?

Hilary This was two o'clock in the morning and her phone was turned off.

Tilly Your own mother like a worm creeping up behind you in a car.

Hilary I was worried about you.

Tilly I'm worried about you – that you're fucking mental.

Hilary You never worry about me, you don't think of me.

Tilly No, because I hate you.

Roland I'm sure you don't.

Hilary They have a gun . . .

Roland A gun!

Hilary A gun.

Tilly Oh my God – that is a joke.

Hilary Tilly was laughing about it on the phone.

Tilly For a joke. No one's going to use it.

Hilary Which is why you are grounded.

Tilly Yes! But it's like the biggest joke – because you can get anything – that is the point – you can get it – it's like a comment – a social comment, it's like satire. Like men having long hair in your day – or women taking the pill.

He is not going to use it.
We laugh. Don't you see?

Hilary No no, I don't see.

Tilly It was a bet. To see if it could happen. To see if Rupert could get one and he did.
Because you can get anything.

Hilary And you are not leaving this house till I know that someone has handed that weapon to a responsible adult. I've made myself clear. I'm giving them a week and then –

Roland A gun is pretty extreme.

Tilly In Japan they've invented a machine – they can place these electrodes on your head and play you back your own dreams.

Roland Wow.

Tilly Mum would love that.

Hilary Why?

Tilly You always want to get inside people's heads.
If they invented this injection –

Hilary An injection?

Tilly Like a small microscopic chip that you can't see, a tracking device – because a mobile phone can be switched off – something they inject into the bloodstream – so we can never be lost. So they – a parent – could always know where we are – would you make me do it?

Hilary I think you'd feel really persecuted.

Tilly I bet you would – there's no way you wouldn't. You would inject your own daughter with some scary technology because you are such a control freak.
Like how fucking sick is that?

Hilary I said I wouldn't.

Tilly Like I believe you.

Roland Maybe, maybe, you know, she's worried about you – she's just being a mother.

Tilly You think that's normal? To think like that? To think the world is such a nuthouse that you need to make your own child into some kind of transmitter?

Hilary This is all hypothesis.

Tilly She'd hunt me down.

Hilary For God's sake.

Tilly You can't control me.

Hilary Upstairs.

Tilly No.

Hilary Don't escalate this.

Tilly LOCKED UP LIKE A PRISONER.

Hilary I GIVE YOU LIFTS, MONEY – CHRIST, YOUR CLOTHES.

Tilly I hope you never get fucked again as long as you live.

Hilary Thank you!

Tilly You're too old anyway. That's what you are, too old.

Hilary Well the world is missing out, that's all I can say. If they can't see what I'm worth.

Tilly OLD OLD OLD.

She exits.

Hilary I'll just check the pasta.

Roland Look, I'm not that hungry. We've got a terrifically long day tomorrow – we're tech-ing. I'll ring you. Come and see the show. Let me know and I'll sort out tickets. Don't leave it too long because the advance is rather healthy.

Hilary Please don't go yet.

Pause.

Roland I feel like – well – I've been so – in such – I've been confused this last year.
I haven't been myself.

Hilary You don't find me attractive.

Roland No no no, that's not it. Of course you are. Very attractive.

Tilly comes downstairs with a gun.

Tilly See.
It's Rupert's gun. It's not loaded. I'm not going to shoot you.

Hilary Oh my God.

Tilly It's just a joke. Don't you see? We take turns because Rupert's dad has threatened to stop paying his uni fees if he steps out of line in any way.

Hilary Give it to me.

Tilly No. Look, it's a joke.

She fires it and it goes off.
She screams. Roland drops to the floor.

Roland I'm okay.

Tilly Oh fuck, that was so weird.

Hilary Drop it drop it drop it.

Tilly Don't freak out.

She drops it.

Roland I heard it go past my ear. A whistling.

Hilary Oh God. You could have killed Roland.
Get upstairs and do some revision.

Tilly No. I need to calm down – I almost just killed someone.

Hilary Get upstairs.

She pushes her.

Tilly Don't touch me.

Hilary GET UPSTAIRS!

Tilly doesn't.

Roland Listen. I have to go. Really, it's been –

Hilary You can't go, you've almost been shot.

Roland (*indicates gun*) Post that anonymously to the police. Best thing.

Hilary I'm really, really sorry. Please don't go.

Tilly Don't beg, Mum. It doesn't work.

Roland I really –

He goes.

Hilary (*to Tilly*) Do what you like. I don't care any more.

Hilary exits. Leaves Tilly alone.

SIXTEEN

Cam and Hilary.

Cam Me and Dad used to sit there like ghosts in front of the telly.
　　The light flickering on his face, and his face was impassive and I was scared to say anything, in case I made him come round.
　　We spent nights like that. Months. I knew it was wrong but I couldn't see a way out.

Catatonic. That's what we were.

Well, that's life. That's what I told myself. You can't expect everything to work out.

And after Mum died I just thought to myself, well, that will have screwed me up but I'll just have to live with it. It takes ages for the fact that it really happened to sink in. Even now I think – maybe it didn't happen. Cognitive dissonance.

Maybe she wasn't knocked off her bike. Maybe she didn't die.

That's why it was so weird when you came in and you'd been knocked off your bike.

That could have been her, you know, a happy ending.

Mind if I smoke?

Hilary No.

Cam Sometimes I think, maybe it's all some kind of practical joke and one day Mum's going to come giggling out of a cupboard and say 'Got you!' We were a family that played a lot of jokes.

Hilary That's just –

Cam My defences. Yes. Once my dad walked naked into the living room with a rose tied to his penis, only it was my gran. Mum had popped to the shop.

Hilary What must you think of me?

Cam I like you, obviously.

Hilary You must think – I mean this is –

Cam Lost your job, it's thrown you off balance. Blame David Cameron. He's a cunt.

Hilary I'd like to blame him – for this – but I'm not sure it's rational.

Cam I wasn't going out with Tilly.

Hilary I know. But you were in a way.

Cam I wasn't her boyfriend. We hadn't got to that point yet.

Hilary I just wanted –

Cam You really wanted me, didn't you?

Hilary Yes, I did.

Cam I liked that.

Hilary Did you?

Cam Yes.

Hilary I don't think we should do this any more.

Cam All right.

Hilary So that's okay with you?

Cam Sure. I mean, have I got a choice?

Hilary Because that's the best thing. I'm thinking of getting back with my husband.

Cam Look, I can take it. I can take anything after Mum.

Hilary I'm too old for you anyway.

Cam What's the point in thinking like that? You like someone or you don't.
  Age doesn't have to come into it.

Hilary That's a good way to think.

Cam Unless you want to have kids. Even now science can do wonders.
  That woman who had a baby when she was seventy but then she died of cancer.
  Do you want a cigarette?

Hilary No. I gave up.

Cam Poor fucking baby. How weird is that. A test-tube dad and a pensioner mum whose carked it. I mean, who the fucking hell would you be?

Hilary I don't know. I don't want to judge those women.

Cam Pussy. Really irresponsible. Do you want to go for a walk?

Hilary I thought you had an essay to do.

Cam I get restless. Easily.
    Well, you've got a nice memory.

Hilary That's a strange way to put it.

Cam How else do you want me to put it?

Hilary I don't know. It sounded a bit punishing.

Cam Yeah?

Hilary Yes.
    Why did you come round again?

Cam I left my jumper. I was passing.

Hilary That was convenient.

Cam I thought you seemed – up for it.

Hilary Don't tell Tilly.

Cam State the obvious.

Hilary How did you meet her?

Cam At a party. Months back. It was just after Mum, and we both were destroyed.

Hilary Destroyed?

Cam Booze. And we talked a lot and went upstairs.

Hilary And you?

Cam I cried. Mainly. Yes. Not much else went on. I tried to, but I was too rammed. She said, 'How do you ever get over something like that? Your mum.'
    She couldn't imagine getting over it.

Hilary Did she say that? About me?

Cam Yeah. Even though you were an alcoholic.

Hilary I am not an alcoholic.

Cam Teenagers speak in totalities. They don't know grey.

Hilary She said that?

Tilly (*voice, off*) Hello.

Hilary (*indicating kitchen*) In there.

Cam goes into kitchen with clothes, closes the door.

Tilly Forgot my purse, free period.

Tilly goes upstairs.
Comes down.

See ya.

Hilary You don't have to rush home after school tonight. If you want to hang out after. That's okay.

Pause.

Tilly Okay.

Hilary I trust you. I'm sorry.

Tilly Okay.

Hilary Give me a hug.

They hug.

I think things are going to be fine. Between us.
What's out there scares me, that's all. I think you're fantastic.

Tilly You don't hate me?

Hilary No, no.

Tilly Okay. Laters.

Exits. Goes out without her bag.
  Cam comes out naked with a flower tied to his penis.

Cam That was fucking close.

  Tilly re-enters for her bag.

Tilly Forgot my –

SEVENTEEN

Hilary with cigarette, mobile phone.

Hilary Voicemail.

Frances You're overreacting . . .

Hilary She would never do this. This long. Never. Never.

Frances She's angry with you.

Hilary No one would put another human being through this, especially their mother.

Frances Oh, I don't know . . .

Hilary Still not picking up.

Frances There was a lot of shouting.

Hilary Obviously.

Frances Because you snogged this lad.

Hilary It sounds terrible when you say it like that.

Frances I don't know how else to say it.
  Fatal Attraction. You ought to watch – Tilly. The competitive thing.

Hilary What?

Frances Snogging her boyfriend. Envy.

Hilary No. Not envy.

Frances Don't kid yourself.

Hilary You never had kids. You don't know what you're talking about.
Anyway, I didn't just snog him, I slept with him.

Frances You didn't?

Hilary Yes.

Frances Whore.

Hilary It's bad, isn't it?

Frances I can't conceive of any possible atonement.

Hilary Really?

Frances No. You were horny and you wanted someone to want to shag you because you're unfeasibly old. She's punishing you. Has she told Mark?

Hilary I don't want her to tell Mark.
She might have done something stupid. Got into an unmarked cab.

Frances She'll be with friends.

Hilary Driven for miles and dumped in a reservoir. Set on fire. Like that poor –

Frances There's no point in going down that route. She's in a club now, dancing to nineties retro music.

Hilary There's a serial killer in Walthamstow.

Frances That sounds a bit glam for north-east London.

Hilary Killed a woman who'd popped out at one a.m. for teabags. Tesco Metro.

Frances Young people move in packs. You told me that.

Hilary You'd think you'd see a woman out with teabags you might have a bit of sympathy. You wouldn't strangle her with her own tights.

Frances A psychopath obviously – ninety-nine-point-eight per cent of men are not like that. He'll be lying low.

Hilary If he's insane he may not be thinking rationally. Can't we move on from bloody Jack the Ripper –?

Phone beeps. Hilary leaps on it.

Mark. Can he come home now?

She punches the keys.

Of course he can't.

Frances Where is he?

Hilary Driving round in a three-mile radius. Searching. I can't bear being in my own skin.

Frances You've rung all her friends?

Hilary Except five of them, we don't know who they are any more. Please don't leave me.

Frances No, of course.

Hilary I can't be on my own.

Frances You're smoking.

Hilary Stopping me from screaming. I could kill her. Why does anyone ever have kids?

Frances Because they're selfish and they don't want to be lonely.

Mark enters.

Mark Two a.m. I'm knackered.

Hilary Are we just going to sit here waiting? We should phone the police.

Mark What are they going to do? It's a teenager – partying at the weekend.

Hilary This is the second night. The second night. This is not normal.

Mark No news is good news.

Hilary Why won't anyone take me seriously?

Mark I'm going to bed. Tomorrow – if – then –

Hilary I know something's happened. I know it.

Mark What happened? Did you argue?

Hilary No. Nothing.

Mark Then we shouldn't panic.

She sits on the floor.

Hilary If something has happened – there's no point in anything.

Frances You don't mean that.

Hilary I do.

Frances She doesn't.

Hilary I'll kill myself.

Frances It was your wedding anniversary today wasn't it? It popped up on Facebook.
Congratulations.

Mark Thank you. We're not – not together at the –

Frances Oh yes. Sorry.

Hilary curls up on the floor.

Shall I make some coffee?

Mark No –

Frances My mother used to flick me with cold water when I got into a state. Like an exorcism. We could do that.

Mark I don't think –

Frances This must be hard for you too. She'll be fine.

Mark Oh, I know.

Pause.

Frances You know my performance that time in Norfolk?

Mark Oh yes?

Frances I've been really working on it.

Mark I don't think now's a good time.

Frances No. I know. No. It's been going really well. The burlesque scene is amazingly vibrant. I've met some really cool women. I've had two actual real live bookings.

Mark I'm really pleased for you. Good luck with that.

Pause. They sit for a long time.

There's no need for you to wait too.

Frances Really?

Mark Yeah. Honestly.

Frances I'd better stay. Otherwise one day she'll hold it against me.

They wait.
  The door opens and in comes Tilly. She is barefoot and carries one shoe.

Tilly Hi. I lost a shoe. Off the pier at Brighton.

Mark Are you all right?

Tilly I needed a new pair anyway. I'm going to bed. I'm so tired.
  Night.

She exits.
  Hilary gets up.

Hilary I'll put the kettle on.

EIGHTEEN

Hilary, Mark. Bedroom.
  Hilary gets into bed.
  Pause.

Hilary That's quite a day. It's strange isn't it? Not waiting for someone to come in.
  How was the drive to the station?

Mark Uneventful.

Hilary I don't think she wanted me to come. I think I made the right decision not to come.

Mark You said goodbye here.

Hilary I offered to go up on the train with her. She said that would be a waste of money. She'd rather have the money.

Mark Well –

  Pause.

Hilary I suppose that's considerate. I'm not working. How's it at your work?

Mark Hanging on.

Hilary I expect we'll survive. (*She gets* Great Expectations.) Where were we? Pip. (*She searches through. She stops.*) Then I said to her yesterday, I said, 'Well it's been a bumpy ride, hasn't it?'

Mark What did she say?

Hilary Nothing. She was packing. I mean what do you say? I was starting to sound like something out of a Powell and Pressburger film. And then I said – 'It's all a journey of self-understanding, of knowing what you want and standing up for it. And that's very important especially if you're a woman.' And that I've tried to pass on those values to her – even though – you know – I'm not perfect.

Mark Yes.

Hilary And she turned to me and she laughed.

Mark What kind of a laugh?

Hilary Well, I was thinking about that afterwards. And I couldn't really – I don't know.

Mark Right.

Hilary I just want her to be all right.

Mark Of course.

Hilary I think she will be. Do you?

Mark Yes.

Hilary As long as she doesn't get into drugs or become the victim of a random terrorist attack or turn into a Tory. As long as she's confident about being a woman.

Mark Yes.

Hilary She will ring us.

Pause.

She took that old toy. That – monkey thing. Jumpy.
    And I was really touched that she was taking it because she never used to be able to sleep without it. And I said, 'Oh, you're taking that,' and she said, 'There's this ceremony at Freshers' Week. They light a bonfire and each fresher burns something that represents their childhood. Like a rite of passage. You drink shedloads and then you

throw this object on to the fire and watch it burn.' She thought she'd immolate Jumpy.

So I tried to be, like we said, not to be too – to hold on too tight. So I said, 'Well, if that's your decision –' and she said, 'God no, what do you think I am, some sort of sick bitch?'

It was a joke.

Pause.

Are you awake?

Mark Yes, I'm awake.

THE VILLAGE

after
Fuenteovejuna
by Lope de Vega

The Village was first performed at the Theatre Royal Stratford East, on 7 September 2018. The cast, in alphabetical order, was as follows:

Gopi Harki Bhambra
Ishani Sudha Bhuchar
Jyoti Anya Chalotra
Mango Ameet Chana
Ramdev Neil D'Souza
Gina Souad Faress
Panna Rina Fatania
Vihaan Naeem Hayat
Farooq Scott Karim
The Inspector Art Malik
Mekhal / Babu Arian Nik
Jacinta Humera Syed
Ved Ragevan Vasan

Director Nadia Fall
Designer Joanna Scotcher
Lighting Designer Paul Pyant
Movement Director Polly Bennett
Composer Niraj Chag
Sound Designer Helen Atkinson
Fight Directors RC-Annie
Casting Director Amy Ball

Characters

Inspector Gangwar
a corrupt policeman

Ved
a policeman

Gopi
a policeman

Vihaan
a young politician

Jyoti
the Mayor's daughter

Panna
a peasant woman

Farooq
a peasant man

Mango
a peasant man

Ramdev
the Mayor of Sahaspur

Ishani
a progressive Hindu candidate

Mekhal
Ishani's PA

Gina
Co-Mayor of Sahaspur

Jacinta
a peasant woman

Investigator

Townspeople

Act One

Airport in Uttar Pradesh.
Inspector Gangwar and two policemen: Ved and Gopi.
They have been waiting.

Gopi
Where the hell is he? Duty Free?

Ved
Buying perfume, two bottles; Dolce and Gabbana.
In Delhi he forgot, but since the death of his pa
He's not only his girfriend to think of but also his ma.

Gopi
'It's my prick, sir, it had to take long piss, sir.
Too much pop on the plane, sir.'

Ved
Air India has facilities, he should have availed himself!

Gopi
Better he has a bladder ache than make the Inspector
    wait.
Student.

Ved
These small courtesies are the lubrication of business.
Doesn't he know, sit, you are Gangwar, Inspector of
    Indian Police?
That should give him some idea of who he is dealing
    with.
If he knew, he'd be sorry for doing as he wants.

Gopi
He'd cack his pants.

Vihaan enters.

Vihaan

Inspector Gangwar? The plane took its time to dock.
Apologies. I thought of you waiting, watching the clock.

Gangwar

Do I know you?

Gopi

It's Vihaan, sir. The one we've been waiting for?

Gangwar

Who asked you? Moron.

Vihaan

I should have introduced myself, Vihaan.
I need to grab a coffee, excuse me.

Ved blocks his way.

Ved

Be polite, neh?

Gangwar

Protocol is old fashioned now? I served your father
    twenty years
Perhaps it's self-flattery to expect respect from his son
    for the battles we won?

Vihaan

He relied on your professionalism
His path would have been steeper without your
    wisdom.

Gangwar

Your father was good company.
I was the glove for his fingers or maybe the fingers in
    his glove,
The hidden partner in his political career.
Now sadly a stroke has snatched him from us
And you are here.

Victory seemed certain at the polls but your father's
    passing
Put any celebrations on hold.

Vihaan

It was very sudden.
Though I lit the pyre, saw him consumed by fire
It's impossible to believe he's gone.
The people flocked to his funeral
Crowding the streets, sending heartfelt cries into the air,
It seemed the whole of the city was there.

Gangwar

It was well attended, even by his enemies I hear –
Sadly business dictated I could not be spared to
    bestow a final greeting.

Vihaan

You requested a meeting. You need me to sign my
    name, releasing funds for your campaign?
Could you drive me to my hotel?
I'm a little wrung out. I need to get my head down,
    shower.
We could talk mañana?

Gangwar

There's no time for that.

Vihaan

I don't understand.

Gangwar

Your father's plan was that you should enter politics.

Vihaan

Really?

Gangwar

When your studies were done.
Now, a little earlier than he thought, your chance has
    come.

You must be the one to pick up the reins, step into
the breach.

Vihaan
What, now?

Gangwar
That's why he paid your expensive fees. Not just a
free ride
But so you could serve your country.

Vihaan
It's just term starts next week.

Gangwar
Forget all that – you're not going back.

Vihaan
Not going?

Gangwar
It seems your stay in UK has left you ignorant of
what's going on.
There are elections to be won.
Our party, BJP, has sworn to end elite corruption,
Boost national production and our biggest test
Cleansing Hindustan of the Muslim pest.
Perhaps you've been oblivious, buried in your
university
Leaving us outside to face adversity.

Vihaan
I am completely abreast of contemporary events –
I'm in the debating society.

Gopi
Good for you. That must get very shouty.

Gangwar
Take his cases.

The policemen go to get his luggage.

Vihaan
I can manage.

Gangwar
We're in a hurry.

Policemen take cases. Vihaan and Gangwar follow.

Vihaan
Where are we going?

Gangwar
Sahaspur.

Vihaan
What's that?

Gangwar
One dusty street and a dog.

Ved
It means courage.

Gopi
That's a joke – It's dead – Nothing goes on in that
place –

Ved
But it's strategically placed near the town of Rampur.

Gopi
Win that town, win the state.

Ved
Win that state, win the country.

Both
India First. Narendra Modi.

Gangwar
In the quiet little town of Sahaspur, a forgotten pocket,
We will plan our campaign undisturbed.
The people there are simple, they hold no views

Leaving us free for what we have to do.
Welcome to your destiny.

Vihaan

There's no gain in me raising my voice
In these matters there's little choice.

They exit.

SCENE TWO

Sahaspur.
  Jyoti and Panna.

Jyoti

One wish. The Inspector would leave Sahaspur forever.
Never come back.

Panna

Jyoti! Be careful. They say the first sign of falling in
  love is hate.

Jyoti

Who says that, Panna? What rubbish.

Panna

It's true. That's what Dimple Kapadia told Rishi
  Kapoor in that old film *Bobby*.

Jyoti

Never heard of it.

Panna

It's a classic! Blame the brain. Love and hate come
  from the same part.
Both make you crazy and both break your heart.

Jyoti

Look at me. I'm about as much in love as that
  sheesham tree.

Panna

    Oh come on. Everyone likes a man in uniform –
        always crisp and neat –
    His trousers end at his feet. Who can say 'I'll never
        drink from that water'?

Jyoti

    I'll never drink from that water. Say I closed my eyes,
        swallowed his lies,
    Laid back and prayed it was all over. Do you think he
        would marry me after?

Panna

    No, I don't suppose so.

Jyoti

    How many girls are there in Sahaspur that trusted him?
    How many have been ruined by him?

Panna

    Six.

Jyoti

    Taken a walk in the wood and come back all belly
        and tears.

Panna

    He quite good-looking for an old man of forty. He
        has teeth.
    There'd be perks – it could be worse.

Jyoti

    He's been pestering me for a month. Sending his
        goons Ved and Gopi
    With pathetic gifts; cashmere shawls and lipsticks.

Panna

    Cashmere? No!

Jyoti

    Shoes.

Panna

I'd love some shoes.

Jyoti

A new silk kameez.

Panna

New! My grandmother wore these. No one ever sends
me gifts.
Even when I swing my hips like Madhuri Dixit.

Jyoti

Gifts won't change my mind.

Panna

You're so refined!

Jyoti

They went on and on about Gangwar, what a great
man he was.
On and on till I was scared,
But they won't sway me, I'm prepared.

Panna

Where did they say this to you?

Jyoti

Down by the stream where we wash the clothes,
Down by the stream six days ago.

Panna

I wouldn't blame you if you told me you gave in.
They say his house has air-conditioning.

Jyoti

If I want to cool down I'll swim in the stream.
Men are overrated, Panna.
Imagine a lad standing here, and over there
A dish of butter chicken, which would I choose?

Panna

Difficult choice; the dude or the food?

Jyoti

It's no contest.
I'd rather wake at an early hour,
Light the fire, put some naan on it,
Sprinkle sesame on top; devour.
Then at noon I'd rather fry some ghee,
Throw in cumin, gently sauté until its splutters,
Mix in a cup of paneer, spice and powders,
Add the cream add the peas
Eat as I please.
Then at sunset – the best yet: Eggplant Bharta
Roast till its flesh is brown, chop it into bite-size chunks
Then fry with ginger, onion and tomato
Season with lemon juice and garam masala.
Doesn't that make your mouth water?

Panna

I'm salivating. My stomach is protesting at being
kept waiting.
My belly only ever knows half full.

Jyoti

That's why my desire is all for a tasty dish,
Lentil patties with vegetables fried.
I'd go to sleep happy and dry-eyed.
Panna, what I say to you
I'd rather spend my nights with a saag aloo.
Food like this you can trust. It fills your belly,
Leaves you content. It tops lust.
Because once men have had us in the sack
They pass us by and don't look back.

Panna

You're right, Jyoti
When men want you they're like flies.
You can't shake them but when they've had you
Then it's too late – they buzz off after crapping on
your plate.

Jyoti

Don't trust any of them.

Panna

That's what I've been telling you all along.
Oh look, here are the boys! Hello!

Enter Farooq and Mango.

Farooq

Mango, honestly, your argument is quite shit.
There's no way I'll go along with it.

Mango

I haven't convinced you then?

Farooq

No, my friend, because your theory is insane,
An undercooked mystery manufactured by your brain.

Mango

Luckily there are some women hanging about who
can judge for us.

Jyoti

Why should we stick around for a dose of blokes
explaining?

Panna

Go ahead. I'm up for a bit of entertaining.

Jyoti

Go on then.

Farooq

So, lovely ladies, are you ready?

Jyoti

You're calling us 'ladies', Farooq?

Farooq

Alternative facts. I want to be on trend,
Look at the world; in America –

He flourishes a newspaper.

Trump says the biggest crowds
Cheered him to the White House.
When TV showed it wasn't true
He swore to God he never lied,
Facts just have a different side.
In UK it's 'Austerity's good for the poor,
Cuts in services will give them more.'
Food banks are alternative shopping
Nothing to do with benefits stopping;
In Russia Putin bares his chest
To prove life's better than in the West.
No need to put truth to the test
Ripple those nipples, remove your vest
And how are we here in Hindustan?
In elections we live free from fear
We don't attack minorities here
See that dead man, head beaten in
Alternative facts say he'll live again.
He's alive actually, how does that work?
Alternative facts will drive you beserk.
A Muslim boy fell in love with a Hindu girl,
It was pure love, no question
Troublemakers from the BJP
Swore it was a case of kidnapping
Tore the lovers apart, broke more than their hearts
No matter how hard they tried
To speak their love, everybody said they lied
Because alternative facts weren't on their side.
Ladies, I could go on.

Jyoti

Please don't. I suppose, Farooq, at agricultural college
Your speech would be applauded.
But here in Sahaspur we'll ignore it.
All this stuff you're stressing
Is terminally depressing.

Farooq

Please infect me with your wisdom, Jyoti.

Jyoti

Is a woman supposed to be adoring
When you're being really boring?
Spouting how truth's so diminished
You've turned into a total cynic.
You think we're so gullible and addled
We'll believe any news that's peddled.
So politicians are sparing with the truth,
That doesn't take a genius to compute,
And if those lovers had more than broken hearts
Perhaps they were better off apart.
Your navel-gazing doesn't impress me
Your pompous speechifying won't repress me.
Life goes round as it's always done.
Winter rain, summer sun.
I work in the fields all day
Cutting sugar cane, milking cows, digging with a spade
Then at midday resting up, dozing in the shade.
My back is strong, my legs are steady,
My hands grow the food that will feed my belly.
Why spend your time moaning and whining?
The sun is shining? What a way to experience life!
Your wife, whoever she will be, will sign up to misery.

Mango

She's demolished you. The tongue of a lioness.

Jyoti

Hurry up then. What's your dispute?
We can't stay here all day.

Panna

We can.

Farooq

It's me versus Mango. Basically no contest.

Jyoti

What's Mango been saying now?

Farooq

It's very wrong but he won't admit it.

Mango

Of course not, because I'm right.
Why would I admit I'm wrong when I'm not?

Farooq

He says there's no such thing as love.

Panna

Mango. Love is in every film! Romeo and Juliet –
That's why they killed each other!

Mango

That's not how it happened, Panna.

Jyoti

No love. That's going a bit far, Mango.

Farooq

That's going a bit mad.

Panna

It's probably because he's a bit fat.

Farooq

Love makes the world go round.

Mango

I think you'll find that's angular momentum.
The earth spins because there's nothing to stop it.

Farooq

I'm talking about pyar love like between a girl and boy.

Mango

Yes, okay, there is a kind of natural love that everyone has.
My hand will protect my face against the slap that
    comes its way,

To stop my body getting hurt my feet will put on
   a spurt.
When my finger sticks in, my eyelid will close,
As I mis-scratch my nose.

Panna

What's picking your nose got to do with it?

Mango

My point, and I do have one,
Is that no one loves anyone more than they love
   themselves.

Panna

Remind me never to fall in love with you, Mango.
I want a passion that's insane.
I want my lover to burn for me like a flame.

Mango

Going out with you would involve some pain.

Panna

You have nothing to worry about, Mango.
I'm after a sexy cane-cutter with a six-pack.

Mango

Isn't that pleasure for the self?

Panna

I hope so.

Mango

See. I hate to crow but I win. There is no love,
Only love of the self. There are no others on the shelf.

Farooq

Jyoti – What do you love?

Jyoti

My freedom, my honour, my papa, my friends, my
   dinner.

Farooq
Nothing else?

Jyoti
No.

Panna
Jyoti would rather eat a biriyani than consider
matrimony.
For her it's a no-brainer.

Farooq
One day maybe you'll suffer from jealousy, Jyoti.
I'd like to see that.

Panna
Why's that, Farooq?

Farooq
I have my reasons.

Enter Ved and Gopi, the two policemen.

Ved
Afternoon.

Panna
Gangwar's men.

Jyoti
His pimps, you mean.

Farooq
Ved, still football mad like when you were a kid?

Mango
And you couldn't afford a ball – just kicked around a tin?

Ved
At training camp we left playground tricks.

Gopi
We learnt to break bones with sticks.

Jyoti

What do you want?

Ved

Is that all the thanks we get, Gopi? After the trouble we've taken?

Gopi

To keep you all secure and safe. Risking our necks.

Farooq

You've risked your necks for us?

Ved

Who gave you permission to speak, Farooq?

Gopi

A son of Mohammad. What are you doing in Hindustan?

Farooq

I live here. This is my home.

Gopi

I think you'll find that's Pakistan.

Farooq

What's Pakistan got to do with me?

Mango

Anyway it's the same DNA. Church, temple, mosque. Just houses of God.

Jyoti

Let's go, Farooq.

Ved

This is where the trouble starts with devious Muslims hiding amongst us.

Farooq

For centuries in broad daylight, living and walking the streets.

Gopi

How can people live their lives in peace?

Ved

Cows can't live their lives in peace.
Cows are sacred. We Hindus don't eat beef.
Imagine you wake up one day and your cow is gone
But the Muslim beard next door is eating burger with
  his son.

Gopi

Something that should not be done.

Ved

An abomination to the Hindu nation.

Gopi

Inspector Gangwar, an honourable man
He heard that things were going down.

Ved

Troublemakers taking over Rampur town.
Fifty miles from here.
So we grabbed our sticks, our guns, the BJP called
  us to arms
To settle the dispute.

Farooq

The BJP betrayed the farmers – won't pay us
For the work we do.
Why would we support you?

Gopi

Mouthy Muslim, aren't you?

Ved

We personally escorted many to hear our candidate
  Vihaan,
He gave a nice preach about foreigners, cows, our
  freedom of speech.

Unfortunately, the Mohammedans kicked off.
We waded in – they had to be stopped.

Gopi

Tell them what happened, Ved?

Ved

By the end a couple of them were – not very well.

Jyoti

Proud of yourselves? Doing Gangwar's dirty work for
  him.

Gopi

Don't bad-mouth the Inspector, he was great.
The night before, he stayed up with us lads till late,
Drank, smoked, cracked a joke,
In the morning, he rolled up his sleeves and entered
  the fray.
Despite his office you couldn't keep him away.

Ved

He looked like a film star – Shashi Kapoor
Not now he's dead but how he looked before.
His uniform ironed to a crisp. Symmetrical the cuffs
  at his wrist.
Bright shining buttons strained over his manly chest.
A roar from his throat primitive and strong.
His stick smashed, splashed droplets of blood
On the white of his collar, his thighs, the streets
As he beat down with love for the people.

Gopi

God willing – come the election, we'll get the results
  we want.
Rampur will be saved.
He's coming now. Receive him with pride.

Ved

Ved and Gopi at his side.

Gangwar enters with Vihaan and the rest of the townspeople.
They sing to welcome him.

Song.

Gangwar
Residents of Sahaspur,
How much I enjoy returning to this humble place
I bring with me a special guest, Vihaan Mukerjee
The future face of our BJP; Bharatiya Janata; Indian
    People's Party.
We're grateful for the love you've shown us here.

Ramdev
We have only shown a fraction of what we really feel.
Sahaspur and the town council
Who you honour here today
Beg you, a little embarrassed I have to say, to receive
    some modest gifts,
I have commissioned a speech.

Mango
I have it here, Mayor Ramdev. Something I wrote earlier.

Ramdev (*reads*)
'Sahaspur, a hick town, down-at-heel, out of luck
But please do not turn up your nose at our truck
Loaded with sugar cane, rice, pickles, a duck,
With mangoes, lychees and sweets for your larder
A goat, ten chickens, that's just for starters,
Round it all off with a hundred parathas.
It would also mightily please us
If you would accept in tribute some paneer cheeses
Which we offer on bended knees . . . es.
To you and your men, we say, eat, eat, bon appétit.'

Gangwar
You have my gratitude, Mayor Ramdev.

Ramdev
Singers, let's have the song again.

Gangwar
That's not necessary.

Ramdev
No trouble. Please. My daughter will sing,
She has a beautiful voice.
You won't regret the choice.

Jyoti
Baba –

Ramdev
Don't be shy.

Song, which Jyoti sings.

They leave.

Gangwar
You two. Wait.

Jyoti
You mean us, sir?

Gangwar
Who else?

Jyoti
Me and Panna?

Panna
Get lost, Jyoti, not me.

Gangwar
Jyoti, you were insolent to me the other day.

Jyoti
But I've never spoken to you.

Gangwar
You refused the gifts I sent.
Do you make it a habit to offend?

Jyoti

Forgive me, that was not my intent.
It's the way in our village that unmarried girls
Keep to themselves and don't accept gifts from strangers.

Gangwar

This is a different case.
I've dedicated my life to keeping you all safe.
Don't I deserve to be shown some respect?

Jyoti

Good day, sir.

Gangwar

Sahaspur wanted to give me more – what do you
    think I should choose?

Jyoti

I'm not sure there's room in the truck for any more, sir.
It's stuffed to the roof as it is.

Gangwar

What if I choose both of you?

Panna

I don't think the mayor meant it like that.

Gangwar

Come inside with me. There we can relax properly.
Get to know each other. Ved?

Ved

Sir.

Gangwar

Encourage the girls to do the right thing and come in.

He exits.

Ved

Don't be stupid girls, get in.
He just wants to tell you tales of Rampur.

Panna
    And hear a clang as he locks the door?

Jyoti
    Ved, let us pass.

Ved
    Cheer up, you've been gifted.
    He deserves better than that shit in the truck.

Panna
    Gopi. Get out of our way.

Jyoti
    Gangwar's had enough meat for today.

Gopi
    It's your meat he's interested in.

Jyoti
    He'd choke on it. Run, Panna.

    They go.

Gopi
    Shit. What message do we take to him now?
    They both ran off, silly cows. He'll pulverise us.

Ved
    It's part of our job as the Inspector's men
    To put up with his crap, now and then. Let's go.

SCENE THREE

Ishani, a progressive Hindu candidate standing in the Rampur election.
    Mekhal, her assistant.
    They are preparing to go in front of a camera for an interview.

Mekhal

You're on in five.
Smile, don't be bullied, let them see you're the boss.
Confident you'll win – that's how you'll come across.
One decaf coffee.

He hands it to her.

What colour for your scarf?

Ishani

Does it matter what I wear, Mekhal?
People are surely more interested in what I have to say?

Mekhal

Sometimes I question, Ishani, your sanity.
It's not a question of vanity; Hillary's pant suits,
Angela's blazers, Margaret's handbag, Indira's hair
They're part of the brand, you barely notice they're there
But subliminally feel a stab of recognition and so
    sympathise with her position,
A female pays a heavy price if she fails to get her
    outfit right.
Too sexy, too frowsy – if the media start debating
    what she's wearing
It drowns out the message the electorate should be
    hearing.
A woman politician has to sartorially plan.

Ishani

God, it would be easier to be a man.

Mekhal

There's a science to colour – it's a code.
Perhaps we should go for a saffron shade,
Reclaim it from the Hindutva gang?

Ishani

Holy colours worn by self-appointed saints.
You say I must be cool and collected

But I feel the hurt done to innocent people personally.
When my supporters stood up in Rampur
Shouted 'Ishani for farmers' wages and a secular
    state'
Those fundamentalist nutters couldn't wait to
    bludgeon a few.
Streets ran with blood.
Now fake news, say they were keeping the peace
But the BJP pays for a corrupt police.

Mekhal

Our sources tell us 'Gangwar' in the name they hear.
Ishani, it won't help you to now appear full of
    agitation and fear –

Ishani

It is they that plant fear in people's minds.
Blame me for the riots, point to the bloodshed
And say this unrest awaits our nation
If you vote for Ishani at the polling stations.
The untruth they want to sell to the Hindu majority,
The Congress Party is controlled by a Muslim
    minority.
Our opponents drag us to dark days!
I must speak up!

Mekhal

Stick to the script.
Play your ace – you have blue blood – your father
    a Brahmin
High Caste – that plays well to the Hindu soul –
Keep them on side,
Put the brakes on the populist slide.

Ishani

My country drives me mad – why has everything got
    to be about religion?
Gangwar, where does he reside?

Mekhal

Sahaspur, in the countryside
It's his playground
From there he controls the areas around.

Ishani

The bastard muscle of the BJP!
There's nothing they won't do
To scare off the people of Rampur who would vote for me
And so turn it to a victory for Vihaan
Who stands a puppet in his father's place,
A smiling front on the fundamentalist face.

Mekhal

God, one minute to go.
Just remember your three key points.

*Ishani turns on the charm – as if she's looking at
a camera.*

Ishani

Here are my promises to you:
One – renew economy by building roads for better
connectivity.
Two – farmers deserve lifesaving subsidy.
Three – ensure religious equality.

Pause.

Four – then we're going to Rampur.

Mekhal

What? On our own – without protection? Even the
journalists have checked out.

Ishani

I've got to ensure a free and fair election.

Mekhal

It's time. Look straight to camera, don't fidget.
Scarf – go for well-behaved in beige.

Ishani

Mekhal, I've got this down.
Then to Rampur – it will be my town.

They exit.

SCENE FOUR

A wood.
Jyoti and Farooq.

Jyoti

Why have you brought me here, Farooq?
Villagers love to snoop and now you give them
    ammunition
Dragging me to the middle of nowhere.
I left the washing half wrung and came away from the
    river.
You want to 'talk'. Couldn't we have done it without
The boring walk?
You know what the whole village is saying
That you fancy me and I've got the hots for you just
    because
You're not like, really minging. You're okay
But that's mostly because your clothes are marginally
    better
Than the average villager. And that's not hard to achieve.
People will be making such a fuss. 'Hindu girl,
    Muslim boy.'
After this there won't be a single person in the village,
    fields or woods
Who won't be whispering that I must be quickly
    married off.
Like that's going to happen!

Farooq

Are you saying you won't marry me?

Jyoti
I'm sixteen. Why would I want to give up my life,
become a drudge of a wife?

Farooq
Beautiful Jyoti, you're killing me with your words.

Jyoti
It's just how I am.

Farooq
Doesn't it give you a pain to see me practically driven
insane?
I can't eat, drink, sleep.

Jyoti
See a doctor, Farooq.

Farooq
How can such a hard heart find a place
In such an angelic face?
I just want us to be together, like two doves cooing
and rubbing beaks in harmony.

Jyoti
What's doves got to do with it?

Farooq
Jyoti, you inspire me to poetry.

Jyoti
No thanks. Though I might have a little bit of an
inclination.
Somewhere. If I can remember where I put it.

Farooq
You must have remembered last night. When we
kissed.

Jyoti
That was because of the moon. I wasn't myself.

Farooq
Am I that horrible? Is the thought of us so awful?
Can't you imagine us being together every night?
My definition of total delight.

Jyoti
I can imagine it – that's what I'm worried about.

Farooq
Jyoti.

They hear a noise, look.

The Inspector.

Jyoti
Gangwar, hunting. You hide. It'll be worse if he finds
us together.

Farooq
No. I'm not leaving you alone with that tiger.

Jyoti
I can handle him better alone. Go on. Go.

Farooq hides.

Gangwar
Not bad to be following a timid little buck
And to stumble on such a beautiful doe.

Jyoti
I was having a rest here after washing some clothes
With your permission, Inspector, I'll just go.

Gangwar
Don't refuse my company again.
Can't we be friends?

Jyoti
I've got enough friends, thank you.

Gangwar
I have feelings too, you know.

Jyoti

I can't leave my washing much longer.
It needs to be hung.

Gangwar

Stay a while this won't take long.

Jyoti

Goodbye, sir.

Gangwar

I could name other women in the village who have
Given in to me with very little persuasion.

Jyoti

Maybe they weren't fussy.

Gangwar

Always ready with the sharp tongue.
There's something about you, it's true . . .
I've been chasing you for a month.
Now in this solitary place
You don't have to save face or play hard to get.

Jyoti

Are you going to force me? Have you lost your mind?

Gangwar

Look, I'm putting my gun on the ground.
I'm not going to shoot you, besides there's a practical
    reason,
I'm going to need both my hands.

Jyoti

Shiva help me.

Gangwar

Relax or you'll make it worse. It's the right thing.
    You'll see.
Then I'll be able to get you out of my head and you'll
    be free.

Jyoti
We don't have to do this now – I'll meet you later –
I promise.

Gangwar
No. Let's get this done.

Jyoti
I'll tell everyone.

Gangwar
You're in good hands.

Farooq takes the gun.

Farooq
Inspector Gangwar. Leave Jyoti. Let her go. Jyoti, run.

Jyoti
Farooq!

Gangwar
Bloody dog.

Farooq
Run, Jyoti.

Jyoti
Careful, Farooq.

Farooq
Go.

She goes.

Gangwar
How many men have you killed, cub?

Farooq
I don't want to pull the trigger.

Gangwar
You're going to shoot me? Then do it. I won't turn
my back.

You'll need to stand up properly – look straight
Down the barrel when you take aim or you'll hit
    a tree.
If you do a bad job I'll be maimed, I'd rather you
    killed me.

Farooq

I'm not going to shoot. I'm quite happy to be alive,
So I'll take the gun and say goodbye.

Gangwar

For this offence and nuisance you will pay.

Farooq exits.

The shame of it. Why didn't I fight him?

He exits.

Act Two

Town square.
  Ramdev and Gina.

Ramdev

The best way for the town to proceed
Is to take no more rice from our reserves in the store
That is how we manage the need. Other counsellors
    disagree
But having food in stock seems sensible to me.

Gina

Not when people are going hungry!
Gangwar's crew have eaten us out of house and home.
How many times can I serve broth made from a single
    spinach leaf?
We farmers already struggle, the government breaks
    its word
And leaves us drowning in debt – this year is the
    worst yet.
The other counsellors ask us to seek the advice of
    a holy man.

Ramdev

We can't afford a good one – a second-rate fortune
    teller will leave us worse off than before.
They talk the big talk – about fate and stars and
    planetary pulls
How Scorpio is a scorpion and Taurus is a bull
Take our money, treat us like fools;
Tell us where and when to plant our crops,
But they mix it up – the bumpkins! They jeopardise
Our mangoes, sugar cane and pumpkins.

Or they say in a spooky voice 'a cow will die'.
And it does, not here but in Chennai.
I may not be blessed with second sight
But I'll take a punt and say after day comes night.
Will we ever be free of our crippling debts?
They moan and sway and say perhaps you may,
Their gift is prevarication – they're masters of
    equivocation.
About as much use as an earache.

Gina

Okay, well we won't do that then.
The Chaiwallah says Gangwar's men demand a
    private tax
As an insurance against attacks! Extortion!
We've been stripped bare by the Inspector,
He'd take the hair on your arms if you let him
And he's dirty – he pesters the women. Even your Jyoti.
Was there ever anyone so corrupt, so venal?
Me? I'd like to see him hanging from that banyan tree.

Gangwar enters with Ved.

A million thanks to God for you, Inspector.

Gangwar

God keep you, good people.

Gina

Please, sit.

Gangwar

You sit.

Ramdev

No, you sit.

Gangwar

I told you sit. Have you some trouble understanding it?

Gina

Okay, sir.

They sit.

Gangwar
Sahaspur always makes me welcome here.

Ramdev|
We do our best, Inspector. We're humble people.

Gina
We may not be the cleverest or the richest
Or the tallest or the quickest or the finest
Or the sharpest or the bravest or the –

Gangwar
Shut up.

Gina
Yes sir.

Gangwar
The women especially make me welcome here.
There is a one hiding behind her door there
Who gave in to me immediately.

Gina
She was wrong to. May her lettuce droop.

Ramdev
I don't think, sir, you should be talking so liberally.

Gangwar
Liberally? What an eloquent peasant. Ved?

Ved
Inspector?

Gangwar
Let's get down to business.
The Chaiwallah's wife – she's usually up for it.
What did she say?

Ved
That her husband hides her away like rice in a bin
But as soon as she's free you'll be the first one in.

Gangwar

The young widow?

Ved

Definitely, she said – if her husband wasn't so recently
   dead.

Gangwar

Panna?

Ved

Getting married – though I can't find anyone who's
   claimed her.

Gangwar

She's stalling.
The peasantry is so boring. It's better in the cities.
There men appreciate their wives being visited.
And the women are amenable, don't make such a fuss
They're delighted to be serviced by one of us.

Gina

That can't be true. In cities there must be honour too.

Ramdev

She speaks for me.

Mango enters.

Ved

I like it when women resist.

Gangwar

That's lucky because in your case it must happen a lot.

Mango

Ha ha.

Gangwar

It's true that pleasure in anticipation is ruined if a woman
Is too forthcoming although it can go too far the
   other way.

There is one here who, how can I say, refuses to grant
    me a wish.
The offender is your daughter.

Ramdev

My daughter?

Gangwar

Yes.
Rebuke her, Ramdev. She is resisting me.

Ramdev

Inspector, we here in Sahaspur wish to live peacefully
Under your command, sir. You mustn't take away our
    honour.

Gangwar

Do you have honour? You let your daughter fraternise
With a Quran–thumper who is ready
To sully our blood with that of his base tribe.

Ved

She's been forced. It's love, jihad.

Ramdev

Not forced.

Gangwar

You say you're concerned to keep your daughter pure.
I found them alone near the river.
A whore is what he'll make of her.

Ramdev

Your words bring dishonour, sir.

Gangwar

Where is Farooq?

Mango

I don't know, sir.

Ved
> Skulking somewhere.

Gopi enters.

Gopi
> I found your gun, sir. Just left outside your door, sir,
> Wrapped up like an old bone, sir.

Gangwar
> That peasant takes my gun with impunity?
> Was about to kill me. He has the nerve to show his
>   face around this place?

Ved
> Jyoti is like his bait.
> Last night I saw someone who looked like Farooq,
> I beat him to a pulp.
> But it wasn't him. I made a mistake.

Gangwar
> I served this country. I've fought scum.
> Now I am threatened by this kid
> I don't know what this world's become?
> If I wanted to I'd tear this village apart.
> (*To Ramdev.*) And you – deliver your daughter to me
>   if you know what's good for you.

Vihaan enters.

Gangwar
> What is it?

Vihaan
> I've been looking for you.
> Ishani is heading for Rampur
> To hold a rally, playing Mother Teresa,
> Telling the people their safety
> Will be assured at tomorrow's polls.

Gangwar
> Impossible.

Vihaan
She guarantees state police will stand
Armed outside the polling gates
To ensure fair elections.

Ved
Does that mean we are going to lose?

Gangwar
Get this rabble out of the square.

Gina
Dear God, we have to go through this.

Gangwar
Back to your holes like mice.

They leave.

Days of restraint are over. We'll take the risk.
We must ensure those that stand against us
Feel our fist.

They exit.

SCENE TWO

A field in Sahaspur.
Mango, Panna, Jyoti fleeing.

Mango
Ramdev instructed me to take you out of town,
Hide there in the wild till things calm down.

Panna
Mango, this will sound strange:
I'm glad you're with us for a change.

Jyoti
Where's Farooq?

Panna

He risked his life to save Jyoti. It's very romantic.

Mango

A good trick. Only now Farooq is kicking his heels
hiding out here in the fields.

Jyoti

He shouldn't be anywhere near. Why doesn't he
realise he needs to disappear?

Panna

He could apologise maybe? Beg for mercy?

Jyoti

Nothing will change his mind. Gangwar has him marked.

Jacinta enters.

Jacinta

Please help me.

Mango

It's the untouchable girl.

Panna

She looks petrified. What is she doing outside the
village?

Jyoti

What's your name?

Jacinta

Jacinta.

Jyoti

What's wrong?

Jacinta

They're after me.
The Inspector's men, on their way to Rampur,
Have taken me for their whore. I can't run any further.

Panna
> They'll find us too then?

Jacinta
> Help me. Hide me.

Jyoti
> How can we? Where?
> Best we go our separate ways – it's safer.
> I need to get to Farooq, persuade him to go.

> *She exits.*

Panna
> I'll try that way.

Jacinta
> Who will help me?

Panna
> Mango will take care of you.

> *Panna runs off.*

Jacinta
> Are you armed?

Mango
> Two arms.

Jacinta
> I wish we had a gun.

> *Enter Ved and Gopi.*

Ved
> What are you thinking, running away?

Jacinta
> I'm dead.

Mango
> Sirs, this poor scrap, a simple Dallit girl – let her go.

Ved
Is this the best you can do, Mango – this shit-shoveller?

Mango
Better a shit-shoveller than an arse-licker.

Gopi
I'll kill him.

Gangwar enters.

Gangwar
What's this?

Gopi
This low-life is protesting, sir.

Gangwar
Really?

Gopi
Shall I stuff his mouth with earth?

Gangwar
No, no, it's worth hearing a citizen's concerns. Go on.

Mango
I have a few suggestions for improvements, sir,
    which I offer up in the spirit of democracy.

Gangwar
And what would those be?

Mango
The constitution of India demands protection of the
    fundamental rights of the people.

Gangwar
Of course.

Mango
In that spirit, sir, punish your men who in your name
Are stealing this woman away from her home.

Gangwar

I've heard what you have to say and I'd rather do it
my way.
Ved, Gopi, tie his hands.

Gopi

Shall we kill him now?

Gangwar

Don't waste a bullet. Make an example of him.
Take him, tie him to a tree, whip him raw.

Mango

Mercy, sir.

Gangwar

Till he bleeds.

Mango

Sir, have I offended you or had anyone in the town?
Ved?
My mother had a soft spot for you, remember?

Ved

Shut up, scum. (*To Gopi.*) Shall I whip him while you
hold him down?

Gopi

Take turns is best. Then when you're tired you can
take a rest.

They take him away.

Gangwar

You, Dallit girl, why are you running away?
Is a farmer better than a man of my worth?

Jacinta

I didn't want to come – your men dragged me to you.

Gangwar

Dragged you?

Jacinta
I'm a Dallit not fit to clean your shoes, nor drink
from the same well or cross your shadow's path. You
don't want me – I'll pollute you.

Gangwar
True.

Jacinta
Thank you, sir.

Gangwar
I'll give you to my men. They can use you.

Jacinta
Some pity, sir.

Gangwar
There's no pity in war.

Jacinta
I'll kill myself after.

Gangwar
Whatever. Get moving.

They exit.

SCENE THREE

Gangwar steps in front of Ishani.

Ishani
What are you doing? Get out of my way.

He doesn't.

You're Gangwar.

Gangwar
That's right.

Ishani

Is this police business? It's irregular.

Gangwar

In the flesh you look younger.

Ishani

What do you want?

Gangwar

A personal audience. A one-to-one.
Where are your plans for today?

Ishani

I think you know.

Gangwar

It's polite to ask though.

Ishani

A rally.

Gangwar

Rally. Really. Yes. It's best you don't attend.

Ishani

It seems I have spooked your man, Vihaan,
So he's sent his crooked cop.
Are you frightened I'll come out on top?

Gangwar

We can't guarantee your safety if you attend.

Ishani

A veiled threat. You can't stop me.
Our country is still a democracy. I have a duty to
   address the people.

Gangwar

What do you know about the people?

Ishani

I've dedicated to my life to serving them – I'm
a politician.

Gangwar

My point exactly. A politician. Spawned from the
Gandhi legacy.
A spoilt rotten dynasty who've never struggled to stay
alive,
Born suckling a silver spoon. Polished up at the best
schools.
My father was a landlord of just two rooms.
For what we had we fought.
I took the lessons he taught.
In the dark I woke – hitched to the airport
Brought back the day's papers crumpled, worn
Ironed them, sold them back on the streets
All so the family could eat
And if I was sick, my father would give me a kick
Send me out again
It made me the man I am – did me good.
I never shirk from unpleasant work.

Ishani

Spare me the Bollywood rags to riches.
You and your Modi are still dining out on those sob
stories?

Gangwar

How is your daughter?

Ishani

My daughter?

Gangwar

Is she enjoying boarding school in Puna? Stay away
from Rampur
And I'll make sure nobody touches her.

Ishani

I'll call the law on you.

Gangwar

I am the law.

Now kiss me on the forehead like my father used to
    when I was a good boy.

He exits.
    Mekhal enters.

Ishani

Where the hell were you, you bastard?

He leaves.

SCENE FOUR

Town square.
    Jyoti and Farooq.

Jyoti

Why have I let you take me home, Farooq?

Farooq

The safest place is here. Gangwar is in Rampur,
Maybe someone will do us a favour, finish him off
    there.

Jyoti

Hold off the curses, people tend to live longer
When you wish death on them.

Farooq

In that case may he live forever.
This buys us some time, Jyoti – be mine.

Jyoti

Farooq – you should have left by now.

Farooq
I want to be where you are.
Nothing else makes sense to me.
You draw me – like the moon draws the sea.

Jyoti
Have you gone completely crazy? You held a gun up
to the Inspector's chest – he won't let that rest.
I don't know how to get that into your head.

Farooq
You love me though, don't you?

Jyoti
Go, why don't you?

Farooq
I gave him back his gun.
Perhaps now Gangwar will leave us alone.
An old married couple.
Don't keep me waiting.

Jyoti
There was supposed to be time – to be young –
have some fun.

Farooq
Marry me, Jyoti, and I'll promise I'll go – I'll run.
Is it because you don't love me?

Jyoti
That's not it at all.

Farooq
So will you?

Jyoti
Yes, if it means you'll go.

Farooq
Let me kiss you for this vow.

Jyoti

Here's my father now – ask him – before I change
my mind.

Enter Ramdev and Gina.

Ramdev

Gangwar has overstepped the bounds.
He has always been corrupt, a tyrant,
But never before has he sunk this far down.

Gina

For a while we can breathe – he's out of town.
He takes girls from the streets.
I'm barely safe in my widow's weeds.

Ramdev

He whipped Mango too.

Gina

No black cloth or ink is as dark as his flesh now.

Ramdev

Don't say any more.
What is the point of our office
If we are so powerless?

Gina

We must go to the temple – pray for better times.
Prayer is the only weapon we have in our hands.

Enter Farooq.

Farooq

It's Farooq, sir.

Ramdev

Has that madman Gangwar done you wrong?

Farooq

That's not why I've come. I hope you'll be happy.
I've come to ask to join your family.

Ramdev
> To join?

Farooq
> I'm making so bold as to ask to become Jyoti's husband.

Gina
> Muslim boy. Who will marry them, Pundit or Imam?

Farooq
> I'd walk round your temple fire
> If it would join us forever.

Ramdev
> Your father was a good man.
> Your grandfather's built the village well.

Gina
> The women brought the stones
> The men dug down
> Until they hit the water that runs beneath our town.

Ramdev
> To join? Hindu and Muslim.
> Everyone will want their say, this is a problem
>   that won't ever go away.

Farooq
> I know.

Ramdev
> As to my Jyoti, I admit wanted a son.

Gina
> But unluckily it was a girl that came.

Ramdev
> From the first minute I saw her
> She had my heart, my daughter.

Gina
> He gave out sweets, ludoos and burfi,
> And we all said, what's up with him,

He's smiling and it's not a son
Perhaps it's the pain has made him deranged.

Ramdev
But they were wrong
And when her mother was gone
She was the one who looked after me, the light of my eyes.
I am happy to accept any son who protected her
As you have done. But the decision is Jyoti's.

Gina
It's a girl's duty if her father accepts the suitor.
Woman must obey man.
My husband's dead, God rest him.

Ramdev (*he calls her*)
Daughter.
She has a sharp tongue, she'll lay down the law.

Farooq
I'm a modern man – I expect my wife to answer back.

Gina
Now you say that.

Ramdev
If she agrees, we can talk dowry.

Farooq
You don't need to.

Gina
Has no one told you before
It doesn't help a couple to be poor?

Ramdev
Jyoti my love, come over here.
It's been a heavy day but now
Farooq has asked me – tell me if you think this is right –
That he be given to your good friend Panna
For his bride.

Jyoti
Panna?

Ramdev
You think she's too good for him?

Pause.

Exactly, that's why I thought he'd be better off
marrying you. The one with the big feet.

Jyoti
You're still making bad jokes at your age?

Ramdev
Do you love him?
You want me to say yes.

Jyoti
Say it for me, Father.

Ramdev
Farooq – you're in luck – Jyoti will have you. And
about the dowry.

Farooq
You're offending my honour.

Jyoti
No, he's not, Farooq. We're taking it.

Gina
Don't say I didn't warn you.

Ramdev
Son,
She'll start as she means to go on.

Ramdev and Gina exit.

Jyoti
What's up now, Farooq? You're not crying?

Farooq
For joy.
I feel so good, Jyoti, when I look at you
Seeing you look at me the same way too.

They exit.

SCENE FIVE

A sleazy bar near Rampur.

Vihaan
She's won. Disaster.
I thoughr you said you warned her off?
Instead she was inspired.
She spoke with redoubled eloquence.
She shamed us. Blamed us for the riots.

Gopi
It's a tragedy.

Ved
Our support really flagged
Even the garlands sagged.

Vihaan
People, she said. I'm scared but I'm here.
Her supporters flocked to sign, those illiterates pressed
their inked thumbs
Beside her name.
The ragbag of independents joined forces and taking
her side
Drowned us in an electoral landslide.

Gangwar
I might as well go.

Vihaan
What? There's no new plan?

Ved

We're going to leave, Vihaan?

Vihaan

You dragged me to this place
Paraded my father's legacy, made me see
My duty.
You persuaded me to make this journey
Only to abandon me?
Now when the fire begins to burn in my belly
Calling me to liberate my country?
Now he tells me!

Gangwar

Vihaan, lick your wounds, look to the next day.
I'll go home, unfinished business awaits me there.
You're young, the lesson is hard won,
The game of politics is a devious dance
You bear the knocks, await the budding chance.
We lost the battle not the war.
Now I've skulls to crack in Sahaspur.

SCENE SIX

The wedding.

Song.

Panna

What a gorgeous song.

Mango

They didn't spend that long writing it though, did they?
Repetitive, I'd say.

Panna

Have you got a romantic bone in your body, Mango?

Mango

I'm sixty per cent chapatti – and I'm happy with that.

Farooq

Go on then, Mango – show them what you're made
of – you sing.

Mango

I'm not in the mood for singing – I've had my buttocks
whipped
So soundly it's taken the spring from my step.
Also they also stuffed an enema up my arse.

Panna

Oh God, less is more, Mango.

Mango

That's what I said as I shat myself.

Farooq

That's how they get their laughs?

Mango

I laughed till I cried, till I was empty inside.

Panna

Oh well, look on it as a spiritual cleansing.

Mango

Can't see it catching on.

Farooq

You complain about the song, Mango – but are you
all talk?
Could you do any better>

Mango

I pray to Bagwan the happy couple
Manage to avoid the usual trouble
At first everything is perfect, rosy
Then one day she thinks, oh lordy
How many times has he told that story?
She wishes they could afford a new mat
He thinks oh why has the sex has gone flat

Last year he swore to mend the chair
She sat on it – her arse went into the air
She fed his dinner to the dog
He sits outside on his favourite log
That pleases them both I'm afraid to report
Cos the person that most annoys them now
Is the one with whom they took their vow
Hopefully this won't happen to you
Because you're my friends
But don't count on it.

Farooq
Pure poetry.

Panna
Your poem is like a doughnut.

Mango
How do you figure that out?

Panna
Or like a jalebi.
You took some dough, threw it in the burning oil
Some bits came out too crispy, some bent
Some burned, a waste of the time you spent.
That's the same way you composed your verse
The pan is the paper, dough the words,
Your hope is the music, like syrup will cover over
The stupid shapes you laid out on the plates
But the only one to eat them will be you.
Because it's only for a tone-deaf person they'll do.

Farooq
Bravo.

Panna
No problem.

Mango
A bit of a poet yourself, Panna, on the sly.

Panna

I try.

Song.

Enter the Inspector with the policemen.

Ramdev

You've come in uniform. Why have you come, sir?
Would you like to sit, sir?

Farooq

I'm dead.

Jyoti

Run, Farooq. Run away.

Gangwar

There's the criminal that stole my gun, threatened me
    with it.
Take him.

Ved

Give yourself up.

Farooq

So you can beat me?

Gangwar

I'm not the sort of man to beat people for no reason,
I represent the law, else these men with me
Would, by now, have smashed you up against a wall.
I've come to take you to prison.

Panna

Sir, he's getting married.

Gangwar

So what he's getting married? What's that to me?

Gina

If he offended you, sir, forgive him
Prove a generous man.

Gangwar
    He's a terrorist. Ved, Gopi – take him.

Jyoti
    No!

Ramdev
    It's not surprising that a young lover will try to protect
    The woman he's in love with –
    You were trying to have your way with his wife
    And so he risked his life for her. Spare him, sir.

Gangwar
    You're a fool, Mayor.
    She wasn't his wife then. You're quick to give your
        consent to it.
    But are you sure she wasn't forced?
    This Muslim scum surely used ill methods
    Stealing our Hindu women is a way of humiliating us.

Ramdev
    No, you're wrong.
    I know my daughter, nothing could persuade her
    Except love.
    As to our community – we have always lived together
        in peace,
    Hindu, Muslim, Christian, Sikh –

Gangwar
    Islam is a foreign religion. Barbarians brought it here –
    It's not even Indian.
    Take away his staff of office. He's unfit.
    This place needs to be purified of multicultural shit.

Ramdev
    Take it, please.

Gangwar
    Bring the prisoner.

Jyoti

Leave him alone. What is he guilty of? Protecting
my honour?

Gangwar

Not even wearing a clean kurta to his own wedding.
You're too good for him, Jyoti.
Think of the mongrel children he would father.

Jyoti

I'm marrying him –
And I'll love him and have him night after night for
the rest of my life.

She kisses Farooq.
Gangwar pulls her off Farooq.

Gangwar

Take him away.

Jyoti

You're obsessed. Farooq!

Farooq

Jyoti.

They take Farooq away.

Jyoti

Here I am dressed as a bride with no husband by
my side.
Perhaps you think I should marry you?
Except that you disgust me.

Gangwar

Slut.

He puts his hand forcibly down Jyoti's top. It rips.
Ramdev averts his gaze. Jyoti gives a cry.

Jyoti

Father! Baba! Don't let them take me. Baba!

274

They take her.

Gangwar (*to Ramdev*)
Perhaps you'd like to watch?

Gangwar, Gopi, Jyoti exit.

Ramdev
Where is justice?

Gina
The wedding's turned to mourning.

Panna
What can we do?

Mango
Say nothing – they have guns and my welts still feel
the whips.
Let that seal our lips.

We hear a last scream from Jyoti.

They exit.

Act Three

Jyoti enters. She is unrecognisable.
  She rings the bell. Slowly the villagers emerge.

Panna

  Jyoti? Is that you?

The village gathers.

Gina

  Better she had died than come back alive
  To face the shame.
  The sin will stick to her, make her hide her face
  Impossible to live with that disgrace.
  Don't touch her. Bad luck can spread by touch it is
      said.
  It's a bad omen for the village.
  Better off if in the extremity of her grief
  She had killed herself.

Panna

  It's like a ghost of Jyoti has come back.

Ramdev

  Is that my Jyoti?

Gina

  That was her lovely wedding dress that we sewed.
  Torn now.

Panna

  How can we help her?

Gina

  We'd all like to – but if someone does
  We may yet feel the Inspector's wrath.

Ramdev

Oh help me. It is my daughter.

Jyoti

Don't call me that.
You let Gangwar's thugs take me
And you stood, soft-limbed, like children
Shuffling, staring, I'll never wipe from my mind
The expressions you were wearing – stunned-eyed
And weak. The men of Sahaspur, what a pitiful bunch
Of cowards you are – as I was marched away
In their vicious grip to be raped and raped.
Doesn't my hair tell its own story?
Or my bloody clothes, my wedding dress of rags
Or my beaten face which was used as a
Space to smash their fists
While they drove into me with their sex
Till my mouth was dry of any cry
Because who would hear it?
Are you my father?
I was your daughter, not yet Farooq's wife
You had the responsibility to protect my life.
Don't you writhe inside to see my pain?
Sahaspur – means courage – never has a town been
So misnamed. It should burn with shame.
Stones, sheep, mice, worms
Yes, that's what you're like – worms –
Blind and buried in the earth, too scared of the bird's
sharp beak to take a peek,
Too timid to raise a shriek
Tigers would pursue anyone who harmed their young
Rip them apart with teeth and tongue
Instead you let us women, helpless, be taken, fucked,
shouldered like sheaves,
While you stood hanging by like rotten leaves.
Tomorrow, Gangwar plans to hang Farooq
No trial, no verdict

Maybe one day his body will be found
Maybe it will never be found.
Gangwar then will turn his vengeance on these half-men
Pick them off one by one. That will do us a favour,
    women –
Because when we are purged of them
We can be Kalis, warrior women – who drink our
    enemies' blood
We have no need for these eunuchs
Better we are alone – a new race to take their place.

Ramdev

Daughter, don't speak like this
My grey hair is bathed in tears.
Jyoti means light.
And now they've snuffed it out.

Jyoti

Don't be deceived, none of you are safe
I may not be the first
But I will not be the last,
This pitiless man
Has an insatiable appetite
To inflict a terrible price on every life.
Nothing is sacred, he'll keep going till
There's nothing left to take
Till we are reduced to slaves.
You have a choice – to resist,
And face this calamity together
Or to submit. Don't make that error.
Let us fight!
What are we waiting for? Pick up your weapons
The stones from the streets.
The tools from our kitchens, our farms
Shall be our arms.

Ramdev

We men will go – march on the gaol.

Mango
> Demand they set Farooq free.

Jyoti addresses the women.

Jyoti
> Women, why are you sitting?
> Knitting, kneading, suckling
> While between my legs a fire burns and in my brain
>   the thought is churning
> What can remove this pain, my honour's stain?
> Can't you see how they are all going to finish Gangwar?
> All the men.
> When it's us women who've been the most wronged?

Gina
> What can we do?

Jyoti
> We have hands, we can pick up stones
> To sate the vengeance nestling in our bones.
> Jacinta, you're my sister in violation
> We can all be a troop of women.

Jacinta
> I'm with you, Jyoti.

Panna
> Me too.

Gina
> And me.
> I'll turn my widow's weeds into a banner
> And march with you.

Jyoti
> We are all in this together.

Ramdev
> Let's speak in one voice
> This way of life has to end.
> Death to the tyrant.

All
Death to the tyrant.

They go.

SCENE TWO

Farooq sits with his hands tied.
  Gopi, Ved, Gangwar. Gangwar is drinking.

Gopi
There's a lot of bloody noise out there.

Ved looks out of a window.

Ved
There's a protest, sir.

Gopi
The whole village is here.

Ved
It's what they call a popular uprising.

Gopi
They appear quite angry.

Loud smash.

Ved
They're trying to smash through the door.

Gopi
Is that serious, sir?

More noise.

Farooq
I could talk to them.

Gopi
Piss off.

More noise, shouting.

Ved
Sounds like they want you, sir – but not in a good way.

Farooq
Ved, lad, It's me they want. You could let me go.
    I could talk them down.

Ved
That's a good plan, sir, they appear to mean war,
They've definitely smashed though the outer door.
Farooq. Mate. You have a chance now to live.
Very straightforward. Show your face, tell them to
    go home.
Then you can expect some leniency to be shown.

Gopi
Is that a good idea? He could fuck off.

Ved
Got a better one, shit for brains?
Remember it'll work out badly for you if you try
    anything.

He lets him go.

They'll turn back when he talks to them. They're weak.

Gopi
But what if they don't?
They feel power for once and it goes to their heads?

Ved
I know these people – I'm from here –
They're not the fighting type, no fear.

*They sit and listen to shouts, noise of smashing.
    Outside, the women gather.*

Jyoti
Women – we have to go in.

Gopi

Bloody noisy out there. That bloody Muslim bastard is doing a shit job.

We should have hung him when we got the chance.

Ved

Sounds like they've broken through the door. What do we do?

Gangwar

We fight. We're men. Not like those creatures we're pitted against.

Dogs, pigs, Dallits all in tow. Let's gp.

Noise from inside.

At that moment Gopi runs out. Followed by Farooq and Mango.

SCENE THREE

Office in Rampur.
Ishani and Mekhal.

Mekhal

They went too far. The villagers took the law into their own hands.

Gangwar is dead.

Ishani

I would have liked a front seat. Is that something I shouldn't have said?

The women led the assault apparently

Tearing at his flesh with their bare hands, like modern day Bacchante –

Mekhal

Gripped by a primitive rage – closer to the surface in the lower classes –

These witches ripped him to shreds with harsh cries,
  screams and cheers.
His largest remaining organs were, they say, his ears.

Ishani

They were angry obviously. Allegedly he was a rapist –
We all he knew he was a creep.

Mekhal

I think you have to be careful that no one outside
  of these four walls
Considers you anything less than totally appalled.

Ishani

He was my enemy and although I can pretend to grieve
I feel relieved. They've done me a favour.

Mekhal

One slip by you over this whole debacle
And I won't need to consult my oracle. You'll be
  political toast.
You must say at the first opportunity he was a great man.

Ishani

That would make me a hypocrite?
Still, I must play the politician and say I'm very sorry.

Mekhal

What's more, you must demand the state brings the
  perpetrators to light,
If not, it gives ammunition to the BJP who will spin
  this as
This as a Hindu–Muslim war and you on the side of
  the terrorists.
The ripples from this heinous act have caused the
  country to react.
It could be the kindling that sets us alight. Riots and
  unrest
May rock India, bring her to the brink of civil war.

It's happened before. In Gujurat – where violence
Was stirred by Modi's lies and thousands died on
   either side.

Ishani

It won't come to that.
Sahaspur is a sleepy little town – a pimple on a pimple.
Relax, Mekhal, news is an invesigator has been
   dispatched
Hopefully that will be the end of that.

SCENE FOUR

The village.
   The morning after the night before.
   Jyoti wears Gangwar's jacket smeared with blood.

Panna

Mercy, he cried, and then we stamped on his insides.

Laughter.

Now his blood has dried on our clothes
But the smiles are still on our faces.
I kept one of his ears.
Here.
You're quiet, Jyoti. Want to hold it?

Jyoti

No.

Panna

What's wrong with you?

Ramdev

Daughter, is there something on your mind?

Jyoti

Sahaspur – listen to me.
The law will come to investigate soon.

Panna
Why don't they just leave us alone?

Jyoti
Because we killed –

Farooq
A beast.

Mango
In uniform.

Jacinta
Three, actually.

Jyoti
One of them Gangwar.

Gina
I was only guarding the door.

Panna
And I'm a Kareena Kapoor.

Ramdev
Jyoti is right. We must come to our senses, face facts.

Farooq
What can we do?

Jyoti
They'll call us a mob.

Panna
I'm not a mob.

Jacinta
Me neither.

Mango
As if?

Jyoti
Say we got drunk on the drug of disorder,
Put us in gaol – throw away the key.

Gina

Foreboding is growing in me.
People like us never get away with anything.
You have to be powerful to commit a crime and walk free.
And that's not a poor widow like me.

Panna

Will there be rats in prison?

Gina

Giant ones with sharp teeth.
When you sleep – they eat your feet.

Mango

A city gaol. Misery. I like to sleep under the stars.
Now I'll wake to prison bars.

Panna

What did we do it for?
We'll be worse off than before.

Jyoti

They'll want to know who struck the first blow –

Gina

Threw the first stone –

Jacinta

Pushed in the first blade –

Panna

What a crazy way we behaved.

Jyoti

I don't want to be separated from you, Farooq.

Farooq

Jyoti, we'll do whatever you think.

Jyoti

If we stick together
When they ask us 'What was it for,

Who did the killing?'
Our answer shall be
Sahaspur.
They can't arrest a whole village
Let's make a pact – we'll all be in it
We'll all say Sahaspur did it.
Are we agreed?

All

Yes. We agree.
We'll do it.
It's the only way.

Jyoti

People of Sahaspur. Are we agreed?

All

Yes, yes.

Ramdev

I'll be the investigator, we can practise what we'll do.
Mango, we'll start with you?

Panna

They're bound to grab you first, Mango, because
there's more of you.

Mango

Okay, I'm ready. Bring it on.

Ramdev

Mango.

Mango

That's me, right.

Panna

Yes go on. And say it nice and loud like you're in the
movies.
Just imagine I'm Katrina Kaif and you're Akshay
Kumar.

Mango
There's a limit to my imagination, Panna, and you pushed it too far.

Panna
I hope they pull your balls off.

Ramdev
Who killed Gangwar?

Mango
Sahaspur.

Ramdev
Break his fingers.

Panna
They wouldn't do that?

Mango
Do what you like, I won't confess.

Ramdev
So again – who killed him?

Mango
Sahaspur did.

Farooq grabs Mango from behind.

Farooq
Who was it?
This isn't a game.

Mango shrieks.

Mango
It wasn't me – I mean it was me plus everyone here. Sahaspur.

Gina
They're here. They've come.

SCENE FIVE

The Investigator, his men and Vihaan.

Vihaan

This was a political assassination. The perpetrators
must be found.
Root them out.
Don't let the guilty go to ground.

Investigator

They'll confess. A crime like this won't go undetected.

Vihaan

A town of savages –

Investigator

We will handle it – the law is clear. We'll find
the culprits.
We won't tolerate evasions. If we have to
We'll employ extra-judicial persuasions.

Vihaan

Do what you have to do.

Vihaan watches as the Villagers are brought on.
The Villagers await their turn in the queue for
interrogation.
Each person for interrogation is taken behind the
Villagers – they are not allowed to look round but are
forced to hear the interrogation knowing that their turn
is next.

Jyoti

Farooq –

Farooq

Jyoti –

Jyoti

I'm scared too you know.

Farooq
Take care, Jyoti – that's all I care about.

Panna
How can she do that? We're all in for it.

Mango
I thought the rehearsal was bad.
You'll be okay, Panna –

Panna
Shut up, Mango.

Ramdev is taken.

Jyoti
My father's first.

Farooq
Jyoti. Be strong.

Gina
Are they going to torture an old man?

Investigator
Tell us the truth
Who killed Gangwar?

Ramdev
Sahaspur.

Investigator
What? I know where we are. I was asking who did it?

Strikes him.

Ramdev
Sahaspur.

Farooq Your father is strong.

Investigator
I know you know who did it. Tell me?
Not saying, old man?

Ramdev cries out as he is hit.

Investigator
Who killed him?

Ramdev
Sahaspur.

Investigator
Enough. He's lost his mind. Now that woman.

Panna
Oh God, it's my turn.

Jyoti
Sister – be strong.

Mango
Be brave. What am I saying? I won't be able to stand it myself.

Investigator
Do not doubt that I will get the truth out.

Jyoti
He's enjoying this.

Investigator
Who killed the Inspector?

Panna
Why are you asking me, sir?

She cries out.

Sahaspur.

Investigator
Is this some kind of joke?

Jyoti
Panna isn't talking, Farooq.

Investigator
Come on – just tell us who killed the Inspector,
Then you can go home and cook your dinner.

Panna
I told you before, Sahaspur.

Investigator
Give her some more pain.

Jyoti
You won't break Panna.

Panna screams.

Investigator
Who was it?

Panna
Sahaspur.

Investigator
Get that one.

Mango
Shit.

Farooq
Mango will confess.

Mango cries.

Investigator
Put your back into it.

Mango cries.

Tell me – who killed Inspector Gangwar?

Mango
I'll tell you –

Jyoti
No, Mango –

Investigator
Squeeze it out of him.

Mango
Stop, I'll tell you.

Investigator
Who?

Mango
Sahaspur, sir.

Investigator
Get rid of him.

Jacinta
They've taken little Ramu – snatched him from his
mother's arms.

Jyoti
He's just a child.

Investigator
Now tell me – you know – and it will go badly for
you if you don't tell the truth
Who killed Inspector Gangwar?

The child screams.

Investigator
Are you going to let me hurt a child? Speak up for
him, one of you. Are you human?

All
Sahaspur Sahaspur Sahaspur.

Vihaan looks like he is about to be sick. Exits.

Investigator
These shits have weak stomachs.
Let's call it quits. We tried, there was much at stake
But Sahaspur won't break.

Disgusted with the whole process, the Investigator exits.

SCENE SIX

Ishani, Mekhal, Vihaan.

Mekhal
Vihaan's here. I told you this day would come.

Vihaan enters.

Ishani
Vihaan. To what do we owe the privilege?

Vihaan
Ishani.

Mekhal
Can I get you some tea?

Vihaan
No thanks. This thing in Sahaspur –

Ishani
Condolences. I won't lie,
Say Gangwar and I saw eye to eye – but one
Has to respect one's opponents – though I'm not sure
What he thought of me.

Vihaan
He didn't say.

Ishani
Maybe it was the best way. He was a great man.
Nonetheless – the women of India have been protesting
    in support of Sahaspur.
They feel his death was justified.
Yes, it's been an outpouring of suppressed rage –
    hashtag MeToo.

Vihaan
That's half the story – the rest is a policeman died on duty.
There's outrage on the streets that more than meets
    the women's cries.

I never wanted to stand. It was always my father's
plan – not mine.

Mekhal

You lost the election, you're a free man.

Vihaan

But then Gangwar's death set me right.
My father's man torn apart and what's his crime?

Ishani

Multiple rapes, I think.

Vihaan

He was never convicted in a court of law.
This is bigger than I had thought before.
A historic moment for our country and my father's
plan party.
You may have won here, but you don't have the
country.
Now I feel it is my destiny to fight on.

Ishani

He's drunk the Kool-Aid.

Vihaan

Will you bring the perpetrators to justice?

Ishani

The village is sticking together – they won't point the
finger at a single ringleader.

Vihaan

Punish the whole village if you must
Or face the consequences in the courts.
The headline: 'Hindu man torn apart by a Muslim
crowd'.
I'll fight you all the way on this. My father's man.
A good man.

Ishani

They have his ears apparently. Although I also heard
That was a euphemism for his cock
Which the women bit off.

Mekhal

Ishani –

Vihaan

This is a mockery. You haven't heard the end of this.

He exits.

Mekhal

Really, was that politic?

Ishani

They killed a rapist.

Mekhal

An *alleged* rapist.
As the minister of Rampur in a story this big
You could either advise that the court pardons them –
Or rather condemns the villagers to death –
If you're seen to be merciful
It gives your enemies the leverage to say
You wanted Gangwar done away.
Be warned if the BJP brings you to court
Accuses you of complicity – their pockets are deep.
And if you're found guilty of terrorist support – you'll
    lose your seat
Face irreversible political defeat. He's right.
There must be a reckoning in Sahaspur.

Ishani

Well, that's where I'll go

Mekhal

What? Why?

Ishani

I have to look them in the eye.

SCENE SEVEN

Sahaspur.
They gather round Mango.

Ramdev
What shall we say to Ishani?

Gina
We should feed her.
I've made a nice chicken biryani.

Mango
I'll say I'm Mango – how do you do – I'm a poet too.
I've written one in your honour.

Panna
Don't read it – you'll send her to sleep
And at the worst – prejudice our case with your verse.
Just get on with it, my love.

Mango
All right, petal. I'll say
That I tried to defend this young woman, Jacinta,
From his people – who wanted to force her – then kill
    her
Then two men set upon my
Buttocks with such savagery – one each – that I
    practically had to have surgery.
I have spent on this prodigious attack money that I'll
    never get back
For ointment fortified with sulphide.

Panna
Which I've been applying to his backside.

Mango
I'll say this much. Panna has a special touch.

Ramdev

We'll ask for clemency – and hope that she will see
mitigation in this case.
Here she comes.

Enter Ishani and Mekhal.

Ishani

So this is Sahaspur
Are these the aggressors? They don't look like
murderers.
You can see my predicament –
Although I can believe these stories of corrupt police
I can't recommend your release from these charges.
There is no proof of what you assert – it's hearsay,
A man is dead and someone must pay.

Jyoti

What do you advise people like us to do?
We are the forgotten, the faceless,
No one was sent here to help us,
So we suffered that brute and one day we stood up
Like people not beasts and said no.
We women avenged ourselves.
We want to know – Do you stand with us?

Ishani

Vigilante justice is not something I can trust.
It's never a legitimate way to proceed.
A politician can't be seen to concede.
Gangwar was never charged in a court of law,
And so he was innocent.

Jyoti

He was guilty.

Mekhal

Not technically.

Ishani

You can't ask that I endorse brute force – for in future
  times
What would protect us from being a victim of its crimes?

Jyoti

But when the law is corrupt, then what?
When justice is impossible because savage force rules
Isn't it our duty to oppose, not stay tyranny's fools?
To fight for our lives, and the rule of law too?
How can you say that's the wrong thing to do?
How can right prevail if people do not take risks
To ensure it exists? Are we supposed to submit to evil?
Obeying the law of a lawless devil?
We villagers said if no one will fight for us
Then we will fight for ourselves – our dignity
Own the right to live decently.
Isn't that what you want for your daughter?
Aren't we your daughters too?

Ishani

That's true –
Mekhal. Where there's no one culprit I can't advise a
  sentence.
That's the law.
The whole town can't be arrested – it's ridiculous that
  that's suggested.
No matter how awful the crime – this time it must be
  pardoned.
These people of Sahaspur will continue their lives
  as before.
And I hope the country sees my point of view.
What's the point of power unless sometimes you do
The right thing.

The Villagers begin to sing in celebration.

Mekhal – have I blown it?

Mekhal
What can you do now but own it?

Song.

Farooq
So – who really did kill him?

Jyoti
Sahaspur.

Farooq
The truth now.

Jyoti
You're scaring me now. Sahaspur.

Farooq
And me – what did you kill me with?

Jyoti
With loving you too much.

Panna
Mango. Why don't you sit down?

Mango
I'd rather stand due to circumstances beyond my
control.

Panna
Mango. You were brave.

Mango
And so were you.

Panna
It's almost like we were in a film. The friends of the
main characters.
Overlooked, but way more fun, and we get together
in the end.

Mango
I'd like to see that film.

RUNE

Rune was first performed at New Vic Theatre, Newcastle-under-Lyme, on 20 June 2015, as part of Hoard – a festival of plays inspired by the Staffordshire Hoard, developed with support from the National Theatre Studio. The cast was as follows:

Marnie Crystal Condie

Director Gemma Fairlie
Designer Mika Handley
Musical Director/Composer Conrad Nelson
Hoard Season Artistic Director Theresa Heskins
Casting Associate Anji Carroll CDG

Character

Marnie
sixteen years old

Marnie Treasure. It's everywhere. It's in the papers. Blokes swill mouthfuls of beer round the word 'gold' and 'hoard' like it was them that found it. Who found it was some loser on benefits whose plimsolls were tied with string, with a beer belly and a shaving rash. He hardly stepped into the field when his machine went off ding! How is that deserving? How is that earned? He should had been at work down Screwfix like everybody else. It's only cos he was a scrounging sod that he discovered it in first place.

Then we had to do it in school in history. The Saxons. They were hopeless cos the Normans trashed 'em. No news there – who'd bury treasure and forget where you hid it? Yeah the Saxons. Then we had to write a poem about it in English.

I went into a field, I pissed about a bit,
I saw something shiny, I almost had a fit.
No more benefits, I'm work-shy now for sure,
Off to bleedin' Spain with a million pounds or more.

My teacher tried to pretend she saw the funny side of it but I know underneath she thinks I'm a chav. Well I am, what of it?

Then we had to have a day trip to see it. It was quite good. I liked the earrings. I was just thinking what they would go with – maybe my new red TK Maxx top – when our teacher, she says it weren't all treasure they found, there were other objects too. And she paused like that was supposed to whet our appetite, like we were educationally challenged. And some of us are, what of it?

And then this bloke from the museum comes and he looks like he ought to get out more. He's wearing sandals and his name is Jeremy and none of the girls want to stand near him but the boys are dorks and they stand around him like tombstones. And Jeremy puts down this box on the table and she says as a special treat we're gonna see something amazing. And Jeremy practically has a hard-on when she says that and he takes out of the box this stone thing. Smooth like a pebble. Like the most boring thing in the museum and she gets us all to look at it.

'No one knows what this was for,' says Jeremy.

There is silence.

'Perhaps it was for counting? Perhaps it was an object of religious significance? Maybe it was for prophecy.' And we all look at this dreggy rock.

'Maybe it was an ancient love egg,' I say. 'Some Saxon bird put it up her hole and got her rocks off on it.'

Jeremy looked like he might throw up. But our teacher laughed with us because she wants to seem trendy and she wants everyone to like her.

'I think it was for prophecy,' she says. 'I think it was a tool of female empowerment.' She's a right effing feminist. Then Jeremy who'd taken a bit of shine to our teacher cos he keeps looking at her tits asks if she wants to hold it. 'Yes,' she said. Like she's having an orgasm.

He puts this stone into her hand, she calls it a rune, and the room goes quiet and everyone cranes their necks to see her standing there holding this bit of Saxon rubbish. Then she says, 'That was profound.' And that seems to move Jeremy because he just nods. 'Thinking of the woman who held this,' she said. 'Who she was. What she saw.'

'You have a go, Marnie,' she says.

'No thanks,' I go.

'Go on, don't be scared. This has lain in the earth for two thousand years. It's practically gone straight from the sibyl's hands to yours.' Jeremy looks a bit freaked out when I say, 'All right.'

So I take it and it's so disappointing. It's like life. You expect it to be good, because everyone seems so set on keeping going you think it must be worth it. But it's not, is it? Well, maybe it is in California – or London – but not in Stoke. Not in my bit of Stoke.

So I'm holding this ball of dullness in my palm and think I might as well have a laugh – so I start making this moaning sound – very soft at first – like this:

She moans.

Then I make it go into a hum –

She hums.

'You have dug me out of the earth,' I say in this spooky voice – 'Why have you brought me forth?' Like the clever ones in our class are laughing and the stupid ones are like looking a bit perplexed. Not scared yet but on the way.

Then I goes –

'WHY! Have you brought me forth?'

That really got to 'em.

More humming.

'My prophecy is this. Germaine Williams, you will never learn Portuguese! Christine Waterhouse, invest in deodorant. Jeremy, if you want to pull our teacher – incinerate your sandals.'

And then I felt this kind of little jolt – just like when you go down two steps on the stairs when you thought there was only one. And just for a second I thought, where am I? Who am I? And the voice came back – 'Marnie, you're not a loser. You're a winner.' And then it was like when you come up for air when you been underwater in the swimming pool and all the sounds that were distant were loud and clear again. And the colours all seemed brighter. And I could see the faces of my class all around me, laughing.

Yeah, that were a good trip.

Anyone want a go?

She holds out the stone.

EXTINCT

Extinct was first performed at Theatre Royal Stratford East, London, on 30 June 2021, with the following cast and creative team:

April Kiran Landa

Director and Dramaturg Kirsty Housley
Designer Peter McKintosh
Lighting Designer Joshua Pharo
Sound Designer Melanie Wilson
Video Designer Nina Dunn
Assistant Director Germma Orleans-Thompson
Design Associate Alice Hallifax
Associate Sound Designer Tingying Dong
Video Design Associate Libby Ward

Characters

April

Suhayla and **Abani**
start out as recorded voices
but are taken over by the actor

Plus the recorded voices of

Helen Burnett
Rob Callender
Sue Hampton
Kay Michaels
Chidi Obihara
Lola Perrin
Leslie Tate
Aaron Thierry
Xanthe
Elise Yarde

CAPTION: *The Anthropocene; the age of human-made climate change.*

I. FUTURE NIGHTMARE

April I want you to imagine me in a crowd of people. The year is 2030 and the mean temperature this summer has been forty degrees Celsius. It's midday. The sun is nuclear hot. There have been spontaneous outbreaks of fires round the country, the closest to us in Epping Forest, a monster conflagration which raged for three weeks. The air still tastes of ash.

It was this year the three breadbaskets of the world in the USA, Central Russia and South East Asia failed due to high temperatures, drought and fire leading to a catastrophic global shortage of carbohydrates. Added to that, unseasonal rainfall here meant that the potato crop which might have compensated rotted in the ground – it was the first time the UK had been subject to rationing since World War II.

And there was panic. Supermarkets stripped bare. Looting began – people convinced that stores of food were being kept from them – nights of smashed windows and marauding gangs. Then onto the streets came the army. There was a shoot-out at Westfield's in the Marks and Spencer's food hall. The government stepped in with a new plan. Since then a fragile peace has descended. Food distribution depots were designated, one member of each household could be dispatched plus ration card to pick up a bag of pasta or flour, a few tins, perhaps some dried pulses. A fortnight's supply. All anyone talks about is food.

People will kill for a sachet of yeast.

I came on my bike which I locked up safely several streets away. Now in the crowd, as anxiety and hunger pricks us, the emotion turns sour. Near me a fight breaks out. People turn on the one who they say was pushing in. The guy is near tears – his kids are hungry, his wife is sick. It turns mean. The thud of fists on flesh. I try to raise my voice but no one hears me. The press of bodies is claustrophobic. Ahead, the iron shutter at the depot is drawn down halfway and a woman appears.

Why have they chosen a woman? Do they think we will forgive her more easily? She asks the crowd to disperse. *The depot is now empty. We will reopen tomorrow at eight a.m. when another delivery is expected.* They can only provide for the last twenty queuers. People mutter. They know they are being fobbed off. The armed security guards at her side look on impassively though I can imagine sweat pricking their armpits. Someone once told me that in cities we are only ever six meals away from starvation but I had dismissed it. I lived a short walk away from twenty fast-food outlets. What about Deliveroo?

Something like a moan rises from the crowd. The unbearable thought of another hungry night, the faces of their disappointed, bewildered kids, their cries of hunger.

There is a sudden jolt forwards. I am caught in a vast river of bodies. Part of me wants to run back to my bike, flee the madness, but another part is thinking – I've stood here for two hours in punishing sun and now to be told to return home with nothing? I too taste anger, bitterness. How has this been allowed to happen? We were not born to go hungry. I'm too far back from the front and I feel guilty – I had stopped off on the way by the canal – there was a lone duck meandering along the puddling water. I wanted the normal so badly as I waited there transfixed to the spot. Wishing myself back

A year, two years, five, a decade – to when there was still time to do something about it.

At the front someone has pulled the woman from her platform into the crowd, she vanishes like a stone into a pond and the first shot is fired.

Lighting changes. The woman is standing alone. We can now see the whole space. She looks at us.

Hello.

Thanks for coming.

I have an hour to convert you to the cause of climate change

So we can avoid the kind of nightmare I just imagined.

So we can change our future.

We live on a finely balanced, beautifully temperate Earth that has sustained human life for two hundred thousand years, But all that, unfortunately, is changing.

As a playwright I ask myself what's the point of me, of theatre, in a time of crisis, if I'm not raising the alarm so that we can avoid unnecessary suffering?

Aristotle's advice to playwrights was: 'Don't make your story so small that it can be consumed in one bite, or too big, like an animal so huge you can't take in both its head and its tail.' Climate change is just like that – a hyperobject – a conceptual fact so large, so complex, like the internet, it can never be properly comprehended.

So I have my work cut out for me.

I'm standing here talking to you

Coming across as quite a rational calm individual

But don't be fooled. Inside I'm screaming.

I'm panicking.

I can see the waters rising over our heads

And I'm shouting, It's the end of the world
But no one can hear me.

Sorry.

There have been five previous mass extinctions.

The most lethal was two hundred and fifty million years
ago when volcanic eruptions released enough carbon
dioxide to warm the oceans by ten degrees Celsius ending
ninety-six per cent of marine life and seventy per cent of life
on Earth. The event known as the Great Dying.

We are now experiencing the sixth mass extinction.

Humans are emitting greenhouse gases ten times faster than
the volcanoes did during the Great Dying.

There is no single peer-reviewed paper
    Published in the last twenty-five years that would
contradict this scenario
    Every living system of Earth is in decline
    Every life support system of Earth is in decline.

I'm feeling that thing where it feels impossible
    Breaking into a sweat
    It's supposed to be that telling people helps to control the
anxiety every time I do this I have to go into it again
    It's not a place I like to go.
    I have to be calm though – no one wants to hear
someone shouting at them hysterically, being emotional.
Getting naked and covering myself in crude oil is not going
to help my cause.
    Still, I want to explain as calmly as I can the shit we're
in.

If I feel really anxious I tend to snack – so I'm just going to
do that now.

    Takes out a sweet – eats it. Then is left with the wrapper.
    Holds up the wrapper.

Is there somewhere I can put this?
Somewhere I can throw it away?

She looks.

I'll come clean. This was planned.
This – what is it – a prop? – it was something in the real world
Now it's kind of standing in for itself
Just like I'm an actor standing in for the writer.

It was something until it became the opposite – nothing.
Something to be forgotten.
Is it recyclable?

She drops it in a bin.

There, forgotten – vanished – someone else's problem
We like to imagine we can throw things away with no consequence.
But we've made 'away' up
Away is somewhere we have been encouraged not to see
Away is our future
And if we don't act until we feel the climate crisis is upon us, we will all beommitted to solving a problem that can no longer be solved.

So in 2018 I went to a meeting of a new group called Extinction Rebellion in the old Limehouse library.
They were concerned about the government's inaction on the climate and ecological emergency.
That we were being kept in the dark.

I expected to find six people and a dog.
I walked into the biggest meeting I had ever attended in my life
We got into smaller groups and went round sharing why we were here
In my group were two local schoolgirls.

One, said I'm here because when I die because of climate change I want to know I tried to do something about it.

The advice everyone gave me was educate yourself. I wanted to know everything.
I did a lot of research.

She gestures to screen.

CAPTIONS:
'The Uninhabitable Earth' David Wallace-Wells
'How to Talk About Climate Change in a Way That Makes a Difference' Rebecca Huntley
'This Changes Everything' Naomi Klein
'On Fire' Naomi Klein
'The Future We Choose' Christiana Figueres
'Falter' Bill McKibben
'Boiling Point' Bill McKibben
'This Is Not A Drill: An Extinction Rebellion Handbook'
'The Great Derangement' Amitav Ghosh
'Corona, Climate, Chronic Emergency' Andreas Malm
'The Climate Majority' Leo Barasi
'Our House is On Fire' Greta Thunberg and Malena Ernman
'We Are the Weather' Jonathan Safran Foer

A little light reading there.

Here's a quote from *This Is Not A Drill*
An Extinction Rebellion Handbook
It's got a lovely pink cover and the comforting penguin icon but don't let that fool you – it's a dead penguin.

'This is our darkest hour; Humanity finds itself embroiled in an event unprecedented in its history, one which unless immediately addressed will catapult us further into the destruction of all we hold dear; this nation, its peoples, our ecosystems and the future generations to come.'

Or as David Wallace-Wells says, 'It's worse, much worse than you think.'

Naomi Klein says our lives will change.
    The choice is whether we are going to be in control of that change
    Or it's going to happen to us in the most terrifying way.

I talked to a lot of activists.

Kay (*voice-over*) I read *This Changes Everything*
    I bloody love Naomi Klein
    I nosedived into it all
    A real light-bulb moment for me – an undeniable need for a massive change in everything.

Chidi (*voice-over*) What's more important than your right and ability to breathe?
    What's more important than having good-quality food to eat
    And clean water to drink?

Lola (*voice-over*) I stayed in my bedroom for six weeks
    That was grief and I literally did not know what to do
    With the heat beating down and knowing people were dying from the heat all over Europe.

Elise (*voice-over*) I remember walking into my first non-violent direct-action training
    And the first thing that popped into my head was like, where are all the people of colour?
    I was actually like, confused by it – like this is Walthamstow, there are brown people everywhere!

Xanthe (*voice-over*) A lot of my friends don't really understand that like, yeah, I live in a field. But they're still supportive, I'm still friends with them.

Rob (*voice-over*) I remember just from school – I'd been to the Amazon, a lucky kid, and found out that one of the places I'd been to no longer exists.

And things like that really made me begin to think obsessively.

Aaron (*voice-over*) One of the things is, collectively sharing our emotions in public
Is a healthy thing to do but it also gives us the language and sense of community we need in order to face up to the realities
Shared – collective grieving.

Chidi (*voice-over*) During COP26 we need to try and convince all one hundred and twenty-six members to stop financing new fossil fuel projects. We have to draw a line in the sand in 2021, we need to stop growing an industry that harms us all physically, economically, biologically, socially. We need to persuade them to keep it in the ground.

Sue (*voice-over*) I volunteered to be an oil-slick rebel, perfect for me cos I don't really feel that I can do something that's very obviously arrestable.

PROJECTION: *Image of oil-slick rebel.*

Helen (*voice-over*) I was arrested on the first day trying to get the ARC onto the bridge – a great symbol
I felt incredibly peaceful when they arrested me. I was in a very prayerful place.

April Before we start, this show comes with a warning
The storyteller's pact
Come with me
We'll go places, sure
But I'll bring you safely back
Home
To dry land
This story is different
I apologise
In advance
I can't tell it
With that same certainly.

CAPTION: *Air.*

The last decade was the warmest ever recorded in the UK. In the summer of 2019 temperatures reached thirty-eight-point-five degrees. Trains were evacuated because of melting overhead cables. Our government's committee on climate change warned we are not prepared for the increase in heatwaves that will come with global warming.

There is now more CO_2 in our atmosphere than at any other time in recorded history – in 2019 humans released forty-three billion tons of it.

Lola (*voice-over*) Like what did CO_2 do?
Someone said, Imagine an orange that you never take the peel off
And I began to visualise it through that
It's the peel, the CO_2 released by the burning of fossil fuels, that traps all the heat in.
Cooks the orange.

April Methane, another greenhouse gas, is also emitted from the burning of fossil fuels, from livestock and farming. Per unit, it is eighty-five times stronger than CO_2 and the second biggest contributor to global heating. In 2020 methane had hit the highest levels ever on record.

These particles which trap heat from the sun are also lethal to breathe. *Globally, ten thousand people daily are dying from air pollution.*

We tend to trivialise the differences between the heating of degrees above pre-industrial levels, one point five, two or four, because these numbers seem so small – but at two degrees, four hundred million more people will suffer from water scarcity. At three degrees, Southern Europe would be in permanent drought. At four degrees, there would be annual global food crises, the Alps would be as arid as the Atlas Mountains
And if we hit eight degrees

A third of the planet would be made unlivable by direct heat.

At these temperatures the human body can't expel heat and basically cooks.

But we won't need to get to eight degrees
to be in serious shit.

Leslie (*voice-over*) It's a terrible experience to realise what's going to happen which, you know, yeah we're doing our best to stop it but we can wipe ourselves out

And our children, our grandchildren, are going to go through terrible experiences.

These temperatures are averages, some places are rising much faster than others.

Aaron (*voice-over*) The Arctic is warming maybe three times as fast of the rest of the planet because you get this amplification process.

April Hot air melts the white ice in the Arctic which then stops reflecting the sun's rays back out into space, and the shiny white mirror is replaced with dull blue seawater which instead absorbs the sun's heat and then the warmer sea shrinks yet more ice. It's called the Albedo effect.

This is an example of a feedback loop.

Hidden ice locked beneath the soils of the Arctic is now starting to melt fast too, and as that permafrost thaws, microbes convert some of that frozen material into methane and carbon dioxide which is released and causes yet more warming –

Incidentally that's not all that could be released – microbes like the bubonic plague and the Spanish flu are lurking in the ancient melting ice – what new pandemics might be unleashed?

As our atmosphere heats, warm air holds more water vapour than cold, providing additional fuel for storms and hurricanes. In addition, sea level rise increases the amount of sea water that is pushed onto shore during coastal storms. In 2018 six hurricanes and tropical storms appeared on radars at once.

We now have 'rain bombs'. In 2017 Hurricane Harvey dropped a million gallons of water for every single person in the entire state of Texas, killing sixty-eight and causing a hundred and twenty-five billion dollars' worth of damage (but they still voted for Trump who called climate change a Chinese hoax to ruin American business).

Suhayla, a journalist, was the last person I met while making this show. She told me her story.

Suhayla (*voice-over*) Bangladesh is at the epicentre of the global climate crisis. Eighty per cent of the country is floodplain and is affected by floods, storms, riverbank erosions, cyclones and droughts. Unless greenhouse gas emissions are controlled now, the situation will become unmanageable.

After speaking along with the recording, the actor speaks directly as Suhayla.

Suhayla My family is from a village in Bangladesh called Kara Mura
   As kids we loved visiting, my brother and me exploring the rice paddies, seeing the farm hands tend the cows, fishing in one of the small lakes or fushkunis, watching my grandmother, Rani, cook one of her famous fish curries.
   As a teenager Ma would bring out the photos and I would wriggle with boredom. Pay attention, Suhayla, she would say, these are your roots. Who cares? I thought. I had important stuff to do, like meeting my friends for the new Spice Girls movie. But I still called my grandmother every fortnight.

The last time we went on holiday to our family bari the road stopped suddenly half a mile away from the village, it was completely flooded. We boarded a small bamboo boat, a nowka, and then meandered down the murky green water for three hours.

Slowly my parents stopped planning to go home to retire
    In Kara Mura the rain was coming at times when it is not supposed to and not coming when it should. The world of their parents, drowning. The last visit they made, they had tried to persuade my grandparents Rani and Ram to come to the UK. The idea appalled them. Leave their home? Your home is leaving you, my father had said. Then we got the news that my grandfather and uncle had drowned in a sudden flash flood, leaving only my grandmother. We were distraught. I told my parents I had to go see Dadi-ma.

So I am thirty thousand feet in the air. Heading to the place Mum and Dad called home.

CAPTION: *Earth*.

Aaron (*voice-over*) So you're watching landscapes which are changing in the space of a generation, you know, like they've not changed for thousands and thousands of years. It's disturbing.
    I spent quite a bit of time talking to the First Nations people in the Arctic, they were in a state of disbelief and quite a lot of trauma at the loss of their heritage, their way of life
    The understanding of who they were in the landscape
    Not being able to go fishing and hunting in ways that they used to.

April Their connection to the landscape being torn from them?

Aaron (*voice-over*) There are these dwarf trees – they can't grow very high because it's so cold – they grow on the permafrost which is only few inches below the surface of the soil which is only really a mat of mosses that the roots are growing through – and now as the permafrost is thawing the trees start falling over but they keep trying to grow towards the light and so you get these wonky trees that are all wobbly and we call them drunken forests because everything is kind of crossing and wobbling everywhere and the ground is all lumpy and bumpy so trying to get across from A to B is like walking through an *Alice in Wonderland* landscape, you're having to zigzag all over the place and you have a sense of it being really eerie, disturbing when you think what it's telling you. Because everything is connected and therefore we should be cautious in how we treat the world – that's something I feel very strongly, this is such a hugely complicated Earth system, that we are dependent on for everything, yet we are going round like a bull in china shop and I think that's terrifying in terms of how we are destroying what we don't yet understand, yet rely on totally.

April Soil is disappearing. Seventy-five billion tons lost each year due to intensive farming practices and excess rainfall. Soil erosion in the UK is currently at unsustainable levels.

More carbon dioxide in the air produces nutritional declines across the board – drops in protein content as well as in iron, zinc and B vitamins
Since 1950 much of the good stuff in the plants we grow – protein, calcium, iron, vitamin C – has declined by as much as one-third. Everything is becoming more like junk food – even the protein content of bee pollen has dropped by a third.
The great nutrient collapse – CO_2 makes plants bigger but dilutes nutrients in the food supply.

Climate change means an empire of hunger.

At two-point-five degrees the ensuing drought would mean the world needed more calories than it could produce. But anthropogenic climate change is already a reality in Africa.

In East Africa, 2011 saw the worst drought in sixty years, in East Africa eighty-two per cent of glaciers on

Kilimanjaro have vanished and rivers are drying up. In Nigeria half the population has no access to water. Catastrophic flooding in North Africa and Mozambique left one million people hungry. Droughts, heat stress and flooding have led to a reduction in food productivity in a continent that was already under pressure. With rainfall below average in Ethiopia, Kenya and Somalia, East Africa faces the worst food crisis in the twenty-first century.

These facts I'm bringing you. They're harbingers. They show us what we will be facing sooner than we like to think. It's hard to believe that our reality, the here and now, could be any different, but to save ourselves we have to begin to try and imagine it.

2. EARTH FUTURE NIGHTMARE

April It's a miracle we had slept through it
I wake up to my husband shouting up the stairs,
We're fucking flooded.
I grab a jumper and some jeans.
Downstairs a stinking, brown metre of water covers the living room
And it's still raining
It has been raining for weeks
Looking out of the window the same fetid brown water is barrelling along the street
I reached for my phone
Every headline. The Thames Barrier has failed. I think of our next-door neighbour and her paved garden. No chance of the soil absorbing the rainwater there. Times that by millions is part of the problem. Bit unfair to blame her for catastrophic global heating but she is handy.

There is no point trying to rescue any of the downstairs possessions – they will be rife with bacteria and need burning.

I feel an overwhelming need to cry. This is my home, my stuff. I try to phone my son. He is living in Rotherhithe, it's low-lying so the rent's cheaper – No answer. A kick of fear in the pit of my stomach.

What can we do but wait it out upstairs – wait for the water to recede? Last time people had died, panicking and fleeing their homes. The metre-deep water was deceptively fast-flowing and losing your balance could be fatal. Stay put was the advice. If that becomes impossible seek higher ground. Last time the water had begun to recede after five days, leaving a toxic sludge over everything. We had got sick – stomach cramps, diarrhoea – just to add to the general nightmare, but we were lucky, our kids were grown up. How parents of young kids managed was beyond me. Mothers shouting Don't touch it – hold my hand – stay upstairs! Little lost faces at windows. No water – sewage had contaminated the reservoirs. We had rescued tins from the kitchen and eaten stuff out of them cold.

Thousands of acres of good arable land had been flooded

Potatoes rotted in the ground, cabbages, carrots, lettuce. There had been a massive fresh vegetable shortage that year.

Awful pictures of those caught on the tube as the water submerged the underground system. People had recorded it on their mobile phones.

I feel a different kind of water rise up in my mind – a dark emotion flooding me –

How could I live like this? I curl up in a ball on my bed – the nightmare is happening again.

I ring my son – his phone is dead. It couldn't mean anything, could it? I had forgotten the stench of floodwater – filled with run-off from factory farms, hazardous chemical waste, sewage and soil. It floats up choking me. Husband comes into the room. The rain's not stopping they say and another storm's on the way. I pull the covers over my head. I don't want to believe it. I want to scream and shout but that frankly would be pathetic. I think we should go now, he says, while we have the chance.

Lights change.

There are a hell of a lot of cows on this planet
 Sixty per cent of mammals are livestock, pigs and cows
 Thirty-six per cent humans
 Just four per cent of mammals are wild
 In Brazil and Australia there are more cows than people
 It takes eight pounds of grain to create one hamburger
 Plus six hundred and sixty gallons of water
 Add the methane farts of cows adding to the greenhouse
effect.

It takes six-point-six-one pounds of CO_2 to produce a
pound of beef
 And only zero-point-zero-three to produce a pound of
potatoes.

In 2018 Jair Bolsonaro was elected president of Brazil
promising to open the Amazon forest to development,
which is to say deforestation for cattle farming.

Deforestation fires have reduced the Amazon by thirty per
cent. A feedback loop. Forest fires release carbon dioxide so
the planet heats up, causing more, bigger fires that consume
more of the forest, and soon we are left with not the biggest
carbon sink but a producer of carbon, the magnificent
rainforest transmogrified to dry savannah.

The wildfires threaten the three hundred thousand
indigenous people who live in the forest. They see
themselves as guardians of that land for all of us. In 2020 a
hundred and ten indigenous activists were murdered.

Eighty per cent of Amazon deforestation is for livestock.

Suhayla It's a bit of a kick in the guts when I arrive – this
time the journey by boat is two hours longer to reach the
village – what's left of it – isolated baris scattered along the
soggy land – people travel by boat now to visit each other. I
call to mind the lush green-gold stretches of rice fields now

vanished. I reach our bari – water lapping at the gate of the farm. Dadi-ma comes to meet me and takes my face in her hands and gives me a blessing. She looks smaller than before and her hair is completely white. She still won't let me do anything, she tells me she's going to make me make my favourite dish. I insist on helping her prepare the meal, she grumbles at me but we slice the fish. Coriander, red onion chopped, garlic and chillis crushed, my grandmother's hands are very quick but I notice a slight shake. On top of the fish she throws the spices then heats the oil, the fish sizzles immediately. The smell is delicious. She picks at her food – she can't eat much now, she says. I musn't worry about her. She tells me that Abani, my cousin's wife, is here with her small daughter, Anya. Abani appears, smiles, she is elegant with a long thick plait of hair. She takes over, shows me my room, watches while I fumble with my mosquito net – she steps in and efficiently sets it up, she tells me because of all the water they are more vicious now. Anya hangs behind but then grows more confident. Three years old, curious, with big bright eyes and fingers into everything. They both help me unpack. Abani and Anya were a double act, I discovered – Anya found the portable charger for my laptop battery and held it up and said, What is it? Abani said, Don't ask so many questions! Anya looked at me, big dark eyes then pointed to my camera, What is it? Now it was a great game. It's my camera, I told her – I'm a journalist. I want to record Kara Mura. Maybe I'll take pictures of you.

Abani says, Will you record my story? Then you can tell people what is happening to us.

Abani – the name means 'Earth'.

That night Rani had gone to bed and Anya was asleep, she came and sat at the end of my bed. We talked till it got light. She married Gopal my cousin four years ago. Anya was born a year later. She asks me if I have children. When I tell her no, she asks me what does my mother say? I say, She says there must be a person crazy enough to take me on somewhere. Abani laughs.

Once she had taught at the primary school in her village. She used to teach the children a Tagore poem.

After speaking along with the recording, the actor speaks directly as Abani.

Abani (*voice-over*) And when old words die out on the tongue
New melodies break forth from the heart
And where the old tracks are lost
New country is revealed with its wonders.

Suhayla Tell me what happened?

Abani At eight o'clock one night, when Anya was just a few months old, the rain began to beat on the corrugated tin of the roof, like hammers. A powerful wind started up, shaking the shutters and doors. We looked out and saw the trees over the road being pushed horizontal by its force. Then with a sickening, grating rip the roof of our neighbours' house was peeled off and tossed away. This storm was different from the storms we had known in the past. We sat in the darkness – then suddenly a mass of water smashed in through the door and Gopal's father shouted that the river had broken its banks. I held Anya close, tiny, fragile, and we fled, running for higher ground in the driving rain and screeching wind. We huddled together with some of our neighbours and watched the river, a swollen monster, black, swift-moving, swallowing everything, houses dragged into its path and destroyed. I prayed what warmth was left in my body would keep Anya warm. The next days the river retreated leaving a blanket of mud where our house had been, the wind had ripped out my father-in-law's fruit trees, carried off rice and tea from the family's small shop and crumbled the mud walls of the house as if a giant had crushed it in its fists. Huge waves at sea had pushed salt water into the river and so the fish in our pond, dead from salt water. The sea is torturing us, Rani said. Huge chunks of land at the edges of the river broke off and the soil was washed away. Your parents sent money and we rebuilt the bari on brick plinths to protect us from floods. Now though we had less to eat. We suffered from skin rashes and pains in our stomach from the salty water, and the village struggled to grow its rice crop and vegetables. We diversified into shrimp farming but it was difficult because harvesting the shrimps gave us very little money. The food we did grow was not like before. I was pregnant again and very sick. I had pains in my stomach, headaches and dizziness. The clinic told us it was the water, it was dangerous for pregnant women. They gave me aspirin and wished me luck. I lost the baby.

Suhayla The light was coming through the chinks in the shutters when we finished talking. I hugged Abani and she went back to her room. I heard Rani call to me. I went into her room and got into bed on my grandfather's side. We held hands and she drifted off to sleep. I lay awake thinking of what Abani had told me.

CAPTION: *Fire.*

April The world is on fire from the Amazon to California, from Australia to the Siberian Arctic.

Do we watch the world burn or do we choose to do what is necessary to achieve a different future?

During the 2019 to 2020 Australian bushfire season, strong winds and extreme heat drove wildfires.

The old ways of fighting these fires are increasingly redundant

Australian firefighters said they were frightened

The idea that a fire could generate a tornado as it did in Australia in 2003 seemed hard for scientists to credit but many more fire tornadoes have occurred since then.

Thunderstorms created by the intense energy of the fire can shoot out lightning that ignites fires twenty miles ahead of the fire's front line. They are known as Pyro-Cbs. Australia generated eighteen of them last year.

Forty-six million acres were burnt, thirty-four people died, as well as three billion terrestrial vertebrates including thirty thousand koalas. One hundred and three billion dollars in economic losses. NASA estimates that three hundred and six million tons of carbon dioxide were released into the atmosphere.

Feedback loops.

As Greta Thunberg says, Our house is on fire. Why aren't we doing something about it?

Because we have too much faith in human progress?
    Because it's not happening to us – not yet anyway?
    Because we are so sociopathically good at collating bad news into a sickening sense of what constitutes 'normal'?

Aaron (*voice-over*) I had one particular meeting with a fireman
    He had just spent the whole summer travelling all over the north of the boreal forest trying to put out these wildfires with his team
    Fires are part of the landscape but they're not supposed to be that common, that fierce
    The biggest city is Yellow Knife and they almost had to be evacuated
    Forty thousand people were told to stay in their houses for a week because of wildfires
    And the air pollution was so horrendous you couldn't breathe
    And the other thing was the water levels in the lakes were so low
        because of the drought
    And the heatwaves, that they couldn't power the city's hydroelectric dam

So they had to set up a system of generators and have a diesel convoy
Endlessly coming from miles away.
Ironic – having to turn to the most polluting fuel in the world which is actually driving the climate crisis.

April We're talking about fire but also air and water.

Aaron (*voice-over*) Like I said.

April Connected, yes.

CAPTION: *Water.*

Rising ocean waters are possibly the biggest threat we face and will completely inundate many coastal land areas in the next three decades.
Places that will be underwater by 2050 include:

PROJECTION: *The Bahamas, Bruges, London. Bangkok, Panama City, Ho Chi Minh City, the Adriatic coast, Alexandria, Mumbai, Shanghai, Manila, Mozambique, Florida Keys, Charleston, San Francisco Bay, New Orleans, New York City and this theatre.*

By the middle of the century the ocean may contain more plastic by weight than fish.

Every year we plough an undersea area twice the size of the United States with trawlers levelling everything on the seafloor.
The overfishing and the dead zones at the mouths of all major rivers where fertilisers pour into the sea, and the gyres of plastic spinning slowly a thousand miles offshore, these are the smallest of our insults to the ocean.

The overwhelming threat comes from burning fossil fuels
Ninety-three per cent of extra heat is actually collecting in the sea
The deep sea is now warming nine times faster than in the 1980s.

Half the coral reefs, once vibrant with colour are now a shade of murk

The volumes of carbon we are producing – it turns out even the ocean is too small to soak up without effect

It turns the sea water into carbonic acid

The oceans have seen their acidity increase by thirty per cent

Increasing ocean acidification, heating and deoxygenation mean our oceans are heading for a tipping point – a qualitative change in a system from which recovery to the initial system is impossible.

Kay (*voice-over*) Anything beyond two degrees we're tipping into tipping points where we could escalate into the four-degree mark and the five-degree mark and it would just go on and on

And society doesn't know if it could survive

And no one's done the work to find out if we can survive

And I doubt it.

April By 2050 all the coral reefs will be dead.

Fish and shellfish will be unable to make their skeletons, their shells

By the end of the century the oceans will be hot, sour and breathless.

One in three people have no access to safe drinking water.

As the glaciers melt the UN predicts a massive increase in water scarcity –

Two billion people will be without fresh water.

England could suffer major water shortages by 2030 due to increasing droughts due to climate change.

London is one of the eleven cities most likely to run out of drinking water.

CAPTION: *The Future.*

To turn on a tap and have nothing come out. The reassuring gush; water, quenched thirst, cleanliness, health. The flow of normal life. Stopped. Ominous. Something big somewhere gone wrong. I remember hearing in 2015 that Cape Town had reached Day Zero and the implementation of level-seven water restrictions. But Cape Town was away. Another continent. It couldn't happen here, could it?

2030 and I'm waiting again. A different queue. Hundreds of us with plastic containers, bottles. The lorry is late. I am about fifty yards back on the line. It's hard to keep positive. To get out of bed to make the front of the queue. I have not brushed my teeth and my mouth feels gummy. The woman behind me has a kid who is crying, thirsty. I try to be nice. It's hard when you haven't had a shower or a cup of tea. When you know you smell. We had been saving rainwater at home for washing our bits but the last week it's been bone dry. Swimming pools are unheard of in level eight.

The woman smiles back nervously at me. I look into her eyes. There are two expressions you see nowadays – numbness or panic. She holds hard to the hand of her toddler. Still no lorry. People are grumbling. Suddenly there is a woman moving towards us from further back in the line – she points her finger accusingly at the woman behind me – You're not from here – you don't live here. She's from Hoe Street! Let's see your ration card. The woman tells them they've made a mistake. Her bag is grabbed before there is anything she can do – her child is whimpering and clinging to its mummy – who is pushed to the ground. I told you, Hoe Street, says the woman triumphantly. My neighbour, Trudi, who is seventy and lovely, says, Does it matter? And helps the woman up. Trudi is a church-goer. She says, If your enemy is hungry give him food to eat and if he is thirsty give him water to drink. I was late this morning and the lorry was only half full, says the young mother. They told me to come here. Fuck off, says her assailant. And then to Trudi, And you can fuck off too, you communist. Then we see our lorry with its tank of water trundle towards us. The woman and child walk reluctantly away. I'd like to say, Stop I'll share – but something stops me. The memory of thirst.

As the queue surges forward, Trudi is pushed aside. I'm ashamed to say I pretend not to notice and push forward too. Those at the back always walk away empty-handed.

Suhayla It was a real moment for me going back and being with my grandma and hearing this story and realising that wasn't the weather anymore – this was different, this was frightening. And I understood why Abani wanted me to tell this story.

Abani Then this year we suffered another storm – they give them names – this one was called Cyclone Mora, which is frustrating – because it gives the impression you can talk to them and say, Come on, Mora, you don't want to do that really, do you? But she wasn't listening.

We ran again. I grabbed Anya, now a toddler, and begged Gopal to leave the animals and come to higher ground but this time your grandfather and uncle went out into the darkness and tried to rescue their remaining cows, the poor animals drowning in the river. Again the water took everything. Our house went into the water but this time also the land it had stood on that was our shrimp farm. The wind picked up anything, helpless and tossed it like a doll. The water seemed to want to obliterate the land, like a dark force. Your grandfather and uncle did not come back. We found their bodies three miles upriver. Grief. Rani was inconsolable. I tried to explain to Anya what had happened but three is too young to understand. Everyday she asks me where are Babu and Uncle – are they coming back today? Not today, I answer.

Aaron (*voice-over*) Climate denial campaigns have been very, very effective in delaying action – undermining the good science that had been done

The system is corrupted by vested interests, fossil fuel companies for example, who are not good faith actors to society

It has strong connections to tobacco campaigns

Some of same people – same PR industries

America had just gone through the winning of the Cold War and they needed a new enemy. Environmentalism seemed like a threat to the free market worldview cos it required government regulation of big business – fossil fuel companies made the most of that because they gave money to institutes so these people got in front of the cameras.

April I heard a story about a scientist who was asked to talk to some major business leaders.

They paid her a years' wages to come to talk to them

She told them the kind of stuff I've been telling you

And at the end of it they said, Well where is the best place for us to go to get away from it?

She said, No, you don't understand, there is no away

Come on, they said, is this place New Zealand or Alaska?

She said again, There is no away

Then they said, Okay – I will build myself a bunker but I have a problem, how do I ensure that my security guards don't kill me and take the code to open my food supplies?

Where are we on AI? Could I employ robots? Or is there some kind of collar I could get my security to wear that will inflict pain if they disobey me?

I don't know what she said but I hope it was Fuck you.

CAPTION: 2030.

It was the day the food distribution depots didn't open. The rusty shutters stayed down bearing a sign: *Please halve your daily rations till further notice.* And that was it. The news is blaming immigrants for getting through the militarised border and using counterfeit ration cards.

At some point that afternoon in the fitful sleep hunger brings I am woken by shouts. I move to the window. The self-appointed patriots' patrol is circling a woman who is talking back to them, her face anguished. Speak English, they bark at her. She carries her child on her back, its thin face, turned like a half-moon, lies silent on her shoulder blade. She turns to the patrol to show the child, suddenly a shot rings out and the woman is on the ground. I run out of the house propelled by an energy I haven't felt in months shouting, No, no.

Another shot.

One of the men turns to me and tells me to get back indoors. I can't move.

Where's Trudi? I need her – and then I remember she had died too. A tick bite. The nasty things had a firm hold in the biosphere due to increased temperatures and it had finished her.

In the road lay the woman and child unmoving and bloody.

They are the first dead bodies I had ever seen and it pours out, all my anger, disbelief, horror.

God knows who is listening but I am past the point of caring and I'm saying things I shouldn't –

Later my doorbell rings. Two men. They show their official status with a flash of their phones. I've heard about this and now it's here at my door. The men, government officials, tell me I have been overheard criticising the government's handling of the ecological emergency. People can have their ration cards removed for six weeks for such infringements. My husband comes downstairs, anxious, he's coughing – a cough that never seems to have an end.

I say that whoever reported me must be mistaken. I don't talk like that. That's not the sort of person I am. Just like everyone else I want my rations. I want food in my belly. A human is nothing without it, and then I look at my husband, who is giving me our 'shut up' signal. It's like I am sounding too radical with my talk of human beings.

I smile and offer them a cup of tea. It's worth the sacrifice of our last teabags to sweeten them up. I make the tea in our kitchen, boiling the water on our one-ring gas appliance. But then there is a flicker and suddenly the power is off. We are plunged into darkness. I search for the candle – why do I never leave it in the same place? I grope my way to the front room. The men have left, taking our ration books pending further investigation. I stand there in the cold, hungry, with the small flickering flame of the candle in front of my husband who is probably dying. It's game over, the thought comes swiftly as a sudden draught guts my candle.

Abani This time our land was washed away, our shrimp farm gone, there is no life for us here anymore.

The land cannot not sustain us.

We have Anya and no choice but to try to find work in Dhaka. Gopal has gone ahead already and we will join him. When I told Anya we were leaving this place we know in every light, every season, she said she would take a photograph with her memory and she blinked her eyes twice like a lizard.

I still cannot cry. I am too numb. Too shocked, too scared. I'm like one of our fruit trees – ripped from the earth by the pitiless water – and now lying frozen – roots bared – sticking out like dead fingers into emptiness. I don't want to go to Dhaka

To live in a room in a Kamrangirchar built over an old rubbish dump for twenty pounds a week. I don't want to work in the garment trade. I don't want to think of Gopal in the brick works. What if Anya gets sick? I am so anxious for her. The air is gritty from traffic fumes and the smoke of cooking fires. The Buriganga river is thick with the slick of chemicals from factories. You cannot wash in it.

There must be another life for us? Ours has been stolen from us.

Suhayla I try to talk to my grandma about her future.

She says, I know what you are up to, child. If you think I will leave the land where I was born, where I have buried my husband and son, you can think again. And she marches off to feed her chickens.

I sit down on the porch to finish transcribing Abani's story, the light glowing on my laptop. I feel helpless. Abani and Anya are packing for their journey to Dakha, but I know that Rani won't ever leave here.

As I write, the first drops of rain begin to fall.

For Bangladesh the one-point-five degrees of warming we have already signed up to will mean more flooding, landslides, poverty, temperature rises and displacement.

A storm was building.

I go to my grandmother. I point to the sky – at the roiling clouds – It's a storm, I say. It's not safe here. The neighbours are good, she says, we help each other. Where else will I get such good neighbours? And that is the last word she will say on the matter. I anxiously watch the sky, the rain is endless. Some people leave on boats while they can, but my grandmother refuses.

The water rises so fast.

A force that could not be commanded. Enraged nature. Abani holds Anya while I help Dadi-ma. Inside there is just darkness, no lights. We are suddenly pushed off our feet by a force of water and Anya is knocked from Abani's arms. She screams her name – I scream into the darkness too, and Abani flings herself after her daughter. Dadi-ma goes limp in my arms. Let me go too, she whispers, let me go. And my heart breaks. I wish myself back to a year, two years, five, a decade. To when there was still time to save them.

Later in London I finished writing Abani's story. I promised her I'd tell it, so I am.

April If the seven-point-five billion people on the planet had the carbon footprint of a person living in Bangladesh we would require an Earth the size of Asia to live sustainably. Our planet would be far more than enough for us. If everyone on Earth had the carbon footprint of a person living in China, the planet Earth would be enough.

But if we all had the carbon footprint of a citizen of the UK, we would need two-and-a-half planet Earths. In the US, four Earths.

I've tried to give you the science.

Stayed stoic – on the whole – while doing it.

Here we are part of a system that is extractive, wasteful, linear, abusive

That takes from the Earth with no heed of the consequences for people like Suhayla and her family

How can we look into the faces of children and tell them what we are doing?

When our media won't tell us the truth, when our politicians pretend they are taking it seriously but lie.

But what if all they think about is the market and their shares in the companies that are profiting from the trashing of our planet?

Why are we letting such a tiny group of people trash our planet for their greed?

And when will the tipping points come that will rock the Earth into a death spiral?

Why aren't we acting like it's an emergency?

Like it's World War Two?

Because this is bigger. This is a thousand holocausts.

And the thing is, we have the solutions. We have them now.

But we also have this.

She picks up a bucket of oil.

Our government says it wants to take action on climate change but subsidises the oil industry giants to the tune of ten and a half billion pounds a year.

The world's top sixty banks have spent three-point-eight trillion dollars financing the fossil fuel industry since the Paris agreement in 2015.

If we want to know why things aren't changing, it's because some people are making a huge amount of money – from this.

April pours the oil over the stage as in a spill. She is affected physically by the oil on her body. She may 'drink' the oil as oil-slick rebels do – impersonating the act of drinking oil.

Chidi (*voice-over*) Shell had arrived in Nigeria in the 1950s and were drilling in a largely under-regulated way
    Millions of people, animals, local flora, have been displaced and destroyed by negligence and greed
    The life expectancy of environmentalists is very very short. One of more famous story is of Ken Saro-Wiwa executed by firing squad by the Nigerian government.
    That execution was based on pressure and financial influence of Big Oil in the region but he is only one of a very big number of people who have simply disappeared
    Big Oil dictates the standards of human rights in certain places.
    Shell wouldn't be allowed to rock up to a small Scottish village
    Mow down the mayor
    And indefinitely pollute the land and waters in the surrounding areas indefinitely
    But they do that in the Niger Delta.

Aaron (*voice-over*) I've had a dark night of the soul.
    I constantly have a sense of grief and loss for what we are losing

346

I was a zoologist, that was my initial passion for the planet and the amazing diversity of life and the sense that already half the Great Barrier Reef has died and every report that comes out, more birds on the verge of extinction, more insect population loss, we're losing the magic of the world, it's heartbreaking

I'm grief-stricken, heartbroken

Full of rage against the stupidity of it all.

Elise (*voice-over*) I can't sit back and look at their lovely little kiddie faces and not do anything about it

I remember thinking they're going to be really proud of their aunty

And one day when they're older and they ask me what did you do?

Cos when everything – hopefully not – not trying to be negative, but when things have turned to shit

And they say you were around at that time, what were you doing?

That they know I tried in whatever way I could.

Things were like this and now they're like this.

I don't know.

Xanthe (*voice-over*) The actual future, I think it's going to be very different

And what people are learning in, like, everyday normal school isn't really gonna help

I think the skills I'm currently learning, like, living in a community will actually be very useful.

Chidi (*voice-over*) We need to move forward to a vision of a better society, our young people need to have a vision of a world they want to see and not be fearful of the world they are in.

CAPTION: *The UK will host the next COP talks in Glasgow 2021.*

It remains to be seen whether governments will take the necessary steps to avoid the continuance of the

*breakdown of our global climate and ecological systems.
Environmentalists are calling these talks 'our' last
chance.*

Chidi (*voice-over*) It's so important to find a group you want
to work with – you'll find a groundswell of incredible people
out there who want to create things you can build on.

Even though you are told by newspapers that are owned
by billionaires that you can't fight billionaires, you just
might find you win.

Aaron (*voice-over*) Radical change
Happens very quickly
There are a lot of signs that the system is close to its
social tipping points in many ways
The fossil fuel industries teetering
Renewable energy is becoming a viable alternative
And if that's amplified by policy and movements
You could start to see the existing system crumbling very
quickly
We need more people putting pressure wherever they can
Each of us has a specialism to contribute – how does it
intersect with the struggle?
How do I mobilise my community to put more pressure
on?
We have to keep fighting because we don't know how
close we are to fundamentally shifting things.
As Nelson Mandela is famous for saying, when he was
finally released from Robben Island, It always seemed
impossible till it was done.

Chidi (*voice-over*) I would urge everyone buy fair trade –
that impact on poorer farmers further down the line is huge
Get a green electricity company
Use a paper bag, a cloth bag
Don't bank with a bank that is bankrolling this kind of
industry, effectively using your money to fund things that
are in your detriment.

Close your account at Barclays
Move your money to an ethical bank
After that go out and find a group of like-minded people
Find your tribe
Join your local XR, your local environmental group
Do fun things that that raise awareness
Things that are enjoyable because of the camaraderie.
Unfurl and develop that personal sense of mission.

Helen (*voice-over*) You have to
Get through the denial to the grief
There was a powerful moment
With my son
We were walking down Southwark Bridge, no idea what
would happen
And that moment when we stepped off the pavement
onto the road
When we took the bridge with all those others
That for me was the start
Actually the road doesn't belong to anybody
We stepped over something
This whole business of obeying
How we have been coerced into something
Subliminally coerced.

Something that had seemed so hard
Was so simple
Powerful.

April Every story has a multitude of possible endings. And
there are always strong clues to where a story is headed.
Warning signs. Moments when characters, groups,
governments, nations, can make choices that will change
everything. And our lives are going to change.
The choice is whether we are going to be in control of
that change
Or it's going to happen to us in the most terrifying way.

Bangladesh is at the forefront of climate adaptation and they've built twelve thousand functioning cyclone shelters, an early warning system, and they've engaged people at a local grassroots and national level. Which has saved millions of lives. They listened to the warning signs. And they did something about it. They managed to change their story.

And as Suhayla promised to tell Abani's story, I promised to tell Suhayla's.

Suhayla The water was rising so fast, we knew if we stayed we would be lost. We struggled through the raging waters, I held Rani, Abani and Anya, and we managed at last to get pulled into a neighbours' boat which took us to the nearest shelter. It was terrifying. But we all survived.

April In 2020 a quarter of the country was flooded, over a million homes damaged, hundreds and thousands of people marooned. Super-Cyclone Amphan was called the storm of the century.

Kara Mura was washed away. They survived, but there was nowhere for Rani to return to. Because no matter how prepared they are in Bangladesh, if rich countries don't stop emitting, then by 2030 one billion people will be displaced by man-made climate change.

So I have brought you back – not to where we were when we started out – not to safety – but how safe was that place?

Two-point-six degrees Celsius of warming is worse than two-point-three degrees, which is worse than two-point-one.

We have to fight for every fraction of every degree. Not just for ourselves but for climate justice.

Abani And when old words die out on the tongue
New melodies break forth from the heart

And where the old tracks are lost
New country is revealed with its wonders.

April I said I wouldn't get emotional but maybe that's wrong. Maybe we should be emotional. Full of rage at what's being done to us and our fellow humans and the Earth and all future life? Maybe emotional is exactly just what we should be.

Climate change is the greatest crisis humankind has ever faced and unless we address it together we will face it alone.

GIN CRAZE!

with Lucy Rivers

Gin Craze! was first performed at Royal & Derngate, Northampton (Artistic Director, James Dacre), on 17 July 2021 in a Royal & Derngate, Northampton and China Plate co-production in partnership with English Touring Theatre. The cast was as follows:

Moll/Queen Caroline Debbie Chazen
Suki/Betsy Rosalind Ford
Mary Aruhan Galieva
Evelyn/Mistress Paula James
Henry Fielding/Jekyll/Constable Alex Mugnaioni
John Fielding/Bartholomew Peter Pearson
Lydia Paksie Vernon
Sarah Fielding/Informer Rachel Winters

Book and Lyrics April De Angelis
Music and Lyrics Lucy Rivers
Director Michael Oakley
Designer Hayley Grindle
Music Supervisor and Arranger Tamara Saringer
Choreographer Paul Isaiah Isles
Lighting Designer Jack Knowles
Sound Designer Tony Gayle
Assistant Director Tian Brown-Sampson
Fight Director Alison de Burgh
Line Producer Tess Dowdeswell
Casting Director Matilda James
Dramaturg Victoria Saxton

Supported by a National Lottery grant from the Arts Council England's Ambition for Excellence fund.

Commissioned by Royal & Derngate, China Plate and English Touring Theatre.

Characters

Henry Fielding

Mary
his wife

Sarah
his sister

John
his brother

Suki Blunt

Thomas Wilson

Lydia Clapp
otherwise Jack

Evelyn Bryant

Bartholomew

Moll Williams

Queen Caroline

Judge Jekyll

Betsy

Customer

Mistress

Constable

Informer

Gin Hawkers, Beer Streeters, Revellers, Rioters, Bow Street Runners, Women in the Court

Note

The roles should be doubled as follows:

Mary

Lydia

Moll/Queen Caroline

Evelyn/Mistress

Suki/Betsy

Sarah Fielding/Informer

Henry Fielding/Judge Jekyll/Constable

John Fielding/Thomas Wilson/Bartholomew

Part One

Song: 'Gin Lane Versus Beer Street'.

Gin Hawkers sell to the audience.

Gin Hawkers Got the hump?
　　　Suspicious lump?
　　　Hands too weak to work a pump?
　　　Got a cold? Got heartache?
　　　Spots, scabies, case of scalp flake?
　　　Lots of fleas?
　　　Creaking knees?
　　　Got a nasty tumour?
　　　Lost your sense of humour?

　　　All your troubles could be past
　　　Lift your lips up to the glass
　　　And drink!
　　　Got a baby just won't sleep?
　　　Give it this, it won't peep
　　　Just drink!
　　　Is your arm in a splint?
　　　Has your cock gone soft and limp?
　　　Got a wound? Got an itch
　　　Passed on by a nasty bitch?
　　　It tames the mad
　　　It's not a fad
　　　It's gin. Gin, gin.

　　　Aggravation
　　　Inflammation
　　　Crippling constipation?
　　　Strangulation
　　　Near starvation?

Got a bit of dry lactation?
All your afflictions will be cured
From bunions to just bored
Got a nasty bloody flux?
Here's a glass you're in bloody luck!

An unveiling of Hogarth's 'Beer Street'.
Henry Fielding and his wife Mary, his sister Sarah and brother John.

Henry *and* **John**
Bonhomie, propriety
The message is crystal clear
A pint with some spunk gets you decently drunk
Let the English all drink beer.

Mr Hogarth has given us a masterpiece
A street scene at the end of the day
Lasses with flower baskets,
Peasants downing tools
Putting pints of frothy beer away.
We want native craft beer, no foreign muck
Buy British is best.
You won't beat your wife or cause any strife
It will give you some hairs on your chest.

Bonhomie, propriety
The message is crystal clear
A pint with some spunk gets you decently drunk
Let the English all drink beer.

A cheeky pint of bulldog makes you warm inside
Puts everyone in good cheer
So pull the pump and get decently drunk
And let's raise our tankards 'to beer'!

Chorus
All your troubles could be past
Lift your lips up to the glass
And drink!

Fieldings
It's safer than water, you can give it to your daughter.

Chorus
The plague won't seem so bad
When you sup your jug of glad
And drink!

Fieldings
Its white frothy head will give you better sleep in bed.

Chorus
Rent's up, you can't pay
Bailiff's due any day
Mounting debts will fade away
If you have a beer/gin today
It tames the mad
It's not a fad
It's gin/beer, gin/beer, gin/beer!

The crowd cheers.
The Beer Streeters try to get rid of the Gin Hawkers:
'Be off with you', 'Nothing for you'.
The Gin Hawkers jeer back. One gives a rude gesture
to Henry.

Henry And so begins our campaign to stamp out the vice of gin. In the future no one will have ever heard of it. How did I do, Mary?

John It's what's called a leading question.

Mary You were perfect, Henry. Your crusade is wonderful.

Henry You're just saying that because we're married.

Sarah Of course she is. If you'd asked me you'd have got a reasonable to middling.

Henry Which is why I must remember never to ask you, sister.

Mary If anyone can encourage the drinking of beer it's Henry Fielding.

Henry Mary, I'm touched.

Sarah I think I'm going to be sick.

John Show a united front, Sarah, we're a family.

Sarah Only when it suits you and Henry, John. The rest of the time we're a hierarchy.

John Lead me, sister.

> *John, who is blind, puts his hand on her shoulder and they exit.*
> *A woman, dirty and dishevelled, approaches Mary.*

Suki Remember me?

Mary I don't carry change.

Suki I remember you.

Mary You've made a mistake.

Suki You're a lady now, is that it? Too good to be seen with the likes of me?

Henry Is she bothering you? Do you know this woman?

Mary No, no, Henry. Get away, you drab.

Henry Run along.

Suki Sir.

> *She moves away.*

Henry I don't like these kind of mysteries. We mustn't give villains the means to slander us.

Mary Of course not, Henry.

Henry Put yourself in my position, Mary – I'm a man who has had the temerity to marry his servant as opposed to merely seducing her and then abandoning her afterwards, for the which I have unaccountably had the more censure. I presume you have no hint of scandal to add to that unfortunate state of affairs?

Mary No, Henry.

Henry Good, because you're carrying our future and he must be born free from the taint of dishonour.

As the party moves off, Suki holds back Mary.

Suki You shouldn't have done that, dissing me. We got history. Don't forget, I know what you was before – a servant in trouble. Like a common whore. How would he like his perfect wife exposed? He wouldn't want the town gossiping. They do love to gossip. Kick its carcass over and over. Vultures. Think of the scandal. The disgrace. Horrible. I'd throw myself in the river. Money is what will buy my silence.

Mary It looks better with us than we are. We're on tab at the grocers and the butchers.

Suki I'll come find you.

She goes.

Song: 'What Does a Woman Have to Do'.

Mary
What does a woman have to do
To get a better life?
What does a woman have to give
To be a mother or a wife?
Always waiting to be found out
When the past comes back to bite,
What does a woman have to do?
I have tried to shape my own destiny
But the truth is buried, hidden
And the weight of it is killing . . .

We go back to Mary's past.

363

SCENE TWO

Mistress rings her bell impatiently. Mary enters her Mistress's room.

Mistress Is that my hot chocolate?

Mary Yes, ma'am.

Mistress What's that supposed to be – a soft roll? Baked hard as a tortoise and the same colour. Lord, what I must put up with. The cup is cracked. I can't drink that. Oh give it here. Wretched girl. Pot. Quick.

Mary Ma'am.

Mistress sits on it to have a shit.

Mistress Did you send for the reverend?

Mary Yes, ma'am.

Mistress When he arrives send him straight to me. I need solace. I spent an unfortunate night at the gaming table and my spirits need biblical fortification. Christ, this is like giving birth. I wouldn't be surprised if it has eyes.

She grunts.

There, that's for you.

Mary Thank you.

Almost barfs and in her unsteadiness splashes her Mistress.

Mistress Clumsy oaf. I did not request you should furnish me with my own piss. Well go on. Don't just stand there.

Mary is queasy.

What's the matter with you?

Mary Nothing –

Mary goes to barf.

Mistress Too delicate for the job? No use to me if you are. Wait. Pale, morning sickly? It's your belly, isn't it? You trollop.

Mary My family – God rest them – were respectable people – I only get out on Sundays to church –

Mistress One wonders how you managed to get into your present state of anticipation?
Harlot! Reverend Wilson?

Thomas Wilson, the curate, enters.

Wilson You sent for me, ma'am.

Mistress Your arrival is timely. My servant is with child. I am not unkind – offer her religious advice, then see to it she is removed. I shall return when less suggestively attired.

Mistress exits.

Mary Thomas . . .

Wilson (*stopping her*) The story of the exile Ruth and her mother-in-law Naomi. Ruth said, 'Whither thou goest there go I.'

Mary Why is it me that has to goest and you that stayeth?

Wilson Sin falls more heavily upon woman due to the transgressions of Eve.

Mary You promised you'd stand by me –

Wilson If the devil didn't tempt me, Mary, through you, his instrument, how would I come to understand my own weakness and thus learn to overcome it?

Mary You didn't overcome it and now there's a baby –

Wilson Think on Ruth. Humble and loyal. Goodbye, Mary, and God bless you and try to remember to say no next time.

Mistress re-enters.

Mistress Excellent advice.

Mary My wages, ma'am –

Mistress Relieve yourself of my presence. And empty the pot on the way out. Reverend Wilson does not want to encounter my morning soil.

Wilson You're most solicitous, ma'am.

Mary But it was Reverend Wilson . . .

Mistress Take your evil tongue, your degraded body and leave my house – nothing foul will stick to a man of God.

Mary throws the pot at them both, the shit sticks to them. Runs out.

SCENE THREE

Mary with baby. She's on the street, begging.

Song : 'I am a Mother'.

Mary
> Don't fret, my child
> This world is so wide
> You will get by
> With me at your side
> I'll never desert you
> Like that bastard man
> And though I'm a woman
> I'll do the best that I can.
>
> And you'll spread your wings
> One day and take flight
> All sorrow and sadness
> Will banish from sight
> And you'll grow strong

366

With my tender care
Here in my arms
You have nothing to fear.

The baby cries.

Suki How can you bear to hear it cry like that?

Mary My milk's gone.

Suki Happens when you hunger. Here. Give it a dram?

Mary Of what?

Suki Gineva.

Mary No thank you.

The baby gives a great wail.

Suki Nothing else is going to soothe it. I know, I've had a few.

She gives a dram to Mary.
Mary hesitates, then gives some to the baby. This settles the baby.

Mary It works.

Suki Mother Gineva don't hang about. Goes straight to it. Told you didn't I?

Mary
I am a mother
That's what I am
I give comfort
And comfort's a dram
You sup the juice
No need to weep
I'll hold you tenderly
As it puts you to sleep.

And you'll drift away
Your sorrows and strife

With just a few mouthfuls
Will banish from sight
And though they'll come back
In the cold light of dawn
At least my dear child
For a while you'll be warm.

Suki What is it?

Mary Girl.

Suki Ah. Pretty dress.

Mary I made it.

Suki What you going to do with her?
You can't feed her. I know someone who might have her.

Mary holds the baby closer.

Mary No thank you.

Suki You should take the chance.

Mary We'll get by.

Suki Take the offer while it's on the table. Someone else will grab it otherwise. Demand is high. Carry on like this what's going to happen, she's only going to starve or die or something.

Mary I couldn't.

Suki A very caring person. Can't tell you who in case you turned up there. Frightened the child. Don't worry, you could always get her back.

Mary I could?

Suki When you set yourself up. Come and find me – Suki. Everyone knows me. I promise you she's going to a good home. I was right about the gineva wasn't I? You trusted me once you should trust me again.

Mary I'd be sure to get her back?

Suki A week's notice. You'd have to give something. For all the clothes and food she's had. The toys, medicines. It's not a free ride.

Mary How much?

Suki Four pounds say.

Mary Take a year to earn that.

Suki But once you get on your feet you can save for it.

Baby cries again.

What do you say?

Mary
> So drink up my dear
> Banish all fear
> Always remember
> Your mother is here
> It breaks my heart
> But what else can I do
> In this cold old world
> But inebriate you?

Mary hands over the baby.

Suki She's lovely. Don't fear about her. She'll be safe with me. I wouldn't hurt her. It's better if you don't look back.

Mary
> And you'll spread your wings
> One day and take flight
> All sorrow and sadness
> Will vanish from sight
> I know you'll grow strong
> Without my tender care
> One day I'll return
> You've no need to fear.

I'll return, don't fear
Remember me my dear
I'll return, don't fear
Remember me my dear.

Mary exits.

SCENE FOUR

Lydia discovers Mary, crying.

Lydia Cheer up, love, spoiling a pretty face. What's your name?

Mary Mary.

Lydia What do you do, Mary?

Mary Servant to a lady. I was.

Lydia Lydia. Watercress and herb hawker. Picking at dawn. Walk into town. Set up my pitch. With watercress you can piss on 'em so they stay looking fresh.

Mary How much does that make?

Lydia Bugger all. But I have ways of supplementing.

Mary I don't really want to live.

Lydia You just come right out with it don't you?

Women are leaving work and heading for the gin dive. They start singing.

Song: 'Gin Dive'.

Women leave your cooking, your cleaning,
    your slaving
Women leave your washing, your sweeping, your old
    man complaining
Come down to the gin dive and sit with girls

Have a laugh, a drink, a good time with the girls
Come down to the gin dive and have some good jest
We'll dance, we'll sing, we'll give our bloody best.

Come on!

Women leave the factory, the shop and your sewing
Abandon your worries, you don't need them where
    you're going
Come down to the gin dive and sit with the girls
Have a laugh, a drink, a good time with the girls
Come down to the gin dive and have some good jest
We'll dance, we'll sing, we'll give our bloody best.

Mary enters. She has never been in a gin dive before.

Mary What is this place?

Lydia Palace of inspiration.

Moll Pit of perspiration.

Evelyn Evelyn. I availed myself of a new opportunity. Two rooms. I sleep in the back – this is my professional premises.

Moll If it had less beetles.

Evelyn Take it or leave it.

Mary grabs a gin.

Mary If I drink enough of this – will I die?

Evelyn Worth a try.

And if our men complain we've left them to go
    out drinking
And if we come back home bloody stinking
Come down to the gin dive and sit with the girls
Have a laugh, a drink, a good time with the girls
Come down to the gin dive and have some good jest
We'll dance, we'll sing, we'll give our bloody best.

Instrumental dance. Mary gets drunker and drunker.

And if they've been moaning we've been taking
   our time
They can stick it somewhere the sun don't shine.
Come down to the gin dive and sit with the girls
Have a laugh, a drink, a good time with the girls
Come down to the gin dive and have some good jest
We'll dance, we'll sing, we'll give our bloody best.

SCENE FIVE

*A room. Lydia and Mary are with an unprepossessing and
very drunk man.*

Bartholomew She new on the streets?

Lydia You are, aren't you?

Mary Yes.

Bartholomew Do you want to see what's in my trousers?

Lydia Yes, that's why she's here.

Mary What?

Bartholomew Want one on my bumhole and one on my
balls.

Lydia You choose, Mary, since you're new.

Bartholomew Then I'll poke her. You did good, Lydia.

Mary What is this? Trust me you said.

Lydia Have another mother, you won't feel a thing.

Mary You trying to get me drunk?

Lydia No. You're already drunk. Just helping you get
through it.

Bartholomew Hurry up. I got a stiffie needs mending.

Mary I won't do it.

Lydia You owe me for the gineva. How else you gonna pay? I don't do it with blokes. So that leaves you.

Mary I trusted you.

Lydia Yeah. You gotta watch that. What you need to know about me is that I won't bring an unwanted brat into the world.

Mary But it's all right if I do?

Bartholomew I got a whopper wants attending to. Sort it or I'll spend my money somewhere else.

Lydia Wait.

Lydia (*to Bartholomew*) Wait, here you go, Bartholomew. Just one more for the road.

Bartholomew I've got hollow legs, I can drink any man or woman under the table. Gineva – don't know what all the fuss is about. It don't touch me.

He grabs Mary.

Mary Lydia!

She grapples alone with Bartholomew.

Lydia!!

Lydia Fuck.

Lydia has to help Mary. He grabs Mary and Lydia prises him off.
They both grapple with him. He gets Lydia in a headlock then he is struck suddenly by the gin.

Bartholomew Aaagh! What's me dad doing here?

Lydia Your dad?

Bartholomew He's dead.

Lydia It's probably not him then.

Bartholomew Are you telling me I'm seeing things, mouthy bitch? He's wearing brown boots.

Lydia Anything else?

Bartholomew Piss off. He's not walking round the afterlife with his tackle hanging loose. You piss me off, Lyd.

He goes to hit her, she ducks, then he is struck again.

Dad, dad!

He collapses.

Mary Is he dead?

Lydia No, he's just flummoxed. Fleece his pockets, Mary.

Mary Aren't we supposed to copulate with him?

Lydia This is better, isn't it?

Mary takes money from his pocket.

Mary We're thieves now.

Lydia It's what I've earned. Fetching girls for him. He never paid me enough. Take off his clothes and all. Sell them too. Easy market in old clothes.

Mary Even baby clothes?

They take his clothes off.

Lydia Good quality.

Mary Won't he come looking for you?

Pause. Lydia picks up the clothes and looks at them.
Puts the shirt up against her.
She puts his shirt on.

Lydia
    Could I
    Could I be
    Could I escape the drudgery

Not a beggar or tart, but taken seriously
Take the chance, Lyddie.

Should I
Accept my lot
Or strike while the iron's hot
You deserve more than this
A woman's life takes the piss
Just take the chance, Lyddie.

What's to lose, it's a million-to-one chance
No longer be led, but I'll lead my own dance,
If you can't beat 'em join 'em, isn't that what they say?
Enough pimping for pennies, it's time I made
   them pay.

Lydia is no more
Dumped like her mother did before
A new start to try
A new star in the sky
I'll show the world I'll not lay down and die
I could be, I could be
A new me.

Mary What are you doing, Lydia?

Lydia I'm not Lydia. Call me Jack.

Mary What will you do? Lyd. Jack.

Lydia Set up on my own.

Mary Doing what?

Lydia Yeah. Something.

Mary Take me with you?

Lydia It's all about me. On my own.

Mary I know your secret.

Lydia Betray me, would you?

Mary We could sell gin.

Lydia Gin?

Mary Yes. Why not us?

Lydia Bye, Mary.

Mary We could make our gineva special.

Lydia Special?

Mary

Maybe
We could be
Witches of distillery
We could hawk day and night
I can charm, you can fight
It's a winning recipe.

What's to lose, it's a million-to-one chance
No longer be led, but we'll lead our own dance,
If you can't beat 'em join 'em, isn't that what they say?
Enough scrimping for pennies, it's time we had our day.

Go on
Take a chance
Two minds can only enhance
You can trust I won't tell
We'll do the hard sell
Mother's juniper berries will get us out of this hell.

We could be, we could be
Good company.

Lydia I'll try you out for a week or so. See how we get. No promises, mind.

SCENE SIX

Lydia and Mary have set up their stall.

Moll You're new here. Taste for free?

Mary Get lost.

Moll I'm not fussy. What's in yours, arsenic, quicklime or rat's droppings?

Mary None of that. With us it's all about the garnish. Nothing Jack doesn't know about herbs.

Moll Nothing I don't know about gineva. Ever seen a pig's brain?

Mary Course.

Moll Coils and coils – like little streets – gineva runs round those coils making it all pure – burning as it goes. Bad thoughts, sadnesses.
      Like a cannonball rolls round the thunder run at the theatre drowning out the noise the actors make.

Lydia When you ever been to the theatre?

Moll I used to blow the understudies. Drury Lane.

Lydia Teach me to ask.

Moll Drink enough mother, burn them out for good. Memories. Give me a sup and I'll stop going on.

Mary I don't want to forget things. You'd lose a part of yourself.

Lydia Give her some, Mary, shut her up. First customer could bring us luck.

They give her a taste.

Moll Nice bouquet. Got a kick to it. Felt that in my fanny flaps. Your gineva has a certain piquant flavour. I think I will avail myself of your beverage with greater frequency.

Mary You'll have to pay next time.

Evelyn Bryant enters.

Evelyn Why don't you two do me a favour and fuck off. You take my customers. I run a dive, not a wanking wheelbarrow.

Lydia Not our fault we have a superior product.

Evelyn Don't cheek me, pretty boy.
   (*To Moll.*) Don't let me see you buying their gineva if you want to trade out of my gaff.

Mary She didn't buy it.

Moll No one's up for screwing me anyway – so no hard loss there. They're all flaccid with drinking your putrid offerings.

Evelyn Could be your charms are flaccid.

Moll Scratch off.

Evelyn Blear-eyed Moll – when was the last time you saw the world straight?

Moll Prefer it bent.

Evelyn You got wheels on your poxy barrow, use 'em.

Lydia We'll move – go down Southwark – catch the people getting off the ferry.

Evelyn Make sure you do.

Mary What are you saying, Jack?

Lydia You heard her.

Mary We always get moved on. Our stuff is better than hers. She don't own the streets.
   We've got to think bigger, Jack. Make a go of it. Get rich.

Moll People start out starry-eyed, then life pokes their eyes out. Gineva's all you can trust.

Mary Mother will give us heart.

378

Lydia What you got to know about me, Mary, is I'm a foundling. I don't do 'us'.

Mary If we had a room, think what we could make then?

Lydia We ain't going to find out because we won't be together long enough.

Mary Why?

Lydia Don't rely on Mary, you'll only be disappointed.

Mary We could make a future together.

Song: 'Lydia's Song'.

Lydia
> The streets are cobbled and paved with woes
> The path I take I travel on my own
> I take the whips,
> I take the blows
> The trail I blaze is the one I chose.
>
> They say that my mother was a whore
> She left me one night by the sea shore
> But I withstood the cold
> That's the story I was told
> Now no one can stop my mighty roar.
>
> Wipe those tears away, smooth your hair
> You're looking wild
> You are your own mother now my child.
>
> And I am strong alone without you
> This tree won't bend I'll see the storm through
> No one to let me down
> To no one I'll be bound
> Then life will treat me fair and true.
>
> Wipe those tears away, smooth your hair
> You're looking wild
> We are our own mothers now, my child.

Evelyn You not gone yet?

Mary We're not going anywhere.

> *A Customer goes by.*
> *Mary holds up a glass.*

Madam!

> *The Customer stops.*

Mary
>> Behold that sight
>> Like crystals in firelight
>> Or moonbeams in a pool of piss.
>> Heavenly
>> Bouquet of parsley.

Customer Fuck me.

Mary That tastes pure bliss.

> *The Customer buys drinks.*

Evelyn They're chancers. Don't try hers, drink mine.

Mary
>> No one wants your poor excuse
>> Her gin tastes like old cunt juice
>> Only good for rats and fleas
>> Tastes like foreskin cheese.

Evelyn I'll have you for libel.

> *Evelyn leaves, the Customer leaves.*

Mary Look, Jack. We made two shillings.

Moll I always knew you'd make a success of it. Lucky for you I've agreed to hitch my fortune to yours.

Mary *and* **Lydia**
>> All your troubles could be past
>> Lift your lips up to the glass
>> And drink!

When your day is looking glum
A swig of this'll make it fun
Just drink!
Buy quick, have a blast
Best be quick, selling fast
Live for now, not the past
The good times may not last
It don't taste bad
It's not a fad
It's gin, gin, gin.

SCENE SEVEN

Street nearby.
   *The naked Bartholomew, who has been asleep all this
time, wakes and exits, passing the horrified Queen Caroline.*
   The Royal Palace.
   Queen Caroline, Judge Jekyll and Thomas Wilson.

Jekyll Queen Caroline has been embroiled in a shocking
and tasteless incident.

Queen Caroline The king is away and usually I am having
very good sleeping on this account. Majesty has a very big
problem with his schnarchen.

Jekyll Snoring, ma'am.

Queen Caroline Yes I said so. But now my dreaming is
infected with something which I am witnessing from my
daily constitutional drive.

Jekyll Her majesty has come upon a great deal of
bestialities in the streets of Westminster.

Queen Caroline It is really doing a bugger with my
sleeping. Who is this Jekyll?

Jekyll Reverend Thomas Wilson, ma'am, a leading proponent
of the Society for Promoting Christian Knowledge.

He bows.

Wilson Your majesty, I hope my visit finds you in good health.

Queen Caroline Are you not listening? I am not feeling a good thing. I have been most verärgert in my daily drive to see things that should never have pierced my eyes.

Jekyll Do make use of the blinds, ma'am.

Queen Caroline But what kind of creature would go in coach and not look the window? One might as well stay home. That is my right surely to look with my eyes?

Jekyll Yes, windows are of course for the perusal of the outside.

Queen Caroline I do not expect to see naked man.

Jekyll No, ma'am.

Queen Caroline I never seen even the king in the Nacht. This man with no trousers lying unempfindlich in the dirt and erbrechen. And then woman showing Busen and shouting to the Queen of England 'Küss meinen Arsch'.

Jekyll You could not have made the point with more persuasion, majesty. Under the influence of this pernicious juice they lose all respect for their betters. Gineva is a peculiarly female drink.

Wilson – and they reward it with prodigious custom. They are consuming five million gallons a week.

Queen Caroline How did this schrecklich habit infect the people?

Song: 'It's the Law'.

Wilson *and* **Jekyll**
    Since Britain's political alliance with the Dutch
    Brought with it a bright new dawn

No more buying in French brandy
For we had our own glut of corn
The distillers and landowners were happy
There seemed to be no cause for alarm
But then this hysteria, by the poor and inferior
Who've gone mad for gineva's charm.

Queen Caroline Ah I see it all went Titten hoch. I am regent and I am putting all my eggs in your basket, Jekyll. What will you be doing?

Jekyll The new bill I propose putting through parliament with your majesty's approval will be more draconian than the last.

Wilson We're introducing licensing. The cost to the sellers will be prohibitive, ma'am. It will be a knock-out blow.

It's the law it's the law
It's the law to help the poor
Heaven forbid they end up dead
When they could work for us instead
It's the law it's the law
It's the strong hand of the law
It's the law they simply can't ignore.

Queen Caroline Gut. For it is my concern for the people of England that they stop with the drinking before they shrivel as a nation. The bricklayers will builden wonky buildings. The women too busy getting betrunken to bring up good healthy children. It is die Pflichten einer Frau to look after her children and love them.

A knock.

God, it is my son – I can't see him now. I can't abide his long face. I must have wine to dull the edge of my repugnance.

She exits other direction.

SCENE EIGHT

Lydia and Mary.
  They have now opened their own place.
  Mary secretes a coin into her pocket. Lydia notices.

Lydia What's that, Mary?

Mary Jack – you crept up on me.

Lydia What is it though?

Mary I put a little bit aside, don't I?

Lydia Do you? What for?

Mary I like saving up. You never know what you're going to need to spend on. Jack –

  Evelyn enters.

Evelyn So you've set up your own dive.
  Next door to mine. Sucked my place dry.

Betsy Well your gin was shit.

Evelyn You drinking here now, Betsy?

Betsy Looks like it.

Bartholomew My day's been biblical. Thrown out me lodgings. Caught leprosy. Stray dog bit off me good bollock.

Moll Usual?

Bartholomew Ta.

  Bartholomew puts his money on the counter.
    Moll gives him a pint of gin.

Moll Drunk for a penny.

  Bartholomew drinks it all down and collapses.

Dead drunk for tuppence. Suffering. It's good for business.

Mary That's the way the world wags.

Lydia (*to Evelyn*) No hard feelings. Drink on the house with me?

Evelyn You think you can win me round that easy, pretty boy?

Moll I'll have one.

Evelyn I want you to be sober when you get the news.

Lydia News?

Evelyn New law. You pay for a licence to sell. A licence that cost five pounds per gallon of gin purchased.

Lydia Five pounds?

Mary We can't make that work, Jack.

Betsy And this is supposed to be good government.

Evelyn Shit innit?

Mary They're trying to ruin us.

Evelyn Twenty-pound fine selling without licence.

Lydia What is that but daylight robbery?

Moll We work hard for what we have, stand all weathers and go through thick and thin, need gineva to keep up the spirits.

Evelyn When was the last time you did an honest day's work?

Moll I never was a woman who spared my carcass.

Evelyn You're right there.

Betsy Jekyll is a cunt and his wife's a cunt and his dog's a cunt.

Lydia The thing is –

Betsy What?

Lydia It is the law.

Betsy What you saying?

Lydia I'm not saying it's right – but it is the law.

Betsy So what you saying?

Lydia Nothing, but it's the law. I'm just saying I'm a constable. And that's what my job is – to uphold the law and that is my duty that I undertook by oath – not for pay – but for all of us – cos someone has to bloody do it and I was the fool that stuck my hand up.

Mary But what you saying? Are you going to hand us in for selling gin?

Lydia Look – I don't want to, it's just it's the law.

Betsy It's the law. I'm your wife, you're not going to hand me in are you?

Song: 'It's the Law'.

> We've always had a talent for brewing
> Ever since Eve got drunk on fermented fruit
> Divinely gifted from Goddess Ninkasi
> We were Alchemists of high repute.
>
> Then the guilds and the church condemned us
> Called us witches to burn, hang and drown
> Took our freedom away, with new laws to obey
> But you can't keep a good Brewster down.
>
> It's the law it's the law
> It's the law to keep us poor
> Heaven forbid we earn some bread
> Without our legs around our head
> It's the law it's the law it's the stinking rotten law
> If we bend 'em they just make up more.

They want us grovelling like rats in the gutter
Fight their wars, do their chores, be their whores
As soon as we're making good business
They make up some new bogus laws.

They say we're all drunk baby killers
Want us sober and pure as a nun
But we'll never give up, swigging gin from a cup
For what is life if it's not any fun?

It's the law it's the law
It's the law to keep us poor
Heaven forbid we earn some bread
Without our legs around our head
It's the law it's the law it's the stinking rotten law
If we bend 'em they just make up more.

London is where we make our fortune
We can be anything we want to be
We don't need the Whig's laws to abide by
We're the masters of our own destiny.

They're afraid of our devilish potions
They're afraid of our drunken displays
But I know we'll weather this storm together
And whip up our very own gin craze!

It's the law it's the law
It's the law to keep us poor
Heaven forbid we earn some bread
Without our legs around our head
It's the law it's the law it's the stinking rotten law
If we bend 'em they just make up more.

So what are you going to do?

Lydia I'd rather swing as a highwayman than be a bloody
constable enforcing this law – against my neighbours.

Cheers.

Mary You're a good bloke.

Betsy Sensible decision.

Moll He's one of us.

They exit.
Bartholomew wakes up.

Bartholomew (*to Mary*) It's you, isn't it? The brim that bobbed me.

Mary Don't know what you're talking about?

Lydia Leave her alone.

Bartholomew The bawd that gulled me. Come here.

He goes after Mary.

Lydia Don't bad-mouth my wife like that. Leave her alone.

Bartholomew Your wife?

They look at each other.

Must have her confused with some other doxy.

Mary Easily done.

Bartholomew goes.

Lydia I had to say something – throw him off the scent.

Mary So my try-out's over?

Lydia So it is.

Mary So we can plan the future then.

Song: 'We Could Have It All'.

> Hello, darling, put your feet up
> I've made a delicious steak and kidney pie
> There's a bun in the oven and a French vintage wine.

Lydia

Why thank you, my poppet
It's so nice to return home to you
With a nursery and our drawing room
And our indoor bathroom.

Mary *and* **Lydia**

We could have it all
Why can't our dreams come true?
We could be a lord and lady
With a family too
I'd do it for you.

Lydia

How's the baby, is she napping?
She looks adorable when she's asleep
Let the servant do the clearing up
Take the weight off your feet.

Mary

Why thank you, my teddy bear
I do deserve a little rest
We've a night out at the opera
And I must look my best.

Mary *and* **Lydia**

We could have it all
Why can't our dreams come true
We could be a lord and lady
With a family too
I'd do it for you.

They kiss.

SCENE NINE

The Royal Palace.

Queen Caroline Reverend Wilson, Judge Jekyll. So you have success to report?

Jekyll Success is perhaps a hyperbole when confronted with the outcome of present legislation.

Wilson 1736 is old news. It's all about 1737.

Queen Caroline What's wrong with old act?

Jekyll People ignored it ma'am.

Queen Caroline My God – what is this country? They don't obey the laws?

Wilson Not when they can avoid them, ma'am.
  One thousand new gin dives have opened in Middlesex alone. Nine thousand children died of gin poisoning in Southwark.

Queen Caroline Dretful. All those little brats.

Jekyll Which is why I am bringing an amendment to our bill. We will recruit informers. Well-meaning individuals who will be remunerated for revealing the transgressions of their fellows.

Queen Caroline In German the word is Spion.

Jekyll The government will now pay the informant five pounds for reporting the purchase of gineva in unlicensed premises.

Wilson And those who cannot pay their fines are sent to Bridewell to be whipped.

Queen Caroline Gut. There is hardly a week, a day that we don't hear of some Mord, robbery or some other dreadful Unfug occasioned by these inflammatory liquors . . .

Can I offer you some refreshment, gentlemen. It's five o'clock but who's counting?

They exit.

SCENE TEN

Mary
> Not long my dear
> And I will return
> This cruel separation
> Makes my poor heart yearn
> I know my promise
> Will one day come true
> I'll never rest
> Till I'm back holding you.

Evelyn has been watching.

Evelyn How long you been with Mary?

Lydia Five months.

Evelyn Not long then?

Lydia Don't say nothing against her.

Evelyn I weren't. Just all those shillings she squirrels away under the floorboards. I keep my eyes open more than you do. Maybe she's planning an escape?

Lydia Don't be stupid. Why would she do that?

Evelyn You're such a baby sometimes, Jack. Don't say you weren't warned.

Evelyn exits.
Mary enters.
She looks at some money and heads to the back room.

Lydia Do you have secrets, Mary?

Mary Secrets? No.

Lydia What you saving for?

Mary It's good to save.

Lydia That don't make sense. Scrimping and saving. We could buy new clothes.

Mary I'm good at mending.

Lydia Sometimes you go quiet. You'd tell me, wouldn't you? Because secrets come out at the wrong time and they spoil things and I don't want anything to spoil us.

Mary Nothing will spoil us.

You follow me round too much, Jack. if I'm going in the back room all I'm getting is a bottle.

Lydia I don't know what I'd do if you left me.

Mary You've got to trust me, Jack.

Lydia Foundlings don't trust easy, I told you. I've had to fight for everything and when I get it I hold tight. No child of mine ever be left.

Mary Your mum might have left you cos she wanted better for you.

Lydia There is no reason big enough to abandon your kid. Bitch!

Mary You can't call her that, Jack.

Lydia I can though, and worse.

Mary You don't know her story.

Lydia Don't you take her side, Mary – that's the one thing I'll never forgive you for.

Mary Never forgive me?

Lydia If she's eating a crust of bread now I hope it chokes her. If she's drinking, let it be beggar's piss. I hope the pox has cankered her, the skanky whore. And she never feels a touch of love.

Mary That's so sad.

Lydia Don't waste your breath. If she came in here now I'd say it to her face.

Song: 'Got Here Without You'.

I'm all right, I've got through
I've survived without you.
Don't think of crawling back
I won't listen to your tales of woe
I'll just tell you where to go
I won't fall into your trap.

I would never do what you did to me
Flung into the path of destiny
How could you shut me from your heart?
There is no reason with love this strong
A mother to leave her child is wrong
I won't be hurt by my start.

Mary

What if you met her one day
In a crowd?
Would you walk or stay?
Would she see herself in you?
Would you see yourself in her too?

Lydia

Like a leaf I went where I was blown
No one to help me and alone
Now I've got a job and a home
A place for a family of my own.
I got here without you.

Informer enters.

Informer Belly's moaning. Give us a quartern of mother.

Lydia You got kids?

Informer Who hasn't.

Lydia Feed them first.

Mary No, Jack, it's business. You got to take it.

Informer Pay my way, don't want charity.

Lydia We're not taking her money if it means her kids get nothing.

Mary Everyone's got a reason not to drink, Jack.

Lydia We're not in this to take out of the mouths of kids. Give her one for free, Mary.

Informer No I want to pay, I ain't a charity. My money's good, take it.

Lydia Haven't seen you around here before.

Informer I'm visiting my sister in Moorgate.

Lydia Oh yeah, whereabouts?

Informer Moorgate.

Pause.

Song: 'The Informer's Song'.

> I'm only asking for a dram of gin
> This is the place in which to purchase?
> It's brass monkeys out there
> My hands are blue
> I wouldn't be surprised if I pissed an icicle.
> I need warming up.

Lydia Who can vouch for you?

A crowd begins to gather.

Informer I don't need no voucher.

Women Ooh listen to her, she doesn't need a voucher.

Informer
>   Well if my custom isn't wanted here
>   I'll simply take it elsewhere
>   Where it is appreciated.
>   They'll be others who take it.

Mary takes her money.
The Informer knocks back her gin.

Ta.

She makes to go.

Evelyn You informing bitch.

Informer Me? I've never informed on no one.

Evelyn You're lying, it's written in your face.

A fight breaks out. The Informer gets the worst of it –
she is badly beaten.

Chorus Damn you, traitorous whore!

>   She's only asking for a dram of gin
>   This is the place in which to purchase
>   It's brass monkeys outside
>   She needs to rest her plates of meat
>   Have a cherry tart
>   She needs warming up.
>   (*Sinister.*) Come down to the gin dive and drink with
>   the girls
>   Have a laugh, a drink, a good time with the girls
>   Come down to the gin dive we'll have a good jest
>   We'll laugh, we'll sing, we'll give our bloody best.

They circle her.

Informer Help, help! I did it to feed my children.
      Suki's the informer – not me.

Mary Suki?

Informer She sets me up to it. 'I can't do it,' she says, 'cos they know me, they don't know you.'

Mary Suki?

Lydia God damn you for a liar.

Moll Damn informing bitch.

Betsy Stop her mouth for good.

They attack her.

> Women informers who try to reform us
> Take heed of our advice
> We're the masters of this house
> Come down to the gin dive and drink with the girls
> Have a laugh, a drink, a good time with the girls
> Come down to the gin dive we'll sniff out a liar
> We'll kick your arse and hang you out to dry.

They realise she isn't moving.
The Informer mumbles.

Moll It's the law.

They all back off as a Constable enters.

Constable She's half dead.

Betsy Informing cow.

Constable I want the truth of this or you're all nicked.

Evelyn (*pointing to Mary*) I saw her take the money.

Constable You know the rules about selling gin without a licence.
Sorry.

Grabs Mary.

Betsy Fuck off, Neville.

396

He grabs Betsy too.

Mary Let me go. Jack!

The Constable exits with Mary.

SCENE ELEVEN

A prison lock-up. The women bang their tin plates.

Sarah Jailer, there's been a mistake. My name is Sarah Fielding. I am not one of these women, I was doing some research for a novel and I was observing a crowd that had gathered outside a lowly drinking establishment and in my eagerness to write down my impressions I failed to leave the vicinity and so I was arrested by an overzealous constable and thrown into this dreadful lock-up.

Bartholomew Shut your face.

Sarah Well, really!

Betsy We ain't done nothing.

Bartholomew That's what they all say.

Betsy He's a right lobcock.

Sarah What's a lobcock?

Betsy He is.

Sarah May I take notes?

Betsy Knock yourself out.

Sarah I'm a novelist of a pedagogic bent.

Betsy Does that hurt?

Mary A novel?

Sarah It's a long, written-down story with a moral point.

Betsy What's that?

Sarah It's when a person sets aside their own interests and acts in the best interest of others. I had a special friend called Jane. She's famous for a book called *The Art of Ingeniously Tormenting*. Very her . . . invited me to live with her in a lady's commune in Wales. The idea was preposterous. What would a group of women find to do together alone all day in Llangollen? Then I missed her. I packed my bag ready to fly to her side and the letter came.

Betsy She was biffing someone else?

Sarah She had passed.

All Awwww.

Sarah Jane's advice to me was always if I wanted to wield my pen to reform the poor, I had to learn about real life.

Betsy It's not very nice. Roast our backs unless we pay four quid. And they wank off while they're doing it.

Sarah What an appalling state of affairs.

Betsy I got the shakes. Anyone got any mother?

Sarah We need water. (*Calls out.*) I think we're all rather hot and thirsty.

Bartholomew Quiet, bitches.

Sarah This is awful. (*She begins to write it down.*) I must write it all down.

Betsy Not water. Once I was dead and someone poured mother in me gob and I came alive again. Give us what we need, you bastard.

They begin banging pots.

Sarah Ladies. It doesn't help to get get into a tizzy. You'll make us all hysterical. Think pride. Think dignity.

Betsy Lost that when I was twelve, you stuck-up whiffle-whaffler.

Mary No. It's good advice, Betsy. It's got a moral point.

Sarah And what's your name?

Mary Mary.

Sarah What a shame you've ended up here in this dreadful prison.
  If only you'd had the chance to read improving literature.

Mary I'd have loved that.

Betsy Stop crawling up her bumhole.

Sarah That's a very distinctive phrase.

  She writes it down.
    Bartholomew enters. He points to Sarah.

Bartholomew You, madam, out.

Sarah I think they've found out my brother is a lawyer. My sojourn here was most informative. Thank you, turnkey. Mary – should you seriously ever consider improving yourself – come and reside with me. Just ask for us – the Fielding house, Bow Street.

Mary I have a friend though.

Sarah Unfortunately I can't rescue everyone. In stories it's always just one person we care about – if there are too many we lose interest. Goodbye.

  She exits.

Betsy Mental.

Bartholomew You're called to the magistrate. (*To Mary.*) Pay your fine or take a whipping.

SCENE TWELVE

Lydia and Mary's place. Smashed up.

Evelyn This place is finished. I warned you about selling without a licence, Jack?

Song: 'Look at Me, Jack'.

> Look at me, Jack
> Look at your Evelyn
> I love you and I always have.
> Right from the first moment I laid eyes on you, Jack
> You're not like most men.
> Most men just want to hurt you.

Lydia I want to hurt you.

Evelyn No you don't, Jack. I've seen you looking at me.

Lydia How could you do that to Mary? You whore!

Evelyn Those words are sexy when you say them, Jack.

Lydia I can't stand to look at you.

Evelyn
> Look at me, Jack
> Look at your Evelyn.
> We have a sympathy
> And when I have the taste of mother the devil gets in me.

She goes to grab Lydia's crotch, but she moves away.

Lydia I'm with Mary.

Evelyn We could start again. We could go into business together – you and me.

Lydia Piss off. Get me a drink, Moll. Just trying to earn a living is all we did. Why should we take it?

Evelyn Don't make trouble, Jack. We should just look out for ourselves.

Lydia But they won't let us.

Moll She's right, Jack. People like us, it's our lot to swallow the shit that's thrown at us.

Lydia No. There's more of us than them, and when we have enough mother inside us we're not frightened. We can do anything.

Moll That's the gineva talking. Big talk.

Lydia What is the one thing that keeps you working women alive body and soul?

Evelyn *and* **Moll** Gin.

Lydia And they're trying to kill the mother off. Are we going to let them do that?

Moll *and* **Evelyn** No.

Lydia Moll, could you lie still enough to be dead?

Moll You want me dead?

Lydia It's acting dead.

Moll Do I have to say words?

Lydia No, not if you're dead.

Moll Piece of cake.

Lydia It will be.

Moll No, can I have a piece of cake? I ain't eaten all day.

Lydia Later.

Moll So I just lie.

Lydia You just lie in a coffin. You're playing royalty.

Moll Never thought I'd get my own coffin. Thought I'd just be thrown in a pit like everyone else.

Lydia Then you get out of your coffin.

Moll Get out? I thought I was dead.

Lydia You get out and you say, 'Mother Gineva refuses to die.'

Moll I can't remember all that.

Evelyn You can say it.

Moll I'll just get into it. (*She does.*) Mother Gineva refuses to – what?

All Die!

Moll I can't be a queen, I'm too smelly.

All Say it.

Moll Mother Gineva refuses to die. Did I get that right?

Lydia That'll do.

Mary returns, having been whipped.

Lydia What happened?

Her dress is bloody.

Betsy Saw the judge six a.m. She got a whipping.

Lydia What have they done to you?

Betsy She didn't want to spend your savings, Jack. Said she had plans for that.

Lydia We could have paid, Mary.

Mary is delirious. She sings a snatch of a song

Mary
 And though they'll come back
 In the cold light of dawn
 At least my dear child
 For a while you'll be warm.

Evelyn Get some hot water, Jack, a cloth, I'll clean her up for you.

Lydia goes.

Give him a hand, She'll need a clean shirt too, poor love.

Betsy and Moll go.
Mary rambles in her shock.

Mary Take the offer while it's on the table. Someone else will grab it otherwise. Demand is high.

Evelyn Demand for what?

Mary You know someone who'd have her?

Evelyn Her?

Mary My baby?

Evelyn What you do to her?

Mary
I know you'll grow strong
Without my tender care . . .

Evelyn You left her!

Mary
One day I'll return
You've no need to fear . . .

Evelyn Shhh now, Jack'll be here. You don't want him knowing.

Lydia returns with Moll and stares at Mary's back.
Hands Evelyn the shirt. Evelyn helps Mary on with the
shirt, it is painful.

Lydia They want a battle. We'll give them a battle.

Song: 'Divine Gineva'.

Divine Gineva, she is our queen
Our queen can never die
She will arise and so will we!

Shame on those who would depose her
We refuse to go unseen
She is our new religion
We kneel and worship our fair queen.
She's our naughty Virgin Mary
Who's fucked around the block
She's our Queen of Scots who keeps her crown
She's all we've bloody got.

Divine Gineva, she is our queen
Our queen can never die
She will arise and so will we!

The women come in armed with pots, pans, metal
spoons. They begin banging.
Split scene – Royal Palace/Gin Dive.
The Queen and Jekyll. Sounds of a riot.

Queen Caroline Jekyll!

Jekyll I have called out the guard – they surround the
palace, majesty. Your royal person is perfectly safe.

Queen Caroline Is the mob near?

Jekyll It's like the fabled hydra, ma'am – it seems to have its
tentacles in every street. They're gin crazed.

Queen Caroline Is it revolution? I can hear them from here.
They howl like a pack of frogs.

The riot.

Chorus
She's subversive, empowering
Our witch, our Halloween
Our Boudicca, Cleopatra
Our own carnival queen.
She will fright the rich in their beds
Lead us to Utopia.
The elite can fuck right off
Along with their dystopia.

Divine Gineva, she is our queen
Our queen can never die
She will arise and so will we!

The Palace.
The Queen is dying.

Queen Caroline A flame once lit can consume die Welt. As my mother would say, Dies ist eine Katastrophe. Perhaps it is better to give up this bill.

Jekyll That's impossible, ma'am – we can't let them win. What would they ask next?

Queen Caroline Mein Blut chills. I need something.

Jekyll A priest.

Queen Caroline Christ no. Brandy.

The Gin Dive.

Mary Where's Jack?

Evelyn Risking his life for you.

Mary I never meant for that to happen.

Evelyn Who are you anyway? A tart left her baby in a ditch.

Mary She's not in a ditch, someone's looking after her.

Evelyn Who'd take a whore's baby? Listen.
I'll do you a favour – vanish and I won't tell on you. Every woman for herself in this world. Go and I'll keep your whore's secret. It's better he has a nice memory of you. I'm doing you a favour really –

Mary Jack. I do love him. Will you tell him?

Evelyn Course.

Mary goes to take her savings.

Don't touch his money, thieving whore.

The Palace.

Wilson (*entering*) Ma'am. Our law has been a failure. They always find a way round it. Who knew they had brains.

Jekyll Cunning, not brains.

Queen Caroline The rabble defeat us.

Wilson For now. Our hand was forced, ma'am. We await our time once more.

Queen Caroline Nein. Ich sterbe. I'm dying. I won't be here.

Jekyll The doctors are hopeful, ma'am.

Queen Caroline Those butchers cut me open and now Blut mit Eiter. Pus.

She shows him. It's awful.

Jekyll Ma'am.

Song: 'Queen Caroline's Lament'.

Queen Caroline
　　Auf wiedersehen mein Rat
　　How the mighty have fallen
　　I've lived a life of righteousness
　　Princess of the provinces.

　　Auf wiedersehen mein George
　　You left me stuck here mit the vermin
　　And now the Pöbel bay for my blood
　　And surround us

Wilson *and* **Jekyll**
　　The mob are closing in
　　Their cries rend the night
　　Bleeding drunken English
　　And your damn rights.

The Queen climbs into her coffin.

Jekyll The queen is dead. Our best ally in the struggle . . .

Mother Gineva arises from her coffin.

Moll Mother Gin refuses to die.

Rioters No gin, no king.

The mob goes wild.

> We'll show those bastard lawmakers
> We won't be weak and quiet
> But march to our drum beat
> And stir up a bloody riot.
> This is what will happen
> When you're shat on from great height
> We'll rise and form an army
> And fight with all our might.

Lydia The soldiers have run off. Mother rules the streets. We're winning – it's our world now. What are you doing, Mary?

Mary In the morning the soldiers will come back. We'll wake up sober and scared, and then what will happen to us? Count me out, Jack.

Lydia You don't know what you are saying.

Mary Goodbye, Jack.

Lydia Mary.

She goes.

Evelyn Drink, Jack, that's the only way to forget. Forget her and think on me.

Lydia, alone, drinks a huge tankard of gin instead of joining back in with the riot.

Rioters

> Divine Gineva, she is our queen
> Our queen can never die
> She will arise and so will we!

End of Part One.

Part Two

Moll as Mother Gineva.

Song: 'The New Queen of this Town'.

Moll
>Could this be me
>Little old me
>With my defective personality
>Who everyone ignored
>Forever poor
>No good for nothing, pushed out every door
>I've staggered on sore legs
>Shagged the dregs
>Kicked out of bed and
>Made to beg
>But I knew it was wrong
>Yes I've been strong
>Success tastes sweeter when you've waited this long.
>
>So come and kiss my hand
>Or you can kiss my arse
>Buy me silken knickers for me nether parts
>I'll work my miracles on you my people
>Bestow on me your riches come on bitches
>Cos I'm the new queen of this town.
>
>I've lived off my wits
>Got off my tits
>Now you can grovel at my feet
>Cos this queen's crown fits
>From the tips of my toes
>Past my arse to my nose
>I'm royalty and from the ashes I rose.

A cunty countess
I'm Pochahontas
My veil and wimple like a sexy abbess
I'm fair but mean
A party queen
Things will change now under Mother's regime.

So come and kiss my hand
Or you can kiss my arse
Buy me silken knickers for me nether parts
I'll work my miracles on you my people
Bestow on me your riches come on bitches
Cos I'm the new queen of this town.

*Underscore for 'Zadoc the Priest' while the crowning
ceremony happens.*

Chorus of Revellers
Hail Queen Mother Gin
High ruler of this sovereignty
Rejoice!
Long live our queen.

Moll
Oh dear Mum and Dad
God you were bad
If only you could see the rise that I've had
Now I've got the power
To send you to the Tower
It's time to make those rich bastards cower.
Am I good enough? Course!
I've even sat on a horse
If your old man's a cunt
I'll grant a divorce.
Now my rules apply
I here decry
If you don't like it you can fuck off and die.

So come and kiss my hand
Or you can kiss my arse

Buy me silken knickers for me nether parts
I'll work my miracles on you my people
Bestow on me your riches come on bitches
Cos I'm the new queen of this town.

A roll of thunder. Sky darkens, Moll hurries off.

SCENE TWO

The Fieldings.
  Mary and Sarah.

Sarah You've made an excellent decision to come to us, Mary. I've a vocation for improving others and having completed work on myself I can now start on you. Before you meet my brother . . .

  Song: 'They'll Never Know'.

There are a few things you should know, Mary
I've learnt a thing or two over the years
They try to keep us in our place
But we must keep our flame alive
Heed my advice and you will survive.
The manuals teach you how to be a lady
To bake a cake or make some bread or worse
But what they don't let on is how to keep your dignity
All the rest is inconsequentialities.

You must crush it down, keep it in
Maintain a tight hold
Lock up your heart and throw away the key
To sail your ship don't make a slip
They're looking for your flaws
But they'll never know the secrets inside me.

So what I'm saying, Mary, is . . .

When you feel the need to scream
Or run or cry or yell

Just smash a plate or coffee cup instead
Wild women are not fashionable
It's the way it's always been
Lead not with your heart but with your head.
Immerse yourself in books and art and theories
I find writing an effective way to vent
My brother enjoys robust conversations
Just as long as you don't run for parliament.

You must crush it down, keep it in
Maintain a tight hold
Lock up your heart and throw away the key
To sail your ship don't make a slip
They're looking for your flaws
But they'll never know the secrets inside me.

If they knew what women were thinking
If they knew our most inner desires
Running through fields of wheat in Llangollen
Staring into her heavenly eyes.

Coming back into the kitchen from the rain, and
drying off in front of the fire, and talking and talking
into the night, saying what we like . . .

If you feel you have no status, no agency, no role
And they snigger when you offer up a thought
Just dig down deep and keep your calm
You are the stronger sex
Don't let them in and you will not be caught.

Modulation.

Mary

Forget about my old life
Look forward not look back
Make the most of this opportunity
Lead with my head and not my heart
No woman can have it all
I could get used to all this finery.

Sarah *and* **Mary**
> You must crush it down, keep it in
> Maintain a tight hold
> Lock up your heart and throw away the key
> To sail your ship don't make a slip
> They're looking for your flaws
> But they'll never know the secrets inside me.

Sarah Henry approaches. Wait there.

Henry and Wilson enter.

Wilson When the poor turn from their lawful pursuits they have nothing to occupy them except sexual intercourse and drinking.

Henry Drunkenness being the most desired, its effects are cheaper and more enduring.

Sarah My brother has a wealth of experience in both so he'll be able to spot them a mile off.

Henry Sibling advocacy!

Wilson You're the man to strike fear into the hearts of sinners, turn them back to hard work and respect for their betters.

Henry Reverend Wilson, I will make a good fist of it.

They shake hands.
> *Wilson exits, Sarah brings Mary forward.*

Sarah Mary Daniels.

Sarah exits.

Henry My sister has made you aware of your duties, Mary?

Mary Yes, sir.

Henry My wife does not always know where she is, please don't contradict her. If she thinks she's a girl again in Norwich then what is that to us?

Mary Nothing, sir.

Henry Norwich may seem a diminished choice – of all places in the world one should expend one's last dreams on – but my wife often thinks of it. Perhaps for one of two reasons; first it was where she met me, second it was where she resided before she met me.

Mary Yes, sir.

Henry Let her spirit wander down those streets, in and out of those ghostly doors visiting her phantoms. I hope she may garner some happiness. It hasn't been easy being married to me. I was often broke, Mary. And I had a prodigious appetite for wine.

Mary Nobody's perfect, sir.

Henry looks at her for the first time.

Henry Would you care to expand on that?

Mary It's just what people say.

Henry But we must pursue perfection – or else languish in depravity.

Mary Perfection seems cold.

Henry looks at her very hard.

Henry Yes. Where did my sister come across you?

Mary In prison, sir.

Henry Naturally. My sister has a selective interpretation of 'finding a regular servant to attend my ailing wife', ah yes, Newgate, of course.

Mary It was a case of mistaken identity, sir.

Henry If I had a penny . . .

Mary I was innocent.

Henry Well, you're here now.

Mary I will look after her, sir, with all my heart.

Henry Yes, I'm relying on you because I am about to be very busy in my new job.

I used to be a novelist, Mary, a profession that could not, in my case, be described as commercially rewarding. Before that I wrote for the theatre. Let's not go into that, but suffice to say that like many of my dearly held enterprises it ended in disaster. As a magistrate for Westminster I trust that my life may be a little less eventual and a little more financial.

Mary I hope so too.

Henry In Covent Garden, you can't walk the hundred yards between the Rose Tavern and Button's Coffee House without risking your life, twice. The reason? A noxious liquid. Gineva.

Mary It sounds awful.

Henry Which is why we magistrates have been called upon to enforce a new policy of prohibition.

Mary Prohibition?

Henry Drum it off our streets once and for all. And excuse me, I'll have to blow my own trumpet here.

Pause.

Why am I telling you all this?

Mary I don't know.

Henry Well I've started. There was a flaw in the old system. Volunteer constables. This is my stroke of genius. My chance to make to make good my name.

From now on they will be trained and paid.

Mary Well, I better . . .

Henry What?

Mary Your wife, sir. Why I'm here.

Henry Yes.

She exits.

SCENE THREE

Split scene – Evelyn's pub/Henry's study.

Song: 'Look at Me', reprise.

Evelyn
> Why don't you want me, Jack?
> Yet another night, you've spent pissing away
>   the savings.
> When are you going to give me what I want, Jack?
> I may be thirty-two, but I still have needs like you.

She moves towards Lydia, who backs away.

> I'm at the end of my tether, Jack,
> I'm sick of wanking myself off every night.
> It's too much work at the end of a hard day.
> Look at me, Jack, look at your Evelyn.
> Drink won't change the fact,
> Mary's gone and she ain't coming back.

> Tell me why there's nothing between us.

Henry Fielding's study.
*   Henry is writing. Mary enters.*

Mary Sir?

Henry You may enquire what I am about scribbling away into the early hours, Mary? A book of mine, *Tom Jones*, the story of a foundling, is being reprinted. I write a new foreword.

Mary The story of a foundling. So it's sad?

Henry No, all turns out well for Tom and he finds himself an heir to a fortune after all.

Mary So it's all made up.

Henry He has a nasty moment when he thinks he's slept with his own mother but luckily that turns out to be a misapprehension.

Mary Yes, because that could have been awkward. I've got something to tell you, sir.

He looks at her again.

Lydia I've got to tell you something, Evelyn.

Evelyn I hope it's a word of love.

Lydia It's in that vicinity.

Evelyn At bloody last.

Henry How is my wife? Is she in Norwich?

Mary No.

Henry One can only suppose that is a good sign. Cambridge?

Mary She's in a tunnel.

Henry A tunnel?

Mary That's why I thought . . . Any changes, you said.

He exits.

Song: 'The Problem of (Not) Having a Cock'.

Lydia You see, Evelyn . . .

> There was once a young woman who called herself
> Mack
> She dressed as a bloke in trousers and cap
> Like most men he hardly took a bath
> And Mack moved through the world with a swagger
> and laugh.

Evelyn What a thing!

Lydia

> He was greeted most sweetly as he walked down
> the street
> Women buzzed around him like flies around shit
> Washed his clothes, made his meals, 'twas a life full
> of joys
> But for one thing that threatened life with the boys.
>
> You see Mack had no way of paying them back
> Because down his trousers, down his trousers
> Was nothing in fact.

Evelyn (*laughs*) That's funny. (*Stops laughing.*) I don't understand.

Henry re-enters.

Henry She's gone. And not in a geographic sense. Charlotte, my wife.

He holds on to Mary.

Hold me.

Lydia The thing is, Evelyn . . .

> Stuffed down Mack's pants was a sock of dried peas
> And all the ladies looked on and were pleased
> The roundness, the hardness and all that it promised
> But the one who looked hardest, her name was Doris.
>
> 'Oh what a fine package!' she imagined inside her
> A prize that only Mack could provide her
> She chased him up, she chased him down
> Through alleyway and all over the town.

Evelyn Poor bloody Doris.

Lydia You're not listening.

Henry realises he has an erection.

Henry I'm sorry, Mary.

The problem of what's down below
It's got a mind of its own
If you're religious, or recently widowed
It tends to pop up when I'm not alone
A cold bath is in order
A smart tap with a tome
What can tame this randy old bone?
I'm ashamed I'm embarrassed
I'm sexually harassed.
The problem of having a –

Lydia

'What's the matter my darling, don't be coy
All I want is my six inches of joy.'
Mack drew out a carrot, said 'What about that then?'
'Don't fucking mess with me.' And stuffed her hand in.

Doris was in for a nasty shock
For down Mack's trousers, down Mack's trousers
There was no cock!

Evelyn What are you saying, Jack?

Mary

Please don't apologise
I'm not offended.
(*Aside.*) My heart can't be touched
All that's ended

Henry I need you.

Mary There's nothing standing in your way.

Lydia

Doris was speechless, she shook with rage
Mack said 'Don't panic! There's plenty of ways
    to engage,
I've a tongue and ten fingers, can't we be friends?'
But Doris refused to make amends.

Mack hadn't planned on a life so complex
The lying and dodging,
Ignoring, avoiding and fending off
All the offers of sex.

I'm a woman, Ev.

Evelyn A woman. That's why we get on so well. Do you love me?

Henry Mary.

Lydia You're not Mary, are you?

Evelyn slaps Lydia.
Lydia goes.

Evelyn Jack!

She is gone.
Henry and Mary kiss.

SCENE FOUR

Family dinner.
Mary enters with John, who is then seated.

Sarah You intend to enforce the law with a band of new recruits. What will they be called?

Henry It's a work in progress. There are alliterative possibilities. I thought perhaps the Westminster –

Sarah Waddlers?

Henry That would scare the living daylights out of offenders. To be pursued by a posse of large ducks.

John No one waits to be arrested – they must be given chase – the Bow Street lads will above all be runners.

Henry Bow Street Runners.

They are happy with this.

Sarah I should like to point to an inconsistency in your character, sir.

Henry I've always been poor.

Sarah I meant you have been arrested yourself.

Henry As a youth.

Sarah For kidnapping your wife.

Henry Ancient history.

Sarah I hope you've thought about this carefully, brother. Passing judgement on others when you are personally acquainted with numerous vices. While we're about it, how many times do I have to propound to you the health-giving properties of lettuce?

Henry Enough times, surely.

Sarah Plato was a vegetarian. That should tell you something.

Henry That makes two things I know about Plato. One day an acquaintance ran up to Socrates and said, 'You'll never guess what I heard about your student, Plato?' Socrates said, 'Before you tell me I'd like you to pass the test of three. First, is what you are about to tell me absolutely true?' 'No,' said the man, 'but it's juicy.' 'Is it good?' 'On the contrary,' says the man. 'It's awful.' 'You're going to tell me something awful that you're not even sure is true? Is it useful to me?' 'Not really,' said his friend. 'Well, if it is neither good, true or useful, what's the point of telling me at all?' The man agreed, and that is why Socrates never found out that Plato was banging his wife.

John and Henry laugh.
Mary drops something.

John The blue plate.

420

Sarah Can you hear the colour?

John No matter, it was cracked.

Henry By what miraculous process of supposition do you arrive at that conclusion?

John Mary gives me the cracked plate because she knows I can't see it.

Mary I . . .

John Which is considerate of other diners. Also to your pocket, Henry.

Sarah I'm afraid that our crockery will never be replaced. Henry never willingly puts his hand in his pocket.

John Though you are a recipient of Henry's generosity, Sarah.

Sarah I have no other means of support. Women like me are not allowed to work.

Mary Henry – Mr Fielding works all hours, diligently.

She has spoken out of turn.

John Are you particularly aware of his comings and goings, Mary? You advocate for him generously.

Sarah Don't bully the servants.

John Perhaps Mary has read *Pamela* –

Henry What a pile of steaming crap that book is.

John 'Diligently' is a word sparingly employed by the servant class not known for their readership. Although one must allow for the possibility she has been talking to a great reader.

Sarah That will be me.

Henry And that is my objection to Richardson. Only a congenital idiot of a man would marry his servant.

Mary deliberately drops something else.

Mary Excuse me.

John Ah, I'm sorry to hear that go. The gravy jug with roses. That was Charlotte's. It's always this time that it leaves the table.

Mary What if she's pregnant?

John Silence.

Sarah What's that, brother?

John The quality of silence in a room. Marry her, Henry.

Sarah Marry who?

John Mary. For the sake of our crockery.

Sarah Don't be ridiculous. Mary is my protégée. Why would Henry marry her? He has just sworn it only happens in morally overinflated novels.

John Lead me, sister.

Sarah All I ask is a little intellectual consistency.

She exits with John.

Mary I'd be a good wife to you, Henry.

Song: 'The Path I Choose'.

Henry
    Footpads, sharpers, cheats and thieves
    Girls with knives up their skirt
    I know the poor aren't born bad
    But they turn the streets to dirt.

    Law and order must return
    I must stop this evil curse
    Bring back sobriety
    Before it gets much worse.

The streets are not for you, my dear
It's a pit of troubled, drunken fools
I feel the job has called for me
To make it my last fight
Is the path I choose
It's the path I choose.

Mary

As your wife, I could help
I'm no use in the shadows
Stamp out this evil gineva
The cause of so many woes.

I lived there, I understand
Some of them were once friends
There's more to me than you know
I want to make amends.

Henry

The streets are not for you, my dear
A pit of troubled drunken fools.

Mary

I feel the job is calling me
To help you win the fight
Is the path I choose
It's the path I choose.

Henry

This is not a woman's domain
We'll play dirty to get them clean
Punishing laws, you're better off indoors
This may have to get mean.

Mary

Let me talk to them as a mother
There's no need for any strife
Stop their endless glass downing
Imagine a sober life.

Henry It's not a bad idea.

Mary We could clean the streets, my dear.

Henry Help these troubled, drunken fools.

Mary
I feel the job is calling me
I can help you win the fight – it's the path I choose.

Mary *and* **Henry**
It's the path we choose.

SCENE FIVE

Street scene.
  Lydia has approached Moll.

Moll You want me to what?

Lydia Miaow.

Moll I'm royalty. I'm not playing a fucking feline. I had a ceremony. You're boring me now. Evacuate the royal presence.

Lydia You haven't got any real powers.

Moll That hurts, Jack.

Lydia So you have to be a cat.

Moll A moggy? How the mighty have fallen. The wheel of fortune takes you to the top to chuck you off of it. What have I done to deserve it?

  Pause.

Oh yeah.

Lydia Get behind the sign of the black cat. And when I say puss puss, you say mew mew.

Moll Easy.

She goes behind the sign.

Lydia Puss puss.

Moll barks.

Song: 'Puss and Mew'.

Lydia

Those lofty souls that live in wealth
Force us the poor to drink in stealth
They'd have us slave with little joy
But we have made a darling toy
Say puss
Say mew.

We once bought gin face to face
The law forbids this to take place
They seek to ban our favourite tipple
Snatch the baby from its nipple.

Say puss
Say mew
Say puss
Say mew.

Racked our brains and we've invented.
A sweet machine to keep us contented
A simple pipe, a little drawer
Attached to a plain front door.

Say puss
Say mew.

Put your money in the slot.

Instrumental. She demonstrates how the machine works.

If they can't see us they can't bang us up.

Moll That's inGINious, Jack.

By this means our cute contraption
Frees us from the law's infraction
And so one step ahead we keep
while those cunts are fast asleep.

Say puss
Say mew.

Moll
Why should they stop us enjoying
Our natural right to employing
For every woman has her right
To have her pleasure every night.

Moll *and* **Lydia**
Say puss
Say mew
Say puss
Say mew.

Whistles.
A customer turns out to have been a Bow Street Runner.

Moll It's the bloody law. Run, Jack.

A hullabaloo – shouts – it's the Runners.
All scatter. Lydia is caught.

Lydia You can't say it was me that sold it to you – you never saw my face –

Bow Street Runner You'll do. You're nicked.

SCENE SIX

Lydia and Henry.

Henry So, Jack Clapp.

Lydia Yes, sir.

Henry How old are you?

Lydia Twenty. I couldn't swear to it.

Henry Your mother gave you no idea?

Lydia I never met her, sir.

Henry Another abandoned lost soul. You're aware I could have you committed to Newgate. Hard labour.

Lydia Yes, sir.

Henry But that would be a waste. I've got a proposition for you, Jack, to turn your life around. I need good men who know these streets. You're quick and strong. You have good sense. Nobody's given you a chance before but I'm giving you a chance now to earn an honest living.

Lydia I won't be an informer, sir.

Henry This isn't about informing. This is about keeping the innocents of Westminster safe in their beds. The men, women and children.

Lydia Well, I agree with that, sir. The children.

Henry Good. You'd get a uniform. The more arrests you make, the more money you earn. Plus a whistle, a stick and a pistol. That's what makes a Bow Street Runner. What do you say?

Lydia I'm flabbergasted.

Henry Crime is astronomical. We've got to come down hard on them, Jack, for their own good. It's tough love. Like a parent disciplines a wayward child.

Song: 'Watch Your Back'.

Henry teaches 'Jack' the principles of becoming a Bow Street Runner.

Arrest them for keeping a bawdy house
Solicitation
Stealing a hunk of bacon

Arrest them for picking pockets
Stealing watches
They break the law
They better watch their back.

Arrest them for having a dirty face
Stealing a piece of lace
For standing in the wrong place
Arrest them for being brazen
Defecation
They flout the law
They better watch their back.

No need for remorse
These thieves are a sorry lot
We're the good guys, they deserve to rot
You better watch your back.

Chorus

The Bow Street Runners are on their way
They don't stop running night or day
The Bow Street Runners, with their cuffs and locks
If you don't watch it you'll end up in the stocks
You better watch your back.

Moll

But you'd never arrest me, Jack,
No you'd never arrest me.
Me and you go way back
You're one of us really.

Lydia

From the hunted to the hunter
I've nothing left to lose
It's just me on my own
Can I really refuse?

I'll arrest you for leaving your baby crying
Your cheating and your lying

Informing and your spying
I'll arrest you for deserting babes in arms
For causing any harm
You mess with me
You better watch your back.

I've got no remorse
You thieves are a sorry lot
I'm the best there is, and you deserve to rot,
You better watch your back.

Chorus
The Bow Street Runners are on their way
They don't stop running night or day
The Bow Street Runners, with their cuffs and locks
If you don't watch it you'll end up in the stocks
You better watch your back.

SCENE SEVEN

We are back at the start of the play. Hogarth's 'Beer Street' is illuminated.

Suki You shouldn't have done that, dissing me. We got history. Don't forget I know. How would he like his perfect wife exposed? He wouldn't want the town gossiping. They do love to gossip. Kick its carcass over and over. Vultures. think of the scandal. The disgrace. Horrible. I'd throw myself in the river. Money is what will buy my silence. I'll come find you.

Mary It looks better with us than we are. We're on tab at the grocers and the butchers.

Suki I'll come find you.

Suki exits.

Song: 'What Does a Woman Have to Do?'

Mary

> What does a woman have to do
> To get a better life?
> What does a woman have to give
> To be a mother or a wife?
> Always waiting to be found out
> When the past returns to bite
> What does a woman have to do?
>
> What does a woman have to do
> When she can't forget what's done?
> How can I ever forgive
> Myself for all the wrongs?
> Is it enough to just get by
> When I dream for so much more?
> What does a woman have to do?
>
> I have tried to shape my own destiny
> But the truth is buried, hidden
> And the weight of it is killing
> Do I search her out, tell her why I left
> And risk losing my position
> All for one desperate decision?
> What's a woman have to do?
> A woman have to do
> A woman have to do?
> How do I find my way through?
>
> Where does a girl have to turn
> When her needs are left to last?
> Where does your childhood vanish to
> When you're forced to grow up fast?
> I have failed as a mother
> What makes me think I'll be good now?
> What does a woman have to do?
>
> What if I find she's on the streets
> Can I bring her home?
> In my heart I'll never rest

Till I know she's not alone.
If I can't live with the disgrace
Can I live with all the guilt?
What does a woman have to do?

I have tried to shape my own destiny
But the truth I've buried, hidden
And the weight of it is killing
I must search her out, tell her why I left
I'll risk losing my position
It's time to make my decision
What does a woman have to do?
A woman have to do
A woman have to do?
I must find my way through.

Henry enters.

Henry, if I was to ask you for some money and not have
you ask me what it was for –
    Would you give it to me?

Henry No. One: I will not give money to unknown ends.
Two: I have no money

Mary But you're a magistrate now?

Henry It won't make me rich, sadly. Though it comes with
a free wig. Friends do take the liberty of cadging a loan but
they usually warm each other up first with flattering
reminiscences.

Mary I'm your wife, Henry. What if you don't like my
reminiscences? You'd still have to be married.

Henry My dear, I'm sure I'm the one with the sordid past.

Lydia enters with a document she gives to Henry.

Lydia Sir.

Henry Here's my best Runner.

He looks at the document.

I'm needed in the courtroom. Sort Jack out with his supper, Mary.

Henry exits.

Lydia You're his Mary?

Mary You're a Runner?

Lydia A good one.

Mary How are you, Jack?

Lydia I'm doing really well. Really, really well. Yes.
Yes. I enjoy my work. I'm good at it. Wiped away my past. Everything. Same as you, looks like.

Mary I'm pleased for you, Jack.

Lydia It's a better life. Just me. You took your chances when you could, hats off to you.
Anyway, I'm over all that. I moved on.

Mary That's good. I'm married, a baby coming.
We used to sell gineva and now we're both on the other side, fighting it. We're still together in a way.

Lydia I'm not hungry, so I'll see you.

Mary I know you hate me, Jack, but you don't know the true reason I left you.

Lydia What do you want, Mary?

Mary Before we met I had a child and I let her go.

Lydia You had a child?

Mary I couldn't tell you. I thought you'd stop loving me.

Lydia Where is this child?

Mary She would have starved. I did what I thought was right. I know she's still alive. I want her back. You're the only one that can help me find her.

Lydia A poor kid in the whole of London?

Mary Suki knows where she is.

Lydia I don't owe you.

Mary I know your secret, Lydia.

Song: 'Got Here Without You', reprise.

Lydia

  I'm all right, I've got through
  I've survived without you.
  And now you come crawling back
  Giving me your tales of woe
  When I should tell you where to go
  I won't fall into your trap.

  I would never do what you did to me
  You had no shred of sympathy
  How could you leave and break my heart?
  I won't keep being strung along
  You must right your own wrong
  We're better off apart.

Mary

  I was scared for you to see
  The shame that burned inside me
  I didn't know what else to do
  No one understands like you .

  Every child who walks by
  Wondering could she be mine?
  To never find her is my fear
  Does she look like me
  Can I see a sign?

  Will she hate me and chastise
  Or can our love reignite
  Will she be the one to recognise
  The mother who left her that night?

> If I could meet her one day
> In a crowd
> Would she walk or stay?
> I don't know what else to do
> No one understands like you.

Lydia

> Like a leaf I went where I was blown
> No one to help me and all alone
> All I wanted was a happy home
> And a family of our own
> Why should I do this for you?

She exits.

SCENE EIGHT

At night.
Moll and Suki outside. Drinking.

Moll Streets are dry as a witch's tit. Don't say you haven't got a dram up your skirts for me?

Suki Dregs.

Song: 'Suki's Lullaby'.

> Always me they come to
> But what's in it for Suki?
> With them it's always the same
> Give me all their misery
> No one ever asks me are you okay?
> It's 'What you got for me today?'
> Feed me, Suki, knock me out
> But what's in it for me?

Lydia enters as a Bow Street Runner.

Moll I haven't done nothing, Officer. Oh, it's only you, Jack.

Suki Your fortune's changed.

Moll Fortunes can change. Once I thought I had to fuck a syphilitic wreck, but he died before I had to.

Lydia Once again it's your lucky day.

Brings out a bottle of gin.

Seized property.

Moll Jack, if I was still queen I'd knight you.

Moll drinks.

Lydia Want a swig, Suki?

Suki If you're offering.

Lydia (*holds off drink*) Mary had a kid once, she says you know where it is.

Suki She's with a mate of mine. My mate needs money though, cos she's been caring for it.

Lydia You're a blackmailer, is that it?

Suki That's harsh.

Moll Are you gonna arrest her, Jack?

Lydia It's a thought.

Suki What favour's Mary ever done you?

Moll Broke his heart.

Lydia Yeah. Screw her. I think I'll come in with you.

Suki Now you're talking.

Lydia That way I might stop hating her – when I've had my vengeance.

Suki That's logical. I'll give you a cut. Let's toast that.

Moll One thing I'll say for gineva, you couldn't give a monkey's bollocks who you drink it with. We're all getting on – isn't it fantastic?

Lydia You ever had a kid, Moll?

Moll Don't ask me.

Lydia Why not?

Moll Cos I can't remember, can I?
   I must have done – it ain't nice but when you're rat-arsed you put things down and you forget where . . .

Lydia Where's Mary's kid though, Suki?

Suki Nearby.

Lydia Where?

   Song: 'Suki's Lullaby' continued.

Suki
      In a house, with a garden
      With dolls in the nursery
      A stream for her to play in
      And a swing hangs from a tree
      Shady in the summertime
      Ribbons in her hair
      Cup of milk at bedtime
      A lullaby sung to her.

      Go to sleep my little one
      Go to sleep my dear
      Your mamma's gone but I'm here now
      There's no need to fear.

Lydia What's she like?

Suki She's gorgeous.

Lydia Is she like Mary?

Suki Spit of Mary. Long dark hair, cute little face. Dark eyes. Actually no, blue eyes now I come to think of it. Blue like bluebells.

Lydia What's her name?

Long pause.

Suki I forgot because, you know, why would I know?

Moll Yeah, why would ya?

Lydia Where is she though?

Suki I told you, she's with my bloody mate.

Lydia What colour eyes?

Suki I need a drink.

Pause.

Lydia There ain't no kid.

Moll No kid?

Suki So I wanted a drink – so I sold their clothes after I done it.

> Always me who has to do it
> Like a china doll to hold
> Better they die quickly
> Than be eaten by the cold
> She put that burden on me
> The heavy weight of shame
> I drink to help me forget
> Something to dull the pain.

Lydia How many have you done?

Suki

> Go to sleep my little one
> Go to sleep my dear
> Your mamma's gone but I'm here now
> There's no need to fear.

Lydia breaks the gin bottle and stabs Suki with it. She crawls around and dies.

SCENE NINE

Henry And so it was discovered that the man was a woman.

Sarah My goodness. You mean she wore trousers?

Henry And lived her life with all the freedoms of a man.

Sarah Why would she want to do that? Oh my God, it's actually obvious.

Henry Mary is quiet. Something preoccupies you?

Sarah Why are you always so suspicious?

Henry I was a novelist. What's the matter, Mary?

Pause.

Mary Nothing.

John Hesitation.

Sarah John.

John Music of a conflicted soul.

Sarah Nonsense. She will not be investigated.

Mary I was thinking that Suki Blunt is killed. What will happen to – the killer now?

John She pursues you. She has skin in the game.

Mary What will her sentence be?

Henry The law has to set an example. If nothing is done to prevent it – cruelty will become the characteristic of this nation. Besides, this case will be the end of gineva. Are you all right, Mary?

Mary The baby's kicking.

They take their places in the courtroom.
    The courtroom is full, Betsy, Mary, Sarah and Evelyn
watch from the balcony. They pass round a bottle of gin,
which Sarah tries.
    Henry and John in the courtroom.

John Margaret Williams.

Silence.

Evelyn That's you, Moll.

Moll Oh, fuck! Yes?

Henry Do you go by other names?

Moll Blear-eyed Moll they call me.

Henry Anything else?

Moll Jenny Gobbler, Betty Blowshaft.

Henry Do I detect a pattern? They're not precisely
euphemisms.

Moll What's that?

John Derived from Greek, the substitution of one word for
another that is less blunt or offensive.

Moll Like 'pork sword' for 'cock'.

John You are a quick study.

Henry You were with the deceased on the night in
question. In the vicinity of St Giles.

Moll We'd been swaffing diddle.

John Translates as drinking gin.

Henry Why doesn't that surprise me?

Moll We was zwaddered, having a laugh one minute and
then . . .

Henry You saw the fatal blow?

Moll I was booze-fuddled, I can't remember nothing.

John It is entirely possible her mind will never regain the property of memory.

Moll I hope so, sir, but I haven't had a dram for three days and I think I'm sober. It's horrible.

Henry Stand down.

Moll joins the women in the gallery.

John Lydia Clapp.

Lydia steps up.
  The women in the gallery cheer.

Henry You are in this court to answer to the murder of Suki Blunt. Do you understand?

Lydia Yes, sir.

Henry Exhibit A.

A broken bottle is produced.

John A receptacle which once held quantities of a beverage named Ladies' Delight.

Moll My favourite.

Betsy Mine's Knock Me Down.

Evelyn Loved a Cuckold's Comfort, me.

Henry Silence. This was your weapon. Do you deny it? When the constable arrived you were still holding it in your hand.

Lydia She was a liar. She deserved what she got. If she wasn't she wouldn't be under the hatches now.

The women agree.

She lied to me and when I confronted her she turned grub. And so now she's in her eternity box – feeding worms.

Henry She's not here to defend herself from your slanders. What conversation did you have with the deceased?

Lydia About a child.

Henry Was it your child?

Lydia No. I was searching for it and Suki knew where it was and wouldn't tell me. She stole that child. You'll have to take my word for it, sir.

Henry How can I take your word for it? You disguised yourself as a man, you were employed as a Runner. You fully and deliberately deceived us.

Lydia Yes, I'm sorry, but I'm telling the truth. I think she wanted me to stick her, sir, she was a guilty creature. It gave her some peace.

Henry Eternal peace, yes. Is there anyone present in the courtroom who could verify any of your assertions of a stolen child?

Pause. Mary looks terrified. Perhaps she feels the first pangs of labour.

Lydia No.

Henry No.
This child is a fiction conjured for the purposes of covering up a drunken brawl. Under the influence of gineva you murdered Suki Blunt, a hawker, in a rage when she refused to supply you. And now you bring us the fiction of an innocent child to forge a motivation. You are a liar, an unrepentant murderer and a cross-dresser –

Moll Wait, I just remembered something.

John You are not in the stand.

Moll I also went by Moll Quickie.

Betsy Why's that, Moll?

Moll It's like when you have to serve 'em two at a time. The old double handshake.

Henry The last piece of evidence is inadmissible.

Sarah Because it suits you, Henry. Like many men of the theatre, you had your rakish nights in the brothels of Betty Blowshaft and Moll Quickie.

Reaction from the women.

Henry You may be family, but any more interruptions and I will have you forcibly removed.

Moll I didn't recognise your honour because you're wearing trousers.

Henry Order!

Sarah Men prove themselves morally inadequate and yet through an iniquitous political system have total power over us – it seems bloody unfair, as Jane would say.

Henry Have you been drinking?

Sarah For research purposes.

Holds up her notes.

Henry We're here to set an example, not to indulge in the principal cause of debauchery.

Sarah But you drink, Henry – port, sherry and brandy. I don't see you giving it up.

The women cheer her.
Sarah stands.

I would like to cite as evidence in the accused's favour Mr Hogarth's picture.

Henry 'Gin Lane'? It's a vision of hell.

Sarah A mother drops her baby into an abyss.

Henry Our capital city falling into chaos. The poor destroying themselves.

Sarah What should be on trial are the dreadful conditions under which these women live – that's what drives them to the comforts of gineva in the first place.

Betsy I lost two babies of sewage.

Women Ah.

Sarah The mother sits alone, but where are the fathers?

Women Yes! We're the ones left holding the baby! Useless bastards. (*Etc.*)

John Do something, Henry, before they start a riot.

Henry I call the court to order.

Sarah Women must create their own society without men and get on with the real business of life – writing educational poetry.

John Pass the sentence, Henry, for God's sake.

Henry Lydia Clapp, I enforce the full extent of the law and pass a sentence of death by hanging.

The women shout from the gallery.

Sarah No, Henry.

SCENE TEN

The jail.
Mary enters.

Lydia Mary?

Mary They don't know I'm here. I've only got a few minutes.
Don't know what to call you.

Lydia Don't matter now, does it?

Mary Thank you for not betraying me.

Lydia No point two of us getting in the shit.

Mary Why did you kill her? Is it something to do with my child? Is she . . .

Lydia She's safe. Suki told me that much. Let her be. Think about your new baby.

Mary My son.

Song: 'We Could Have It All', reprise.

Lydia
> How's the baby, is he napping?
> He looks adorable when he's asleep
> Let the servant do the clearing up
> Take the weight off your feet.

Mary
> Why thank you, my poppet
> It's so nice to return home to you
> With a nursery and our drawing room
> And our indoor bathroom.

Lydia *and* **Mary**
> We could have it all
> Why can't our dreams come true?
> We could be a lord and lady
> With a family too
> I'd do it for you.

Lydia Goodbye, Mary. You'll be a good mother. Toast me when it happens.

Mary I can't do that. Gineva. That's what ruined us.

Mary exits.

SCENE ELEVEN

Lydia is pushed on a wagon on the way to the gallows. She is allowed down to stop off at every drinking establishment along the way, including Evelyn's tavern. The following lines weave around the song.

Evelyn Off the wagon one last time now. It's Beer Street here. But I thought gineva today for old times' sake.

Lydia Thanks, Ev.

Song: 'This World Stinks'.

> So it's my time
> To say goodbye and sing my last song
> Yes I was wild
> I drank and fought and loved but all that's gone
> And now I should say sorry
> Repent all of my sins
> Look my maker in the face and beg for mercy
> But I won't
> Cos this world stinks.
>
> This is goodbye
> To all my friends to the laughter to the tears
> I'd wish I'd seen
> More of this world to think what could have been
> But this life is what has made me
> I won't be kept like a caged bird
> A woman of the streets and always will be
> Now that's gone cos this world stinks.
>
> Women, remember this is my story
> Standing together is our path to glory.

Moll Here's a dram to see you on your way.

Lydia Thanks, Moll.

Bartholomew Back on the wagon, Lyddie.

Lydia Coming, Bartholomew.

Bartholomew No hard feelings.

Lydia No.

The baby starts to cry.

Mary
A little boy
Bringing light into this world full of pain
A brand new life
Bringing hope and a chance to start again
You're one of the lucky ones
Many don't get a fair hand
Deserted by their mother
And left to hang
Now she's gone
Cos this world stinks.

Chorus
Mother Gin won't let you down
Mother Gin wears the crown
Mother Gin won't stop you now
Mother Gin, Mother Gin.

Mother Gin won't let you down
Mother Gin wears the crown
Mother Gin won't stop us now
Mother Gin, Mother Gin.

Women, remember this is our story
Standing together is our path to glory.

Lydia To the mother I commend my spirit.

She is hanged.

SCENE TWELVE

Mary
You've got to crush it down, keep it in
Maintain a tight hold
Lock up your heart and throw away the key
It's not working
You've got to crush it down, keep it in
Maintain a tight hold
Lock up your heart
Lydia.

Sarah Were you friends like Jane and I?

Mary Yes. Lydia lied in court to save me. And I stood by. Henry hung her but there was no moral point.

Sarah gets out a massive bottle of gin. Familiar green bottle.

Sarah The Gordon family saw a business opportunity. It's quite fashionable now the poor can't afford it.

She pours two glasses.

I'll shall write the story of the gin-drinking women of England. Your story shall never be forgotten. Not as long as my name is remembered – Sarah Fielding, author of *The Little Female Academy*, the first novel in English for children.

Mary (*toasting*) To Lydia.

They both drink.
We hear a ghostly reprise of the 'Gin Dive' song.

Chorus
Come down to the gin dive and sit with the girls
Have a laugh, a drink, a good time with the girls

Come down to the gin dive and have a good jest
We'll laugh and sing and give our bloody best.

The End.

Final song:

So when you pour your G&T
Think of us in history
And drink
Don't brand us as pariahs
While you swig Bombay Sapphires
Just drink
We're the mothers and the givers
Despite our ulcerated livers
We're the ones who made the fuss
You should thank the Lord for us
We drank the most
So raise a toast to
Gin, gin, gin!

The Real End.